Praise for
How Cool Brands Stay Hot

"To win the consumer revolution, all brands should have the ambition to become a Lovemark. This book explains brilliantly how you can gain the love of Generation Y. A must-read for all generation Y marketers and for all brand marketers together, since Generation Y leads to all the other target groups as well."

Kevin Roberts, CEO, Saatchi & Saatchi Worldwide

"If you get this book, you will certainly crush your competition!"

Gaëtan Van Maldegem, Country Director, Belux at The Coca-Cola Company

"I am generally not a big fan of marketing books and particularly not when they touch so-called youth marketing. But this one was refreshing and informative, more observing and sharing a frame of thinking on the evolution of generations instead of an absolute theory on 'how to get after those young consumers'."

Gert Kerkstoel, Investor and former Global Business Director, Nike SB

"It's actually quite a cool book on youth and brands and very relevant for my day-to-day international marketing and branding practice!"

**Peter Van Overstraeten, Global Marketing Manager,
Beck's & Hoegaarden at AB Inbev**

"This youth generation is more socially empowered than ever. A brand today needs a strong DNA that is capable of constantly surprising youth with novelties to keep them interested while staying recognizable and true to its legacy. You're either a cool brand or you're not, but you can't TRY to be cool. Coolness is the result of delivering the real deal to your customers. Sometimes you will have to lose a few smaller battles to retain your credibility and win the big battle. *How Cool Brands Stay Hot* taps into these areas of tension that hold the key to success in youth markets."

Joris Aperghis, CMO G-Star International

"It's been said that if Victorians looked at the world through rose-coloured glasses, then the 20th century looked at it through jaundice-yellow glasses. What will the 21st century bring? Nothing draws a sharper, more incisive and still warm, caring picture of how to reach Gen Y consumers than *How Cool Brands Stay Hot* does. Values are emotionally-laden, and cause marketing is but one manifestation of what it will take to grab and hold onto the heartstrings – and pocketbooks – of today's youth and younger adults."

Dan Hill, President of Sensory Logic Inc and
author of *Emotionomics* and *About Face*

"The 'R' from the CRUSH brand model has confirmed to us the importance of having a modern or attitudinal interpretation of authenticity in our marcomms. It relates better to the current consumer climate as well as to specific Generation Y expectations. A lot of hot takeaways for cool brand builders in this book indeed."

Dirk Van Kemseke, Global Marketplace Insights Manager, Levi Strauss & Co

How Cool Brands Stay Hot

Branding to Generation Y

For my two Generation Z daughters, Vita and Jina who haven't lost much of their muchness yet

Joeri

For my grandmother and role model Lilly, who has the wisdom of a 99-year-old but the heart and mind of a teenager

Mattias

How Cool Brands Stay Hot

Branding to Generation Y

JOERI VAN DEN BERGH
and MATTIAS BEHRER

Foreword by Gert Kerkstoel,
Investor and former global business director, Nike SB

KoganPage

LONDON PHILADELPHIA NEW DELHI

Publisher's note

Every possible effort has been made to ensure that the information contained in this book is accurate at the time of going to press, and the publishers and authors cannot accept responsibility for any errors or omissions, however caused. No responsibility for loss or damage occasioned to any person acting, or refraining from action, as a result of the material in this publication can be accepted by the editor, the publisher or the author.

First published in Great Britain and the United States in 2011 by Kogan Page Limited

120 Pentonville Road	1518 Walnut Street, Suite 1100	4737/23 Ansari Road
London N1 9JN	Philadelphia PA 19102	Daryaganj
United Kingdom	USA	New Delhi 110002
www.koganpage.com		India

ISBN   978 0 7494 6250 5
E-ISBN   978 0 7494 6251 2

British Library Cataloguing-in-Publication Data

A CIP record for this book is available from the British Library.

Library of Congress Cataloging-in-Publication Data

Bergh, Joeri Van den, 1971–
    How cool brands stay hot : branding to generation Y / Joeri Van den Bergh, Mattias Behrer.
        p. cm.
    Includes bibliographical references.
    ISBN 978-0-7494-6250-5 – ISBN 978-0-7494-6251-2   1. Young consumers.   2. Young adult consumers.   3. Generation Y.   4. Target marketing.   5. Product management.   6. Consumer behavior.   I. Behrer, Mattias.   II. Title.
    HF5415.332.Y66B47 2011
    658.8'27–dc22

                                                                                        2010036704

Typeset by Graphicraft Ltd, Hong Kong
Printed and bound in India by Replika Press Pvt Ltd

Contents

07   Happiness: Gen Y's adoration for branded emotions 181

List of figures

List of tables

Acknowledgements

We would like to thank some of the many people who have helped us along the way in writing this book. Thanks to the more than 20,000 Gen Yers who have anonymously participated in the various global research projects that gave us the required inspiration for this project. We thank the wonderful people at Kogan Page: Helen Kogan, Jon Finch, Liz Barlow, Julia Swales, Cathy Frazer and Ben Glover. Thanks also to project editor Sara Marchington and copy editor Lynda Watson.

Joeri's words of thanks

In *Alice in Wonderland*, the Mad Hatter keeps confronting Alice with the riddle: 'Why is a raven like a writer's desk?' Alice sighs and answers: 'I think you might do something better with the time than wasting it on asking riddles that have no answer.'

I'm very grateful to my partners (Kristof, Steven, Niels, Tim, Christophe, Sam and Filip), my clients and all my colleagues at InSites Consulting for giving me the chance to waste some time at my writer's desk. In these challenging economic times, I should probably have been using it for more profitable occupations. Thanks to my Macbook Pro, no raven feathers have been hurt during the production of this book.

I would also like to thank the MTV Networks people for believing in this project from the very first day I spoke to Veerle Colin and Patrick Alders about the idea. Many of MTV's sympathetic global staff have been extremely helpful in supporting and endorsing my work: Emma Norström, Helen Rose, Lisa Cowie, Sebastian Barth, Ralf Osteroth, Emelie Wahlström, Ann Hoeree, Pascale Engelen, Anne-Elise Jardinet, Chenling Zhang, Tina Verpooten, Laura Vogelsang, Menno Wagenaar, Frank Bakker, Lieselotte van der Meer, Tobbias Dettling, Dora Szemadam, and many more.

Mattias's gratitude

I would like to thank all my wonderful colleagues at MTV, particularly those already mentioned by Joeri as well as the following people: Antonio Campo Dall'Orto, Dan Ligtvoet, Ben Richardson, Kerry Taylor, Philip Bourchier O'Ferrall, Nicolas Declercq, Hanna Hedberg, Alejandro Romero, Marta Pinilla, Benedikt von Walter, Hugo Pinto, Sofia Fernandez, Tanya Leedekerken, Mar Mayoral, Jurgen Hopfgartner, Rasmus Dige, John Jackson and Georgia Arnold.

*

Producing this book would certainly have been impossible if it hadn't been for the help of the following people: Isabel Raes for being the Vancouver Style Reference/Figures expert; Tania Van den Bergh for proof-reading and editing; Annelies Verhaeghe for sharing the produce of her own marvellous brain cells and writing some texts on youth's brain cells; Michael Friedman for his terrific research work on the CRUSH model and the go/no go distinctive asset study, and Niels Schillewaert for his valuable input for the model; Anke Moerdyck for the marketing support that would easily exceed any agent's efforts; the patient reviewers of the script: Barbara Verhaegen, Sanna-Mari Salomäki, Veerle Colin, Patrick De Pelsmacker, Gaëtan Van Maldegem, Vincent Fierens, Marc Michils, Gert Kerkstoel, Dennis Hoogervorst, Dennis Claus, Steven Van Belleghem, Niels Schillewaert and Kristof De Wulf. The interviewees and their colleagues and connectors: Dennis Birk Jorgensen, Anders Gam, Anja Ballegaard, Clara Buddig and Thijs Luyt (Bestseller/Jack & Jones) & Saskia Neirinckx (former Bestseller, now VF); Satu Kalliokulju, Bjorn Ulfberg, Ann Van Dessel and Jurgen Thysmans (Nokia); Jörgen Andersson and Sara Svirsky (H&M); Emelie Wahlström (MTV Sweden); Patrik Söder, Thomas Brenemark and Olle Johansson Bergholtz (DDB Stockholm); Joris Aperghis (G-Star International); Avery Baker, Sanne Krom and Jeroen Vermeer (Tommy Hilfiger); Gert Kerkstoel (former Nike); Derk Hendriksen, Cristina Bondolowski, AJ Brustein, Joanna Allen, Susan Hines, Judith Snyder and Gaëtan Van Maldegem (Coca-Cola); An Martel (Diageo); Sanna-Mari Salomäki (Kuule); Matti Rautalahti and Virve Laivisto (Cancer Society of Finland); Ellen Vermeulen (Procter & Gamble); Dirk Van Kemseke (Levi's); Joe Beek (Channel 4); Mia Venken, Kris Stevens and Peter Vandermeersch (De Standaard, Corelio); Carolijn Domensino (The Fish); Dan Hill and Joe Bockman (Sensory Logic).

Foreword

An awful lot has been written recently about new technology and how it is changing communication with consumers. Social media and consumer interaction are often at the forefront when discussing brands these days. It has always been the case that when new methods of reaching consumers become available, no marketer wants to miss out on the 'miracle' solution. The newest gadget or technique sooner or later finds its way into the marketing plan, at the very least as 'a test project'. But understanding the changing habits and behaviour of a generation is more important than hoping to capitalize on new technology or new media. The real question is, how do you evolve your brand, or even reinvent it, to ensure its appeal crosses generations? How do you establish and retain a real connection?

This book will help you to consider the evolution of different generations in society and what's important to them. Read through the research, get some insights from the interviews and the anecdotes about current brands, refresh your memory on some of the theoretical concepts that you may have forgotten about and discover some newer ways of thinking. It will become very clear that brands have to re-think their relationship to consumers. Either that or become old and obsolete to their current customers.

To make a product, give it an image, ask an agency to find a creative angle to make it memorable and carpet-bomb until you reach the desired awareness levels, might not work anymore. Consumers might not listen or even care. The main drivers of your brand are now the people that actually know about it and use it. Who knows about your brand, uses it and what they say about it, has become much more influential than the message you are broadcasting.

As far as I am concerned, the main elements that help to build strong brands have not changed. What has changed is that weaker brands can't get away with it anymore and that any mistakes that are made cost more. A strong, consistent identity for your brand has always been important. But as you have less control on how your brand is presented on the internet, it becomes even more important that you don't confuse people by changing personality and tone with every new re-launch.

Strong brands always had a more interesting and unique point of view to share with consumers. But today the depth and the authenticity of the stories behind a brand, and the skill with which they are told, have become more important because brand stories have become part of everyday conversation, be it real or virtual. More people are aware of your brand, more people have a strong opinion about it and every day more people find out the many new ways to share that opinion with others.

As current society moves towards total transparency, brands need to know what they stand for and who should care about them. This book delves into how the current generation feel about brands, and interact with them. It contains many practical insights and situations that I recognize from my own experiences, especially when I was helping to build the Nike Skateboarding brand. Here are a few insights from the book that I can testify to:

- The incredible importance of product and brand design to make your unique style visible and easy to recognize.

- The vital and growing role of channel management: where can a product be found, where can you really experience it and who are your true partners? Retail as a logistical middle man simply does not make any sense in a future where everything is so easily available.

- The power of story telling and original content, leading to a situation where there is no need to tell your own story because others are doing it for you. Relevant and exclusive information is really the new social currency.

- The power of collaboration and association between like-minded people and brands as opposed to the old-fashioned idea of us against the rest of the world.

I could continue but it all starts with one absolute insight: the key to brand survival over generations is authenticity and connectivity.

The essence is to let the organization BE the brand. Do not compromise your brand DNA, your history, your deepest conviction about why the brand exists. At the same time you must have a relationship with the current Generation Y that enables you to to understand their spirit and true habits, and let that guide the creative evolution of your brand. Capturing the spirit of an era to help evolve the core of a brand is very different from catching the next trend.

And that is what this book is about. I do not consider it part of the trendwatching or cool hunting industry. It is just a valuable tool to help you to understand the spirit and the habits of a generation. Nothing more, nothing less. It doesn't describe a model for capturing a younger audience. There is no way to manipulate youth. There is no menu of tips on how to 'seduce the next generation'. But it should encourage you, as a brand manager or marketing professional, to be yourself, to sometimes take inspiration from seemingly random information, to lose yourself in interesting stories and characters that might have nothing to do with your daily routine. And let this all lead you to an idea, a test, a project that fits your brand.

I guess it's being creative.

Gert Kerkstoel
Investor and former global business director, Nike SB

Introduction

When we were young, marketing to teens and young adults was really rather easy. We, Generation Xers true to type, were eager to tune ourselves to global brands and definitely wanted to start our yuppie careers in a famous multinational. The big corporations radiated the proof of the ultimate success. Just imagine... when we were 16 we'd be able to buy those big cool brands ourselves! And that's exactly what all brands were shouting at us. Buy us and you will be so cool! And oh yes, we loved it... we even believed it. Brands were projecting cool and aspiring images in their ads. They were setting the goals we all desired to achieve. They dictated how to dress, behave, walk and talk. We didn't doubt for a minute what the marketers were telling us. We even adored TV commercials, because we were the first generation to grow up with commercial stations and it was all so new and glamorous to us. Like forbidden fruit. Our parents and grandparents gave us an allowance from time to time and we all spent it hastily on Depeche Mode or Talking Heads vinyl records, just saving enough to buy a pair of Docs or All-Stars and some hair gel.

Today, things have dramatically changed. This youth generation has been bombarded with commercial messages from their birth. They have learned to filter out all those loud messages and they have been empowered by their parents and teachers to have an opinion of their own and never merely believe whatever somebody is proclaiming. But the global brands are still there. So are the commercial media. And there must be countless times more choice of both. Instead of new wave or synthpop records Gen Yers can choose and mix dozens of music genres at last.fm or iTunes, and what brand of gel, wax, clay, gum, spray, whip, cream-mousse, pomade, paste, texturizer, balm or lotion will they use to style their haircut tonight? To survive in the current cluttered and fragmented environment, today's teens and adolescents use collective peer wisdom and social connections. They believe what their best friends and parents are telling them and self-consciously want to explore what roads they should take.

And what are brands to do now? Shouting how cool they are isn't working anymore, that's for sure. Brands have lost their role model or oracle status. Whispering might be an option, but you still need to convince the confident teen to remove his white iPod earplug and bother to listen to you instead of to all the other teen whisperers. The main point is that you have to earn youth's respect, before you can even start the conversation about your brand. This book is all about connecting with a new generation who will determine how consumer markets evolve in the next three decades.

Although Generation Y still embraces cool brands, the ones that just claim they are cool, won't even reach their radar. It takes a great deal of effort to be cool and to stay hot for this consumer group. In working with media and advertisers in our day-to-day jobs, we have often experienced some insecurity in addressing youth markets. Of course, the pressure for marketers is high when they have to deal with the most marketing-savvy generation of teens and 20-year-olds ever. The huge number of competitors that join them in trying to convince this age cohort heightens the stress levels and kindles the battle between brands in youth markets. Unfortunately, this rat race often ends in a brand's mere surfing on youth fads and hypes. Many research agencies seem to have limited their youth insights to trend-watching and coolhunting. Although a youth brand needs to be aware of what's hot and what's not, just to stay in touch with its environment, we believe that there's much more to the equation.

Creating brands that touch their hearts implies a true knowledge of the underlying youth drivers and needs. In this book, we will explain the five key attributes of successful youth brands to you. Together they form the acronym CRUSH:

- Coolness;
- Realness;
- Uniqueness;
- Self-identification with the brand; and
- Happiness.

Each of these traits is the main topic of a chapter in this book. The CRUSH brand leverage model is based on five years of intensive youth research and consulting grounded in a daily connection with 13- to 29-year-olds. By optimizing your brand's performance with regard to the five characteristics of engaging youth brands, your brand too will enjoy an uplift in terms of satisfaction, peer-to-peer promotion (conversations about your brand) and purchase preference.

We have illustrated our youth brand vision with inspiring case stories from the past as well as the present including Sony Playstation, Axe/Lynx, Vans, Quicksilver, Red Bull, Levi's, Doctor Martens and many more. The CRUSH model was tried and tested through new international research as well as interviews with global marketing executives of successful brands such as Jack & Jones, Nokia, H&M, Nike, G-Star, Coca-Cola, and Tommy Hilfiger. If you're not working for a global and mainstream brand, it might be relatively easy to become cool for a while for parts of Gen Y. But the marketers and brands we have interviewed have managed to stay relevant for the entire youth market year after year. On the other hand, we have also inserted a number of 'unusual suspects', not-for-profit organizations connecting with youth in a low budget yet very effective way. A few examples include the Swedish Armed Forces and Cancer Society of Finland.

We first kick off this book by debunking some Millennial myths and explaining how this generation differs from others. What are the specific characteristics of adolescents that will affect the way they connect with brands today?

The impact of our vision on youth branding is explained in the second chapter, as an introduction to the subsequent parts that will deconstruct each of the five CRUSH dimensions.

The third chapter explores what being cool means for a brand. Is it necessary to be cool and is it possible to become a cool brand in every product category?

In Chapter 4 on real brands we will prove that brand authenticity really makes a difference for the critical Generation Y. But being authentic means completely different things for Gen Yers than for other generations.

Gen Yers are on a mission to become special or unique. That's why they are also looking for unique brands that help them to stand out. But how do you make your brand unique in a post-modern world full of choice? The fifth chapter tackles this subject.

Contrary to previous generations, Gen Yers were brought up in an atmosphere of equal relationships and co-decision making and that's exactly what they expect from brands today. This also means that brands should have a better knowledge of the values, interests and opinions of different youth lifestyle groups. The new consumer combines brands in an eclectic way to express his/her own individual identity. In Chapter 6 we will fully delve into the topics of identity development and self-identification with brands.

Today's youth generation is more emotional than ever. The last chapter deals with the way brands can offer them magic moments and arouse feelings of happiness.

Although in marketing there are never one-size-fits-all solutions, we are confident you will recognize the brand attributes that might need focus in your own market approach. Perhaps this book will even confront you with the blind spots in your current offer. By reading this summary of our findings, you will explore the Generation Y world. You will understand why the five brand components are essential for Gen Y and how your brand can tap into them.

We know that trying to capture the mindset of an entire generation is quite a vain endeavour. And although the world and this generation are more globalized than ever, we still feel it would be a bad idea to generalize too much. But we hope that by sharing our passion to understand and connect with these mind-blowing consumers, we will challenge you to develop relevant youth strategies and brands. Although the real difference will be made in your own creative marketing approach, we trust this book will help you to get a better grip on this fast-moving target group without losing your brand's identity in the next small trend. After all, it's all about staying true to your roots, but adapting to the changing environment and constantly finding new angles to keep this stimulus-oriented and emotional youth on board. We wish you an inspiring and exciting journey and look forward to hearing your feedback and thoughts via **www.howcoolbrandsstayhot.com**.

Last, but not least, on behalf of The Staying Alive Foundation we would like to thank you for buying this book. A quarter of the book's royalties are donated to the global HIV/AIDS charity that empowers young people. You can read more about the Foundation at the end of the book.

Joeri Van den Bergh and Mattias Behrer

Chapter One
Defining Generation Y

Today's youth are getting the most out of their lives. Youngsters do recognize that they are raised in an affluent world flooded with choices. For most of them, the question is not how to get something but rather what to choose. In this highly competitive society, brands realized that they had to increase marketing investments to be heard above the noise of the advertising clutter. Generation Y is not only aware of being marketed to but has grown up in an environment full of brands and commercial media; it's all they have ever known. The rise of digital media allowed youth to create their own personalized world. They are able to live their lives through new online and mobile communities. Today's 13- to 25-year-olds grew up in a world where mobile phones for children and teens became commonplace and the internet was being used at school. They are so conditioned to use these internet, MP3 and mobile technologies that deprivation of one of them would feel like having a limb removed. The way youth socialize, build relationships, shop and make career choices is heavily affected by the era they have been raised in. There is an ancient saying that bears much truth: 'people resemble their times more than they resemble their parents'. Gen Yers are children of the cyber revolution. Just like the industrial revolution changed lifestyle and culture by the end of the 19th century, the omnipresent connectivity and digital advancement has reshaped the social DNA of our current and future youth generations.[1]

The oldest part of Generation Y is already entering the job market, getting married and becoming the heads of households. If you haven't already targeted this cohort, now is an important time to introduce them to your brand.[2] A better understanding of what makes young consumers tick will improve your brand positioning and marketing to the target group. Whatever business you are in, this generation will make or break your market success. The long-term flourishing of your company depends on how well your brand strategy responds to the demand of this new consumer generation.

In this chapter, we will dive into the characteristics of Generation Yers. More than half of the world's population is under the age of 30. Gen Y is currently one of the largest demographic groups and will soon outnumber the Baby Boomer generation. In the United States alone, there are over 70 million Gen Yers with over $200 billion in purchasing power. Their generational impact on society, culture, business, politics and economics in the next three decades will be similar in magnitude to that of the Baby Boomer generation. We will indicate how the arrival of this new consumer group affects branding and marketing. Of course, there are as many differences within generations as there are among generations. It's never a good idea to generalize too much, especially with a youth generation that has never been so ethnically and lifestyle diverse as today. Still, certain aspects of society and parenting will influence the way your marketing and branding campaigns are perceived by young consumers.

WTF do you think you're doing?

In the early years of the new millennium, peer-to-peer file sharing networks such as KaZaA and Napster were popular among youngsters for uploading and downloading MP3 files. When Madonna launched her April 2003 album *American Life* she decided to fight internet piracy. She flooded the file-sharing communities with digital decoys that looked like tracks from her new album but were actually recordings of her cursing and snarling at the illegal downloaders. Only a few days after the decoy files were released, new versions of Madonna's a cappella started to pop up on the networks with new backing tracks and music underneath. Soon radio stations and clubs around the world were playing the many pirate remixes of Madonna's unintended new single titled *WTF*. Dmusic.com started a competition to find the best version of *WTF*. Fifteen of the best illegal remixes were compiled and released on an album by an independent label. On 19 April 2003 Madonna's official website was hacked and every real track from her new album was pinned to the homepage free for anyone to download. Across the homepage, the hacker posted a response to Madonna saying: 'This is what the f**k I think I'm doing.'[3]

X, Y, Z: three youth generations

Generational labels are usually the result of popular culture. Some are linked to a historic event, others are derived from drastic social or demographic changes or from a big turn in the calendar.

Millennials

Millennials belong to the third category. The term refers to those born between 1980 and 1996, although different authors use different data. It is the first generation to come of age in the new millennium. 'Y' was chosen as a popular label as they are the successors of the Generation X, but there are many synonyms such as Generation Why, Generation Search, Generation Next, the Net generation, the digital natives, the dot.com generation, the Einstein generation, Echo Boomers, etc. They are the children of the throngs of Baby Boomer parents, which explains why there are so many in spite of the declining fertility rates. Baby Boomers gave birth at a later age (average mum aged 30) and were consequently more mature in their role as parents and tutors. They have raised their children as coaches with one central notion: individual empowerment. Gen Y children have been taught that all opinions are equally important. Boomers included the view of their children in every discussion or decision. Parents gave their Gen Y children the chance to learn and experience a lot of different things (in travel, sports, art, music...). The result of this upbringing is that Gen Yers are more critical and cynical and generally difficult to wow. As 'stimulus junkies' they have a shorter attention span and an irrepressible need for instant gratification. If they have an idea, they will immediately want to execute it. Their parents have served them hand and foot, and that is what they will expect in life, work and relationships too.

Generation X

Generation X consists of people who were born from 1965 to 1979. Other labels for this generation include: the Baby Busters, Post Boomers, Slacker Generation, indifferent, shadow or invisible generation and Lost Generation. Ironically, the Generation X label was popularized by Douglas Coupland's book *Generation X: tales for an accelerated culture* describing a generation that actually defied labels – 'just call us X'. Not only did the label stick, it has also produced labels for the next two generations – Y and Z. Xers began their career in the early 1990s when there was a recession and much downsizing of the work-force. They adopted the work ethic and focus of the Boomers but were more individualistic and pessimistic.

Baby Boomers

The Baby Boomers' label is drawn from the post-Second World War spike in fertility that began in 1946 and ended in 1964 as a result of the commercial launch of birth control pills. They grew up in an era of economic growth and full employment. The austerity from the Silent Generation was replaced by technological advancement and increasing freedom and leisure time. Boomers have lived through years of incredible change and are therefore very adaptive and flexible.[4]

The Silent Generation

The Silent Generation covers adults born from 1928 to 1945. They are the children of the Second World War and the Great Depression. Their 'silent' label refers to conformist instincts and contrasts with the noisy anti-establishment Boomers.

Differences between generations

Pew Research Center found that the majority of generation members believe they own a unique and distinctive identity. In Table 1.1 you will find the spontaneously uttered reasons of each generation for feeling distinctive. Although the previous youth generation X also cite technology as their generation's source of distinctiveness, just 12 per cent (half the amount of Gen Yers) say this. For Generation Y, technology is more than just their gadgets; they have fused their social lives into it.[5] In InSites Consulting's global social media study, more than 70 per cent of the 15- to 24-year-olds have created a profile on social networking sites, compared with 31 per cent of Boomers and less than 20 per cent of the Silent Generation.[6] Of Gen Yers who use Facebook, 56 per cent visit the social network every day, compared to 47 per cent of Gen Xers and 38 per cent of Baby Boomers.

One third of Yers access the site using their mobile phone. Among Baby Boomers, this is a mere 13 per cent and it's 24 per cent with Xers.[7] Technology makes life easier for Millennials and is bringing family and friends closer together. On the other hand, if parents join Facebook and invite their son or daughter to become friends, this might lead to uncomfortable situations. Online confrontations between generations happen, especially because older generations are often unaware of the implicit social rules (tagging, wall postings, etc). Two young girls created MyParentsJoinedFacebook.com to collect screenshots of the awkward situations that happen when parents invade their online community and break the implicit rules of privacy or 'friending'. Or, as they sarcastically mention on the website: 'Congratulations! Your parents just joined Facebook. Your life is officially over.'[8] For Boomers, work ethic is the most prominent identity claim, for the Silent Generation it is the Second World War and the Depression that makes them stand apart.[9]

TABLE 1.1   What makes generations unique?

Generation Y	Generation X	Boomer	Silent
1 Technology use (24%)	Technology use (12%)	Work ethic (17%)	WWII/Depression (14%)
2 Music culture (11%)	Work ethic (11%)	Respectful (14%)	Smarter (13%)
3 Liberal/tolerant (7%)	Conservative (7%)	Values/moral (8%)	Honest (12%)
4 Smarter (6%)	Smarter (6%)	'Baby boom' (6%)	Work ethic (10%)
5 Clothes (5%)	Respectful (5%)	Smarter (5%)	Values/Morals (10%)

SOURCE: Pew Research Center, Jan 2010.

It's not just technology that is shaping the personality of our youth, it's actually also the other way around. If you reverse the direction of causality, it's a perspective that helps in explaining technological evolutions. The Boomers were a generation that was very much concerned with self-sufficiency and they took the mainframe computers from their parents and turned them into personal computers in the 1980s, supporting individual work on everyone's desk. Generation X took that individualism to a next level. They were interested in making money by buying low and selling high. Gen Xers introduced online auction sites such as eBay in the 1990s and they have boosted e-commerce in general. Today it is because of the social needs and the peer tethering of Generation Y as well as their high need for me-marketing that the web has turned into a network of social communities.[10]

Generation Z: the new kids on the block

And what about the generation following Gen Y? This new generation was born after 1996. They are the children of Generation X and still preschoolers and primary school children today. Hence, not much is known about them at this point. Some have called these children Generation Z as the normal alphabet successors of the Y and X Generations. You can be pretty sure we will see a bunch of new names popping up over the next years. Larry Rosen of California State University, has already coined 'iGeneration' in his book *Rewired: Understanding the iGeneration and the Way They Learn*. The 'i' is not only referring to the popular Wii and iPods but also to their need for customization and individualizing. Thanks to digital TV, they can watch whatever they want at any time, stop live television and fully customize their media consumption. They were born in a society in which constant connectivity and individual mobile devices are normal. They started using the computer mouse at the early age of 18 months. They don't see technology as an instrument, for them it is just a part of life. The way this will affect their thinking and behaviour is not clear yet, but they will certainly adopt new learning styles focusing on knowing how to gain access to every piece of information, synthesizing it and integrating it into their life.[11]

How permanent are generational characteristics?

A question often heard during speeches on Generation Y is: aren't those youngsters just in a life stage, a mindset that they will outgrow when they age? Well, the answer is: NO! Experience with previous generations such as Gen X has shown that the mindset of youngsters won't change when they reach the age of 40. Generations do not change over time to look identical to their parents at the same adult age. A generation is a product of current times and obviously the technologies, media, social markers and events that uniquely shaped them. Values, attitudes and priorities set during youth will remain identical in the rest of their life.[12]

Facebook prompts giant snowball fight in Washington DC

When in early February 2010 a snow blizzard covered the East coast of the United States, someone created a Facebook page inciting social network members to have a snowball fight near the White House two days later. More than 2,000 people turned up to participate in the giant fight, causing unseen traffic problems in Washington DC. Live reporting of the fight could be followed on Twitter and on YouTube where more than 400 videos of the snowball fight were posted. Traditional media had much more trouble reporting the event with TV reporters being the ultimate target for the snowball throwers.[13]

The ten commandments and seven deadly sins of Gen Y

At the end of 2009, MTV Networks International conducted a large study to understand the values, hopes and dreams of young people in Europe. The study, named 'Youthopia', made a snapshot of contemporary youth values. Seven thousand Gen Y participants (aged 16–34) from seven European countries participated.

In order to understand better how Gen Y values compare to those of previous generations, MTV Networks International came up with a creative exercise that enabled participants to rewrite the Ten Commandments and Seven Deadly Sins for the modern age.

The first key difference was that young people today stressed that their commandments should comprise a list of 'Dos' rather than 'Don'ts'. It was also interesting to note that despite the global recession and reports of record youth unemployment, the hopes and dreams of young people remain surprisingly intact. Across Europe, their overall outlook and codes for living life were overwhelmingly positive.

The **Ten Commandments of Youth** include:

- Have faith in yourself.
- Respect your parents.
- Be honest.
- Take responsibility for your own life.
- Live life to the full and be passionate.
- Keep your promises.
- Work hard to succeed but not to the detriment of others.
- Be tolerant of others' differences.
- Be happy and optimistic, even in adversity.
- Create, don't destroy (yourself, others, the earth, values).

The **new Seven Deadly Sins** include:

- Racism.
- Dishonesty.
- Bullying.
- Greed.
- Adultery.
- Anger.
- Envy.

Through an emphasis on understanding Gen Y values, Youthopia highlighted the inaccuracies that exist today in how young people are portrayed in the media versus how they see themselves. Old-fashioned stereotypes and terms such as lazy, rebellious, promiscuous, hedonistic and celebrity-obsessed have been replaced with industrious, optimistic, family and friend-focused, choosing conformity and respect.[14]

A cause without rebels: the new parent–child paradigm

Surprisingly, Pew Research Center's survey revealed that 79 per cent of the US population believes there is a 'generation gap' in society. This is 5 per cent higher than the 74 per cent that saw this gap in the roaring year 1969. But the modern gap is mostly about the different ways in which old and young are using technology. Only about a quarter of those surveyed saw conflicts between young and old in the United States. Among today's Generation Y, 52 per cent say becoming a good parent is one of the most important things in their life. That's 10 per cent higher than youth in 1997 (Generation X). Eight out of ten youngsters applaud the classic ideal of getting married and starting a family.[15] Gen Y get along well with their parents. They report fewer fights with mum or dad than older adults say they had with their own parents when they were growing up.[16] Six out of ten US teens say their family eats dinner together at least four nights a week. Eighty five per cent identifies a parent – rather than a peer – as their best friend. Of these, 53 per cent call Mum their best friend versus 32 per cent who say it's Dad.[17]

Little Emperor Syndrome

For many parents of Gen Yers, getting their teen's approval is the most important thing in their lives. They treat their children as friends rather than subordinates. A major explanation for this is that the average number of children per female has drastically dropped, while the divorce rates have gone up. Gen Y children get far more attention than previous latchkey-youth generations. It's the Western variant of China's 'Little Emperor Syndrome'. Parents project high hopes for a better future on their only child and turn him or her into the major focus of the family. As the family tree increasingly gets smaller (with fewer branches of brothers, sisters, cousins, aunts and uncles), the bonds between parent and child are strengthening. Moreover, Baby Boomer parents have shifted away from the traditional disciplinarian role as a reaction to their own relationship with their parents. Today's parental environment is one of open democratic dialogue and negotiation, rather than conflict, rebellion and resistance. Two-thirds of parents claim to ask the opinion of their children before making big decisions such as choosing holidays. According to parents, this openness is the glue to keep the family together and an investment in the future. Three-quarters of parents claim their relationship with their children is more open than the one their own parents had with them. Discipline has been replaced by tolerance. Today's young people simply don't need to be rebellious and difficult anymore.[18] Unilever has created DontFretTheSweat.com to help parents to navigate the many physical and emotional challenges their adolescents face. With community partners, they assembled a panel of experts who are giving advice on the educational website. The site is endorsed by three deodorant and antiperspirant brands of Unilever: Dove, Degree and Suave.[19] Dove's 'campaign for real beauty' also successfully connected Millennials with their mums.

Helicopter parenting

Youngsters are often shielded from the realities of life. 'Helicopter parents' increasingly try to protect their Gen Y children from growing up too quickly. They are called 'helicopters' because they are always hovering to have a permanent view on what their children (even if they are older than 20) are doing and to manage their lives as a coach or manager. The mobile phone has become a new and indispensable body part of youth. A substantial 83 per cent of them sleep with their mobile phone turned on in their bed. The device has also received the function of an umbilical cord for their worried parents. Through texting and voice calls they are able to contact their children at any time and check on their safety. Unfortunately, in our discussion groups, the youngsters often admit they don't pick up their phones if they see it's their old folks.

Boomerang children

Parents are increasingly replacing monthly or weekly allowances with need-based money handouts. This change resulted in a 'want it now' generation that is not learning the real world value of money and will take longer to live independently. The trend of young people delaying departure from the family home ('Hotel Mum and Dad') has been boosted by the economic recession. It has also led to an increase in 'boomerang children', returning to parental homes after a period of independent living. In 1980 in the United States, 11 per cent of the 25- to 34-year-olds were living with their parents. By 2008, this figure had risen to 20 per cent and according to the Pew survey, 10 per cent of young adults, aged 18 to 34, have moved back with their parents during 2009 because of the recession. The portion of 18- to 29-year-olds who live alone has declined to 7.3 per cent in 2009, compared to 7.9 per cent in 2007.[20]

A consequence of Gen Y's closeness with their parents and the boomerang trend is the increasing and enduring influence of young-sters on the family purchases. By staying at home, Gen Yers are get-ting a lot of perks. Parents are covering their bills, food, toiletries, rent and travel and acting as chauffeurs, cleaners, cooks and laundry services for them. Where young adults used to leave home in search of independence, today they are quite comfortable in bedrooms that are mini-flats stuffed with their own TV, DVD and game consoles.[21] For many important decisions in life such as a job, housing, banking or a car, Gen Y will automatically turn their heads towards their parents. HR managers and university selection committees have even reported an increased presence of parents during the interviews. It is the new paradox in youth sociology. Kids are confronted with the adult world at an earlier age because parents want them to be stimu-lated to explore the world. This phenomenon is called 'KGOY' (Kids Getting Older Younger). On the other hand, they are much slower in taking independent decisions. More than 8 out of 10 youngsters report that their parents are always available for them 24 hours a day.[22] For parents, being an adult has become dull and unattractive. Youth is everything. They want to remain youthful as long as they can. Many Gen Yers admit their parents want to wear what they are wearing, adore co-shopping and they even regularly swap clothes. The line between parents and children is increasingly blurring.

Insane in the brain: teenage neurology

Teen brains are still under construction. Their hardware is to blame for the unpredictable behaviour that is led far more often by their emotions than by their logic. Neuroscience is slowly discovering the secrets of teenage brains. Scientific studies indicate that adolescence is *the* period in which habits and behaviour are shaped. Two pro-cesses are responsible for this blueprint. On the one hand, we see an explosion in the creation of grey matter.[23] This boost in thinking power gives teenagers the opportunity to excel in all kinds of areas. The more they engage in certain behaviour, the better they will become at it and the more skills will be anchored in their brains. At the same time, cells that are never used are eliminated. The 'use it or lose it' theory dictates that if teenagers do not engage in certain activities during their adolescences, they will never do this anymore simply because the neural connections will be absent for these activities. For example, if teenagers are not exposed to a healthy lifestyle, their brains will be built up around the famous sex, drugs and rock 'n' roll mindset.[24] Because teenage brains are still very flexible in this period, it is an important moment for brands and products to communicate to this target group. If people are consuming a certain product or brand in their young years, their brain will be programmed for similar behaviour when they are adults.

Emotional roller coasters

However, not all communication will have an equal effect on the adolescent brain. Neuroscientists have revealed that some strategies work better to connect with teenagers. Teenage brains function like an emotional roller coaster. Brain researchers have uncovered that this is a direct consequence of the brain growth. Unlike adults, their frontal lobes are still in full development. This brain area is responsible for taming the wild beast reflexes in us. It suppresses emotional and primitive reactions and makes us behave like good citizens. Frontal lobes also help us with logical reasoning. They are directly related to another brain structure called the 'amygdale', the source for emotional processing. In the adult brain, the frontal lobe is in control and triggers coming from the amygdale are largely ignored. It is only in case of dominant emotional stimuli or when we sedate the frontal lobe, by drinking too much alcohol for instance, that emotions take the upper hand. With teenagers the amygdale is in the driving seat. Because the frontal lobes are still immature, they will show more emotional and impulsive behaviour. Research has also shown that adolescents are more eager to respond to emotional stimuli.[25] Emotional information is more likely to be noticed, processed and remembered. In terms of consumption, they are looking for stimulation of their positive emotions.[26]

Identity construction and brands

Although the amygdale and frontal lobes play different roles in teenage brains, it is exactly the interplay between them that is responsible for their most important development: the creation of an own identity. Adolescence is typically the stage in life where you start reflecting about the self. Youngsters spend a great deal of their time trying out different roles. By engaging in different activities, they try to shape their identity. Their self-concept is shaped by past experiences. Positive life experiences such as getting positive reactions to a new outfit, good grades at school or positive feedback on your guitar play, help in building a positive self-concept. Failure or negative feedback leads to a more negative self-concept. All these experiences cause emotional reactions in the amygdale. The amygdale reinforces the positive experiences by sending a signal to the frontal lobes that will give it more importance within the self-construct. For marketers it is important to realize that consumption can play a powerful role in shaping one's identity. If young people get positive feedback when consuming your brand, it will be more likely to find an emotional connection with them. This will lead to a stronger place of your brand in a youth's self-identity.

Idealism and activism

The frontal brain lobes are also capable of going from the concrete to the abstract world. A consequence of the abstract mind is idealistic behaviour. Because abstract thinking capacities are growing, teenagers at a certain age will finally be able to understand how the world works. By reflecting on the world, they will be capable of envisioning a perfect ideal world. During that phase, youngsters can become very critical about the actions of past generations. At first, this idealism is often reflected in endless discussions with their parents and teachers. When growing up this idealism is often transferred into activism. Youngsters join animal rights movements, become a member of political parties or organize social actions with their youth movements. Brands and products are not spared from their critical judgements. Company processes, origin of goods and advertising are studied and can be used as a symbol of protest. Other brands embrace this idealism by explicitly supporting good causes.[27]

Since 2008, H&M has brought the collection 'Fashion Against Aids' on the market (see Figure 1.1). They have joined forces in the battle against AIDS in cooperation with Designers against AIDS and celebrities such as Rihanna, Timbaland and many more. It was the right moment to take action. To this new generation of youngsters AIDS was something that had happened to Freddie Mercury in the 1980s and the number of HIV infections was on the rise again. A quarter of the collection's sales are donated to youth HIV/AIDS awareness projects to promote the message of safe sex. By April 2010, over £2.6 million had been raised.[28]

FIGURE 1.1   The H&M Fashion against AIDS collection

Risk-taking behaviour

During puberty, teenagers often involve themselves in risk-taking behaviour. Many parents can verify that they have caught their son or daughter taking drugs or secretly drinking alcohol. Boys and girls that were known as quiet kids, decide to sneak out in the middle of the night, hitch a ride to a party and terrify their parents who notice their absence in the morning. Teachers are confronted with youngsters who decide to hang around in pubs rather than attend classes and principals wonder why they decide to make a small fire in the school bin. It seems that at a certain age, teenagers lose their senses and have an irresistible urge to indulge in stupid and dangerous behaviour. Again... their brains are to blame. Risk-taking behaviour is something we all involve in on a daily base.[29] To be successful we need to engage in new and unknown behaviour: if adults do not dare to take up responsibility for a certain job at work, they will never feel the resultant gratification. If you never start talking to unfamiliar people, you will be stuck in your small network forever. There needs to be a first time to drive a car or bike. Both adults and youngsters need to take risk in order to achieve something in life. There is however more than achievement alone as a reason to engage in risk-taking behaviour. We seek danger also for the thrill of it. Surviving risky behaviour leads to pleasure. Think of the feeling when you exit a roller coaster or the kick you experience when you have successfully addressed a large crowd. There is one specific substance in the brain called 'dopamine' that has been associated with pleasure seeking. Experiments on rats have shown that taking away the dopamine systems leads to passive and lazy behaviour. The test animals showed no intention to explore their environment. Dopamine stimulates adults as well as youngsters to take action that leads to pleasure. The more it is activated, the more you will seek out pleasure and the more you will take decisive action to find new thrills. So far, it is clear that risk taking and pleasure seeking is a human proclivity. How can neuroscience explain why youngsters seem particularly eager to undertake stupid things? Research has shown that dopamine regulation in the developing young brain is out of balance.[30] Some studies have found evidence for an overproduction of dopamine that turns youngsters into mega pleasure seekers. Other research claims rather that the risk behaviour would be caused by a sudden decrease in dopamine production in comparison with childhood output. In order to reach the same levels of reward, adolescents are condemned to undertake more risky behaviour. Again there is an important relationship with the premature development of the frontal lobes. The adult brain suppresses dangerous behaviour because its frontal lobes can make an estimation of the consequences of their actions. However, youngsters live in a physiological situation where their brains tell them to take risks but cannot stop their urge for pleasure. Risk-taking is a theme that many successful youth brands are using. In 2010, the clothing brand Diesel embraced this concept in an advertising campaign on the theme 'be stupid' (see the following Box).

Be Stupid

Diesel, the international jeans brand, launched 'Be Stupid', a campaign that encourages consumers to take risks and move beyond the smart and sensible track of life. The campaign, developed by Anomaly London, includes online, press and outdoor advertisements featuring 'stupid' acts, a digital recruitment campaign for the Diesel music video/2010 catalogue, and viral activity outlining the company's Stupid philosophy.

The Diesel Stupid Philosophy is translated on their website (**www.diesel.com/bestupid/**) as follows:

> Well, we're with stupid. Stupid is the relentless pursuit of a regret-free life. Smart may have the brains... but stupid has the balls. The smart might recognize things for how they are. The stupid see things for how they could be. Smart critiques. Stupid creates. The fact is if we didn't have stupid thoughts we'd have no interesting thoughts at all. Smart may have the plans... but stupid has the stories....
> So, BE STUPID

The Diesel Stupid philosophy taps into youth's proneness to pleasure seeking and taking risks. It fights rational frontal lobe thinking and encourages youngsters to not suppress their emotions and impulses. David Ireland, Diesel's Vice President of Marketing in the United States, commented: 'In the campaign, "stupid" actually means "brave". We're really getting back to what Diesel is all about. "Be Stupid" is not an ad campaign, it's a manifesto.'[31]

Stimulation junkies

Today, anything is media. Everything and everyone is constantly spitting out messages whether it is on Twitter, SMS or Facebook. Young people were raised in a cocoon with their anxious parents often being afraid to let them go out. It is no surprise this generation has embraced technologies to build new communities through tweeting, texting and friending. Equipped with a bunch of portable media Gen Y is never alone or out of touch with their friends. By analysing more than 40,000 monthly US mobile bills, Nielsen determined that US teens sent on average 3,146 texts a month during the third quarter of 2009. This equals more than 10 texts every waking non-school hour.[32] Youngsters get addicted to this constant entertainment and distraction. They can't think of a life without stimulation and variation. If they are for some reason disconnected, they feel boredom more than any generation before. Constant connection and compelling content are no luxury, they are fundamental everyday life expectations. iPhones are affecting the daily routines of youngsters, telling them when to get up, what to do, what their friends are doing, etc. The first thing many youngsters do when they get up is to switch on their computer, if they still switch it off to begin with.[33] Their mobile is always on, unless the batteries have run down.

The triumph generation

Ask a Gen Yer when adulthood begins, and chances are high he/she will answer 30. For this generation your early twenties are a time to move around, try different things and date different people.[34] This need for stimulation and instant gratification is also translated in consumer behaviour. Generation Y shows a relaxed attitude towards consumer purchasing and debts. In *Gen BuY. How tweens, teens and twenty-somethings are revolutionizing retail*, Yarrow and O'Donnell state that shopping is 'the new weather'. Talking about clothes, music, cars and the latest techno gadgets brings Gen Y together and keeps them engaged. Buying fashion and entertainment items are vital to leading a happy and hedonistic life and shopping is just another form of exciting entertainment to them. Shopping provides a 'mental vacation'. To de-stress from their busy lives, they will search for pure indulgence. Shopping plays an important emotional role and helps youth to calm anxiety during the many life transitions they have to cope with.[35] The large amounts of non-essential purchases are justified as 'deserved' or a 'reward'. Sometimes, buying a gift for someone else is a good reason for a 'treat' of their own. For this reason, Gen Y is sometimes also dubbed the 'triumph' generation. They are spoiled with parental attention and expect a lot of feedback and attention at work too. This perception of 'entitlement' has changed the perception of credit card usage and lending services with this generation. After all, finances are of secondary importance to the pursuit of happiness through consumption.[36] Although Gen Yers have also suffered from the global economic downturn – the youth unemployment rates are the highest since the Second World War – they don't seem to panic. In a report of PricewaterhouseCoopers only 25 per cent of Gen Y consumers say the economy has significantly changed their spending behaviour, while 36 per cent of Generation Xers and 37 per cent of Boomers say it has changed their shopping habits.[37] They are more compulsive shoppers than the former generations.

A fragmented world

Through online technology, youth get what they want without having to look too hard. They live in a culture of convenience, consuming snippets devoid of ever seeing the entirety. There's no need to research a topic when you can just Google it to find the answer. This short cut way of life is something they have been brought up with. Instead of knowing a few topics in depth, they have a little knowledge about everything. This affects the society more than you might think. The length of a *Time* cover story has dropped from 4,500 to 2,800 words in the past 20 years. Average news sound bites have slipped from 42 seconds in 1965 to a present-day low of 8 seconds. We want more entertainment better and faster.[38]

Bite-size commitment

Youngsters pick and mix individual parts of media to create their own personalized products and services that fit their individual needs. There's no need to buy a whole album on iTunes, you can create your own. Bite-size formats in a much wider variety have replaced mass and uniform media formats. Gen Y is only bite-size committed. The good side of this is that they are much more open to hop between different styles. They listen to different music styles and festivals offer six to 10 different performance stages to fill in the needs of variety and style switching. RSS feeds on the internet allow you to make your own personalized multimedia news medium. But this doesn't mean that traditional media have lost their meaning to Gen Yers. When chilling out, a newspaper or TV programme caters much better for their need of de-stressing and relaxing. In one of our studies on the use of newspapers among youngsters, we have found that a traditional daily is linked with 'pyjama moments'.

A friend's focus

Now that online tools enable youth to achieve social interactions, the broader offline community has eroded. Students listen to lectures without having to attend the sessions together with fellow students. They are less and less interested in connecting with those around them that are outside their immediate inner circle of friends, family and relatives. New forms of online communities, MMORPGs (Massively Multiplayer Online Role Playing Games such as *Runescape* and *World of Warcraft*) and belonging to groups like those on social networks have filled the void created by this hyper-fragmented environment.

This generation has different technologies, media, brands and a number of different core friendship groups of which they select the right ones according to situation, event, time and mood. Friends are fun to be with, more understanding than anyone else and can be tribally differentiated for different needs and moments.[39]

Implications for brands

Brands targeting Gen Y should offer the same degree of choice and allow young people to interact with the brand elements they like. Gen Yers are creating their own personal brands by combining competitors with personality traits that reflect their own identity. Youngsters are more fickle today but they tend to be selectively loyal to those elements of brands that touch their hearts and that keep their promise. It is up to brands to fit into the complex identity of youngsters today rather than the other way around. Brands aren't dictating styles or image anymore.

Another result of the fragmentation is that competition for brands has surpassed the traditional category borders. Brands need to tap into the need for new cohesion and group belonging by bringing youngsters with shared passions together.[40] In 2006, Nike launched Nike+: technology that tracks data of every run and connects runners from all around the world at the **nikeplus.com** website. They log on and sign up to register their running programmes and goals. The key development to bring runners together on the web was the Sport Kit sensor that synchronizes with an Apple iPod or iPhone and tracks runners' speed, distance and calories burned. When runners dock their iPod the data are automatically uploaded on the nikeplus community. On the website different tailor-made training programmes are available and members can check out the most recent activity of runners in their own neighbourhood. They can either try to achieve their own goals or be more competitive and challenge others in the community. The success of the community has also translated into sales results for the company. Before Nike+, the brand accounted for 48 per cent of all running-shoe sales in the United States. Two years later, in 2008, the share had grown to 61 per cent. Of course, this growth cannot be reduced to the success of Nike+. Although product innovations play an important role, choosing running shoes is very much connected to habit and the Nike+ community and tools stimulate runners either to stick with Nike shoes or to buy a pair when they were used to another brand.[41]

From living in a fragmented world that is giving them continuously more freedom and opportunities, Gen Y also feel more concerned and insecure. More freedom equals more responsibility and finding out what's right and what's wrong. Youngsters feel the need for more meaningful things in life: stability, harmony and authenticity. This search can really feel like a burden to them and that's why they want to be connected with their friends.[42] Brands need to acknowledge this search for authenticity. Although Gen Y favours peer-to-peer reporting (Twitter, social networks and blogs) over traditional media, they still see TV and TV commercials as the most trustful medium that is suited for brand building. They know that TV advertising is expensive and it is therefore a sign that a company or brand on TV must be stable and successful.

You are worth less than one-tenth of a Whopper!

Early 2009, ad agency Crispin Porter & Bogusky created the 'Whopper Sacrifice' campaign for Burger King. The Facebook application promised a coupon for a free burger if participants deleted 10 friends from their list on the social network. If you were unfriended, the app sent a notification explaining that your friend had more love for the whopper than for you. The campaign was a huge success. In only a few days' time, the application was installed 60,000 times, more than 200,000 people got unfriended and nearly 20,000 coupons were distributed. After 10 days, Facebook disabled the Burger King campaign claiming that it was violating user privacy. Of course, the ban led to even more buzz for the viral social media campaign.[43] 'Unfriending' was elected as 'word of the year 2009' by the *Oxford Dictionary*.

Crowd sourcing and co-creation

Open source is a technique used in the development of computer code. It means that the coding allows other participants to cooperate and build better software and applications. The 'open source' idea is very much in line with the expectations of Generation Y. It has evolved much further than just software and computer code and is the backbone of many Web 2.0 applications. Wikipedia for instance is an open source encyclopaedia and dictionary that is not only constantly building better definitions but is also updated amazingly fast. Less than two hours after one of Michael Jackson's employees called 911 on 25 June 2009, Wikipedia reported Jackson's cardiac arrest. The open source site had beaten the CNNbrk Twitter stream by 18 minutes and was updated more than one hour before the first mainstream news article appeared on **MSNBC.com**.[44] Wikipedia servers received 1.24 million requests for the English article about Michael Jackson in the first hour only, 8.7 million in the first 24 hours and 14.4 million in the first seven days.[45]

Tony Whoop-de Doo Blair

At the end of 2009, the online encyclopaedia Wikipedia had to struggle for life. As a non-profit organization, they urgently needed 5.5 million euros. The fans of the online knowledge bank managed to rake in the required amount in less than eight weeks. Google added 1.5 million euros to the banking account as a mark of honour to what Sergey Brin, co-founder of Google, named 'one of the biggest triumphs of the internet'. The encyclopaedia is 10 years old. At first, it was named 'Nupedia' but the publishing admission process seemed to be too strict and lengthy, resulting in only a few articles online after several months. In January 2001 Wikipedia was born. The encyclopaedia gave power to the users by offering wikis, a software application that allows multiple users to contribute to the same text simultaneously. Nowadays, Wikipedia provides more than 14 million articles in 270 languages. More than 300,000 unique visitors a month find their way to the site. The whole concept relies on the mutual trust of the Wikipedia users. In the past, there were some stories about the CIA editing Wikipedia entries or the BBC adding 'W****r' as George Bush's middle name. Jokers were able to include in Tony Blair's entry that he has Hitler posters hanging above his bed and his official name really was 'Tony Whoop-de Doo Blair'. The site suffered from April Fool attacks each year. Meanwhile, articles on living personalities can't easily be changed anymore and the English version is experimenting with editors.[46]

User-generated content

Generation Yers like the idea of being in full control of everything and don't passively accept what is given to them. They embrace ownership of content and want to be able to edit and change their environment every minute. Youth marketers should adapt the same 'open source' philosophy. A brand is not what a company wants it to be, it's what Gen Y consumers want it to be.

Online tools have made it possible for youth to create their own unique support structures through interactions with friends. They have a constant open feedback channel with their peers that will help them make decisions, no matter whether they are choosing a movie to watch, a new pair of jeans to buy or a boyfriend to date. These connections are as real to Gen Yers as offline supports. They often claim they have 200 friends on Facebook who they know personally, which would be quite difficult in the offline world. Although it is hard to understand for older generations, these new 'passive' type of friends are very valuable to them. Gen Yers around the world have 140 Facebook friends on average, compared to 91 among Gen Xers and 64 among Baby Boomers.[47]

Trusted brands become friends

Gen Yers are cynical about the way brands behave and are no longer willing to trust anything based solely on faith. They would rather trust unknown peers than brands and have the tools to undercut the authority of brands and advise each other. Word-of-mouth marketing is therefore more effective as they tend to trust their friends' opinions. Online friends don't replace traditional real-world friendships. They are an extension of existing friendship groups. An offline friend will call them on their birthday, while an online one may write a message on their online space. The online world is Gen Y's entertainment, it is not their life. Media that reach them through their peers' filter are automatically relevant. Facebook is one of the main filters for young people today. It delivers content that is almost always relevant and organizes many aspects of their lives: events, music, photos and communications. It's Gen Y's diary.

Of Gen Yers that are active on social networks, 4 out of 10 befriend brands, compared to 31 per cent of Gen Xers and 27 per cent of Baby

Boomers.[48] Brands on social networks should behave like friends connecting with them, not just like distant brands. But they should not try to act as a friend in the traditional offline form, rather as one of the passive friendships that exist and develop in online social networks. Just like with their other passive friendships they will get to know you through watching and gaining an insight into the brand's online life. Appealing brands do not dictate but engage them by providing involvement and perceived control over the brand. Gen Y wants a less top-down and more equal relationship with brands than Generation X. Brands in social networks should offer them tangible services or sponsored utilities instead of advertising. Youngsters are turned off when a brand is seen as an uninvited intruder into their space.

When a brand's behaviour is not transparent to them, they will assume it is hiding something from them and is dishonest. The increased marketing savvyness means that they are now demanding something back from brands. Brands need to work harder to build a connection with young target groups and authenticity is key. They are not just seen as product providers but as life and lifestyle supporters. This youth generation has a much greater emotional attachment to brands which display that they really understand their lifestyles and make themselves relevant by supporting their needs. Gen Y puts much more emphasis on brand experience and brand credibility.

Machinima mania

Machinima are user-generated computer animation videos that use the 3-D graphics of video games. The name is a contraction of machine cinema and originates from recordings of gameplay in first-person shooters such as *Doom* and *Quake*. When storylines were added 'quakemovies' were born. MTV has made machinima a mainstream trend by airing *Video Mods* on MTV2. The broadcast featured music videos using characters from video games such as *The Sims* and *Need for Speed*. Machinima is a good illustration of the open source philosophy of Gen Y. Although this Gen Y way of thinking is criticized a lot because of copyright claims, it spurs creativity and innovation.[49]

A soap called 'ME': youth's new narcissism

Generation Y has also been dubbed 'the ME generation'. Indeed Gen Y sculpts, crafts and storyboards their lives in social networks to present campaigns of themselves. Eyes are always on Gen Yers. They are stars of their own soap operas in which all their friends play their parts with comment boxes and status updates as the scripts of the soap. Youngsters increasingly look at their world through a journalist's lens trying to find an interesting story. With every photo taken, they wonder whether it could be their next profile picture. Youngsters who are still formulating their belief systems are attracted to well-defined and authentic brands that help them to strengthen their values and reinforce the identity they are building.[50] Jean M Twenge, Associate Professor of Psychology at San Diego State University, is convinced that narcissism is much more common in our recent youth generation. According to her studies, the average US college student in 2006 scored higher on narcissism scales than 65 per cent of students in 1987. In other words, in less than 20 years, the number of college students with a high narcissism score has risen by two-thirds. The professor mainly blames our education systems designed to raise the self-esteem of youth.[51] In her 2009 book *The Narcissism Epidemic*, she even suggests treatments for what she deems an epidemic.[52]

Celebrity worship and the 15 Mb of fame

The constant stream of media updates in youngsters' social networks and on their mobile phones means they are always aware of what their friends are doing and their friends know what they have been doing. Youngsters have never had so many live benchmarks as today. The media celebrate the young and successful whether it's sportsmen, actors or singers. In 2005, Kaiser Family Foundation came up with a quite remarkable finding. Not less than 31 per cent of US teenagers were convinced they would become famous one day.[53] In the same period, UK policemen had to cope with a trend of youngsters taping 'happy slapping' movies and posting them on YouTube. More recently, a 19-year-old made the global news headlines by creating a video in which he and his friends are demolishing a brand new iPad with a baseball bat. In an interview with the *LA Times*, the young videographer said he was a big Apple fan and bought two other iPads that he didn't pulverize. He just thought the stunt would be funny. Within less than two days, more than 765,000 people had seen the video on YouTube.[54]

Today, there are so many tools for micro-celebrity: being a studio spectator, talk-show guest, reality TV participant, appearing on YouTube or talent-scouting TV shows such as *Pop Idol*, etc. In his book *Hello, I'm special*, Hal Niedzviecki states that pop culture is creating the myth of instant stardom. TV shows such as *The Osbournes* demonstrate the ordinariness of celebs and in a climate where Kate Nash and Lily Allen are discovered on MySpace, everyone can elevate themselves to new heights. Psychologists at the University of Leicester have identified a mental disorder named 'celebrity worship syndrome'. Their research claims that one in three youngsters in the UK suffer from some derivative of the disease. For most of them this is luckily limited to casually following the careers and lives of certain celebrities.[55] According to Jake Halpern's theory in *Fame Junkies*, this interest in celebrities and the tendency to form para-social relationships with them is fuelled by loneliness and the innate desire to belong. The more lonely and under-appreciated an adolescent feels, the more he/she wants to befriend the ultimate popular guy or girl. Proximity to the famous is a way of receiving recognition and status for the self. Nothing's new. In US high schools there are two main routes for teenage girls to belong to the elite group: either become a cheerleader or become a friend of a cheerleader.[56]

However, these authors may be exaggerating the phenomenon. Recent research found that very few Gen Yers consider becoming famous an important life goal. Just 4 per cent consider it very important and this is not different from older generations. The vast majority (86 per cent) say fame is not important to them.[57] Celebrities have always had a big appeal to the general audience, whether it was Marilyn Monroe in the 1950s or Lady Gaga today. Nevertheless, we do acknowledge that this generation has a higher self-esteem and a higher need for self-realization and uniqueness than former generations. The continuous media and peer benchmarks, as well as society and parents stimulating Gen Yers to turn their life into a success story affects their thinking and behaviour.

Status anxiety

Youth today have unrealistically high expectations of becoming a millionaire before they are 30. Media often portray the successful 20-something CEOs of their own companies endorsing the 'you can be anything you want to be' mythos. The increased importance of self-esteem and self-importance also shows up in increased materialism. Back in 1967, 45 per cent of Boomer freshmen said it was important to be well-off financially. By 2004, 74 per cent of Gen Y freshmen agreed.[58] This is translated in high starting salary and working life expectations. A mere 31 per cent of employed young people say they earn enough money to lead the life they want. However, they are more optimistic than other generations about their future earning power. Among the ones who say they don't earn enough money, 88 per cent think they will be capable of earning enough in the future. Being financially secure is also a concern for 7 out of 10 teens aged 13–18 around the world.[59] But the negative aspect of this status anxiety is an increased self-imposed pressure and an increase in fear of failure among youth. Youngsters feel ashamed that they can't live up to their own high expectations. The midlife crisis of the current Generation X is actually already taking place transformed into a quarter-life crisis among Gen Yers.

The social network voyeurism and exhibitionism has also created a more hedonistic culture. Youth problems such as binge drinking are increasingly justified as youngsters feel comforted by the fact that everyone else is doing it too. The more extremes happen in their lives, the more content they have to post on their Facebook walls. Experiences in the offline world provide content (the new social currency) for online life. They know that their behaviour is being recorded and will pose for pictures with the specific intent of uploading these on social networks.

Social networks allow Gen Yers to support many more and much deeper passive friendships than previous generations. They value social relationships and love to work, shop and date collaboratively a lot more than previous youth generations. Gen Y seems to be more loyal to people than to companies. This is not only important for HR programmes but it also urges you to put enough emphasis on the social aspects of your brand. The store personnel and your employees can really make a difference. They are the advocates of your brand's DNA.

Playing God in a virtual dollhouse

In most video games players are heroes saving the universe or reckless racers or just David Beckham dribbling his way through the defence and scoring five top goals. In the most popular game in 10 years, *The Sims*, youngsters merely play a normal character that is doing ordinary everyday activities. You design your own virtual dollhouse and then you are responsible for the well-being of all the occupants. 'It was a latent need which was not fulfilled with existing videogames 10 years ago', says Lucy Bradshaw, co-designer of the game. 'Until then gamers were used to play the concepts and storylines created by others. *The Sims* was the first game to break with that tradition. The entire content and storyline of the game is owned by the gamer.' Most of Bradshaw's colleagues at Electronic Arts (EA) were initially laughing at her idea at the end of the 1990s. Back then most gamers were teenage boys. When she brought up the idea of 'Dollhouse' (the project name of *The Sims*) together with game designer Will Wright, they thought she was pulling a joke. But soon the first sales results came in and *The Sims* was immediately a bull's eye. More than 100 million copies of the game (including *The Sims 2* and *3*) have been sold since the launch in 2000. Together with the release of *Sims 2* an online community was created in which players could share the objects and their own creations. The game was truly a precursor of the user-generated content trend that was first adopted by Generation Y. *Sims* players are able to change the rules of the game, that's why these kinds of game are also named 'God games'. It was the first game to attract girls to gaming. In *The Sims* they can decorate their own house and choose fashionable outfits. The Swedish brands IKEA and H&M have already sponsored expansion packs of the game, offering their real-life catalogues within the virtual *Sims* world. Since *The Sims* many other God games were introduced. Lucy Bradshaw is now working on EA's *Spore* franchise. *Spore*, a game launched in 2008, allows players to let a creature evolve from a single-celled organism to an intelligent being that is capable of visiting planets far away.[60]

Millennial myths: debunking conceptions of Gen Y

Youth behaviour typically sets many tongues wagging; especially older generations, such as Generation X, who have many prejudices against Generation Y. We would like to challenge some of the common misunderstandings.

Gen Y only put trust in peers

Generation Y are allegedly only capable of trusting their own friends. It is true they do attach a lot of importance to their peer's opinion and word-of-mouth and have more real-time channels to connect with them. This doesn't mean that they only listen to peers. In a survey InSites Consulting did for Levi's Europe, we asked what would be the most trusted source to decide what new pair of jeans to buy. The results are shown in Figure 1.2. Although 74 per cent prefer the opinion of their best friends, shop personnel are trusted too. They even put a higher trust on commercial staff than on their own mum. Still, mum remains an important source. This confirms the better relationship between Gen Yers and their parents, although dad doesn't seem to be the fashion style specialist. Brochures and commercial websites of the jeans brands are as important as reviews and objective forums on the internet. So although they are marketing savvy, this doesn't automatically imply that they don't trust commercial media anymore.[61]

FIGURE 1.2   Most trusted opinion to buy jeans

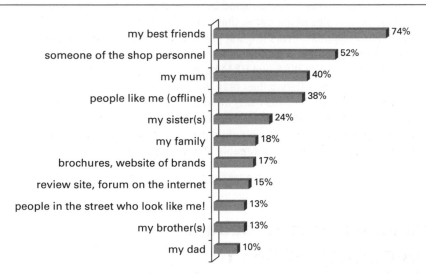

They reject global brands and mass marketing

After four years of researching 'cool brands' among Gen Yers, it is safe to conclude that they are not the 'No Logo' generation at all.

Global mass advertising brands such as Coca-Cola, Nike and Nokia are still among their most beloved brands. The advertising and marketing strategies of these brands changed to appeal to the new consumer though. Coke's 'happiness' campaign, for instance, is much more emotional and on an equal level with the consumer than the 'real thing' or 'always Coca-Cola' campaigns of the past.

The global presence of brands radiates a sense of power with which Gen Y is happy to affiliate. Because they seek reassurance for what they perceive to be a chaotic world, they are looking for security. Global brands are a safe haven because they have proven to be able to survive. If they had not been delivering high quality and reliable offers then they would surely not be around today. Great brands are always one step ahead of the rest and are continually innovating and updating their products. Although some of the brands in youth's preferred list such as Levi's, Apple, Nike and Coca-Cola have a US origin, this is no longer the ultimate rule. Scandinavian brands such as H&M and Nokia, German brands such as Adidas and Italian fashion brands such as Diesel were able to conquer global youth's trust. As children of a media-dominated society, Gen Y love excellent visual communication from their beloved brands. They tend to adore ads that:

- portray openness;
- express closeness, warmth, caring and harmony;
- show that a brand is natural and stays true to itself (authenticity);
- support the simplicity of the brand;
- have witty humour;
- provoke controversy.[62]

More than 7 out of 10 youngsters say they are critical towards advertising in general.

In Figure 1.3 you will see some interesting results from our brand authenticity work for Levi's Europe. Most youngsters like humour and irony in advertising and they want to hear the unvarnished truth. Although Gen Yers are stimulation junkies, it remains important for brands to stay consistent in their messages. Youngsters today generally reject image-oriented advertising.[63]

FIGURE 1.3 Gen Y's attitude towards advertising

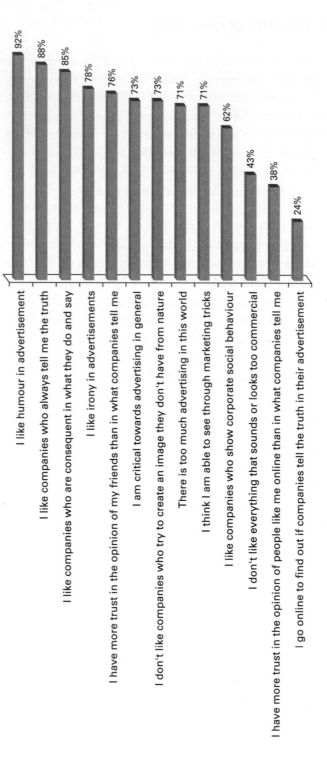

I like humour in advertisement — 92%

I like companies who always tell me the truth — 88%

I like companies who are consequent in what they do and say — 85%

I like irony in advertisements — 78%

I have more trust in the opinion of my friends than in what companies tell me — 76%

I am critical towards advertising in general — 73%

I don't like companies who try to create an image they don't have from nature — 73%

There is too much advertising in this world — 71%

I think I am able to see through marketing tricks — 71%

I like companies who show corporate social behaviour — 62%

I don't like everything that sounds or looks too commercial — 43%

I have more trust in the opinion of people like me online than in what companies tell me — 38%

I go online to find out if companies tell the truth in their advertisement — 24%

They are ethical consumers

Ethical, green and charity issues are of growing importance for this generation. However, the media have made them feel numb for many of these messages. Footage from the developing world, wars, and nature disaster zones are projected on the same screens they watch movies and play games on. They have become another fiction, far away from their own real words. They only take these issues into account when they are directly affecting their immediate social circle or local world. Gen Yers transfer all ethical responsibilities to organizations. Although they will try to avoid buying unethical brands, they will rarely deliberately choose a brand because of its charity programmes. Being ethical is important to them as a principle, but it is not their utmost concern when choosing favourite brands and they will rarely compromise the convenience of their own lives to make a difference. A brand's socially responsible image will never make up for poor quality or other basic issues.

Because eco-claims became just another advertising strategy in the first decade of the 2000s, Gen Yers are cautious in really believing what a brand is telling about protecting the environment. In April 2010, sports fashion brand Puma worked together with Yves Behar's Fuse project to design a shoebox that would reduce its environmental impact. Many Gen Yers reacted rather sceptically on blogs. Puma claimed in a movie that using a bag instead of a box reduced the use of cardboard by 65 per cent, eventually resulting in lowered usage of paper (trees), energy, water and emission of carbon dioxides. Youngsters called it propaganda, questioned the positive impact of the design, uttering that 77 per cent of the carbon footprint in shoes come from the raw materials (leather, rubber and cotton) and only a mere 5 per cent from packaging.[64]

Protecting the planet is not a typical Gen Y thing, it is the result of our zeitgeist. They recycle as much as the other generations and they will buy environmentally friendly and organic products as much as other generations.[65] More important to Gen Yers is that they don't just get bombarded with traditional charity programmes but that they can make a difference by owning the values and choosing how and where charitable contributions will go.[66]

Pepsi, a company that used to spend most of its marketing money on TV commercials in the United States, decided to go for a $20 million social campaign at the start of 2010. They replaced their traditional

Superbowl opening ad position and created the Pepsi Refresh Project. The project is about the online social community nominating projects that need funding in local communities. On the website of the project everyone is able to upload their video or project profile and get votes to win funds ranging from $5,000 to $250,000. Funding ideas can be related to health, arts and culture, food and shelter, the planet, neighbourhood or education. The voting engine allows youngsters to select projects near them, catering for the local identification needs of Gen Y.[67] Through the Pepsi Refresh Project, *Desperate Housewives* actress Eva Longoria is appealing to her fans to support PADRES Contra El Cáncer, a non-profit organization supporting Latino families in the United States dealing with a child's cancer diagnosis. Longoria is also endorsing Yo Sumo (I count), a Pepsi initiative encouraging Latinos to participate in the 2010 census and to share their personal experiences, dreams and contributions as they help shape the United States. The stories will be compiled in a documentary directed and produced by the actress.[68]

They are lazy

Gen Y are believed to be lazy because they mostly take the shortest way to get what's needed. But that's simply the way they were educated, attaining the objectives with the least possible efforts in a smart way. Most youngsters will express a strong work/reward ethic. Nine out of ten believe you will get your rewards in life when you work hard enough. They do know they have been spoiled by their Baby Boomer parents and realize that when they move out as adults they will have to work hard. Failure is assumed to stem from laziness. Most teenagers will only select role models and celebrities that have worked hard and really earned their success.[69] Barack Obama and Britney Spears are both often quoted as people who are admired for their work ethic and for achieving great things from humble beginnings by overcoming adversity to maintain their success.[70]

They are multi-tasking wizards

A common misunderstanding about Generation Y is that they are multi-taskers.[71] With the rise of new technologies and social media they are showered with information. The easiness with which youngsters follow people on Twitter, answer text messages or communicate via MSN or Facebook astonishes adults and might lead to the false conclusion that Generation Y is particularly good at processing multiple streams of conversation and information. Research, however, has evidence for the opposite: until the age of 22, youngsters are less good at multitasking. They have more difficulties than adults in distinguishing relevant from irrelevant information and have fewer abilities to park a certain chunk of information for later usage. Although they are exposed to more information channels than before, this does not lead to an increased absorption of this information. Only strong and short messages are able to pass through the stream of information. There is a limit to what our brains can actually process simultaneously. While we are able to perceive multiple stimuli in parallel, we cannot process them simultaneously. This is especially the case when the different messages are non-related. Young people are actually not attempting to process non-complementary messages simultaneously but rather switching back and forth between different activities.[72] Steve Johnson, author of *Everything bad is good for you* calls this strategy to cope with information overload 'telescoping'.[73] Johnson claims that younger generations have got smarter in using these strategies by evolutions in popular culture: not only gaming but also soaps on television. The latter increasingly have complex narratives with instead of one main plot, several separate alternating storylines. TV series used to have 'pointing arrows', clues in the plot that clarify what will happen next. Recent popular youth TV series such as *24*, *Heroes* or *Lost* lack these pointing arrows and there isn't even a clear distinction between good and bad characters anymore. There's a bit of the dark and white side in everyone. Leading actors unexpectedly die in the midst of the series. Youngsters have learned to analyse these series as puzzles. They don't need to study medicine to understand the rather medical scripts of *Grey's Anatomy* or *House MD*. They simply deduct the meaning of the difficult terms from the context. This is exactly what they do when they learn to master new technologies or tools. They don't read manuals, they just 'probe'. Youth master the skills of deduction, probing and telescoping. They don't multitask.[74] In April 2010, only a few days after Apple launched its iPad, MTV Networks released interactive iPad apps for *Beavis and Butt-head*, *MTV News* and *VH1 To GO*. MTV is also investing in co-browsing apps, meant to be used while youngsters are watching TV, to run on the iPhone or Android devices. The goal of these apps is to make chatting with friends more user-friendly by facilitating conversation without your eyes abandoning the on-screen action. The idea is that mobile devices are easier to use while watching TV than laptops or desktop computers, and the iPad tablet is the perfect in-between.[75]

Conclusion

Of course a number of elements of Gen Y's behaviour are more linked to their young life stage than to their generation. The fact that their brains are still under development is one of these universal features. This explains why generation after generation of youngsters adore freedom, push their limits and are involved in risk-taking behaviour. They want to explore the world around them and discover novelties. Identity construction and the need for self-expression are also universal adolescent themes. Madonna sang: 'Music makes the people come together.' This is specifically true for youngsters. And although every lifestyle group and every generation has different genres, festivals and music carriers, music will always remain one of their main preoccupations.

You can also see Generation Y as the ultimate products of our postmodern society. They are both individualistic and very sociable. They have traditional family values but are very tolerant and open as well. For instance, they are more sexually and ethnically permissive than former generations. They do have a strong work ethic but want a balanced life and lots of leisure time as well. They don't want to make the same mistakes as their Baby Boomer parents who traded in a fair amount of their spare time to succeed in life. They have seen the downside of their parents' success in terms of broken marriages, absentee parenting and stress-related illnesses.[76] Many youngsters take a sabbatical year after they have only been working for one or two years. They want to get rich and believe they will earn a lot, but at the same time enriching experiences are even more important. They cherish their local roots and love brands with local anchors but at the same time they think very globally, in career as well as in friendships and travel.[77] Generation Y is a more positive generation than Generation X with a stronger belief in a better future and a better world.

The specific characteristics of Gen Y we have discussed in this chapter will affect the way you should conceive your marketing and branding targeted at this group. Gen Yers will only stay interested in your brand if it succeeds in whetting their curiosity. Keeping your brand cool by incremental innovations is the key to winning their loyalty.

While constantly renewing your brands and products, staying real and true to your own brand DNA and unique identity is essential. Gen Y are more marketing savvy and will immediately see through fake marketing strategies. Honesty and transparency are important aspects of successful youth brands. Again, both the uniqueness and honesty Gen Yers look for in brands are nothing more than a reflection of the times they were raised in. They were born in a society that celebrated individual success and were stimulated to become unique and special. Twenge has also highlighted that the younger generation has a compulsive honesty. If you're not true to yourself and you conform to someone else's rules, you might be seen as dishonest. Gen Y appreciate directness. Instead of making image claims in advertising, brands should demonstrate what they stand for by their deeds. For Generation X, brands were communicating status and had to express that they were winners. For Generation Y, brands are tools for communicating who they are.

Baby Boomers gave their children many choices and taught them to make their own choices from early childhood on. Think of preschoolers choosing their own clothes in the morning. Even if they ended up wearing terrible combinations, that was okay because they were expressing themselves.[78] Brands and products are seen by this generation as important in creating their own personal and unique narrative. Your brand needs to mirror the values and identity of the youngsters you are targeting. Brands that communicate a similar view of life will be more appealing.[79]

Brands provide them with a way to stand out from the mass. Brands stimulate discerning usage. At the same time, successful brands have to bring social acceptance for youngsters in their reference groups. A youth brand will only be a youth brand if Gen Y can participate, co-create and co-shape the brand identity while they receive the most important youth currency: content for offline as well as online conversations. To experience brands in exciting environments contributes to arousal. Positive emotions are one of the most important reasons why this generation of stimulation junkies will be loyal to your offer.

Those companies and marketers that adjust their branding strategies to address the needs of this emerging segment will find themselves better connected with them and thus more successful.[80]

Hot takeaways for cool brand builders

- Gen Yers are stimulus junkies who look for individual empowerment (control) and instant gratification in the hot brands they choose.
- Gen Y fuse their social lives in technology, not the other way around.
- Content is the number one social currency for them.
- Hot brands continuously bring new cool content.
- Friends are the relevancy filter through which Gen Yers process brand messages. Hot brands embrace social media and peer-to-peer strategies in which they don't dictate but engage youth by offering them control.
- Gen Yers put more trust in people and social connections. Hot brands value the role of employees, shop personnel and ambassador clients to defend and spread their DNA.
- Gen Yers have a bigger influence on family purchases as a consequence of the hotel mum and dad and boomerang trend.
- Gen Yers select and mix the right snippets for the right moment and need. Brands should cater for this variety of moments and needs and offer choice.
- Hot brands don't just offer products, they are the supporter of Gen Yers' lifestyles.
- Brand affection and self-identification with the brand is built during adolescence as a result of brain development.
- This consumer generation is searching for anchor brands that provide them with stability, harmony and authenticity. Brands need to have a well-defined, transparent and consistent meaning and a clear vision.

Chapter Two
Developing a brand model for the new consumer

The idiom 'Friend of a friend' or FOAF is often used when someone is not sure who the source of a certain story is and the story cannot be confirmed. 'I know it from a FOAF' or 'it happened to a FOAF'. Rodney Dale, a British writer specializing in urban legends, coined the term in his 1978 book *Tumour in the Whale*.[1] No, The Great Wall of China is not visible from the moon. Toilets and bathtubs don't drain differently in the Southern hemisphere and ostriches just run away when they sense danger. They don't bury their head in the sand... These are all examples of urban myths. They perfectly illustrate the power of human narratives.

The power of word-of-mouth

As stories are so embedded in human nature, they tend to express both our rational and emotional selves.[2] From a research point of view, it is therefore interesting to analyse the stories that Generation Y would spontaneously tell about brands. After all, brands only exist in their minds. This generation of consumers do not passively receive the brand stories told by companies, they co-create the meaning of brands.[3] For marketers this means that the old trick of shouting how fantastic your brand or using your brand is, won't work anymore. Today, listening to these young consumers and understanding how they are fitting your brand into their lives and lifestyles is crucial. The good thing is that this generation *are* talking a lot about brands. In its TalkTrack survey among more than 2,000 US teens aged 13–17,

The Keller Fay Group found that youth have on average 145 conversations a week about brands. That is twice the rate of adults. They are also talking about the advertising they observe. The amount of citations from advertising and media was 10 per cent higher than in the adult population. Brands that were leading the conversation in the study were Apple, American Eagle, Dr Pepper, Chevrolet and Nintendo. The broad categories that were most talked about were: media and entertainment (mainly TV content), sports, recreation and hobbies, technology, telecom and food and dining. Gen Yers are three times more likely to use online tools (texting, instant messaging, e-mail, social networks, chats or blogs) than adults. Most of the teen conversations (58 per cent) about brands are positive.[4]

In our own youth brand conversation research, we saw that 13- to 29-year-olds have more conversations on topics such as mobile phones and operators, games and game consoles, as well as MP3 players and cars. The 15- to 17-year-olds had more talks on portable game consoles. Girls talk more often about beauty care and chocolate, boys about beer and spirits. But both genders' chats contain on average an equal 2.5 different brand mentions. Although the net generation is indeed using online media more than the 30+ population, 86 per cent of brand conversations are still taking place in a face-to-face situation.[5] A Japanese study based on the responses from more than 1,700 teenagers between the ages of 13 and 18 years revealed that face-to-face word-of-mouth elicited stronger affective brand commitment than mobile-based.[6] About half of the Gen Y population said that peers were frequently telling them about their experiences with products and brands. The same amount are regularly sharing their own brand anecdotes with their friends. A substantial 43 per cent of youngsters aged 15–24 are even actively recommending certain brands.[7] For this generation, word-of-mouth, specifically through peer conversations, has a strong impact on buying preferences. Six out of 10 brand conversations between youngsters will change one of the participant's opinions. In one third of the talks, they will incite someone to try a product or brand for the first time.[8] Observing Gen Yers' talks about brands both on- and offline is therefore an important new task of youth marketers today. Word-of-mouth measured through a brand's share of conversations is increasingly replacing old school key performance indicators (KPI's) such as share of voice (a brand's relative advertising spend).

The research base: 5,000 brand stories can't be wrong

Because listening to Gen Y's own creation of brand meaning is the only way to learn what it takes to sustain a successful brand, we invited more than 5,000 14- to 29-year-olds across different regions of Europe – the UK, Germany, France, Spain, Sweden, the Netherlands and Belgium – to participate in our brand research. We asked them to share their most and least favourite brands with us in three different product categories:

- clothing;
- mobile phone devices;
- sweet snacks (chocolate bars or sweets).

Then we randomly showed them their most desired brand in one of the three categories and invited them to write a short story of at least 750 characters about that brand. They could write whatever they wanted about their preferred brand.

Results for clothing brands

Gen Yers came up with no less than 646 different beloved clothing brands. This illustrates how fragmented Gen Y's world is today. As more and more competitors are each taking their chunk of the pie, many brands have to expand into new and growing segments or markets as the only option to grow. Nike, for instance, needs to launch products for new sport disciplines. Table 2.1 shows the top-mentioned brands in this category.

Of course, every country or region has its own local hero brands. TopShop is conquering H&M in the UK, Zara triumphs in Spain and G-Star in the Netherlands. But H&M overall achieves the biggest international success in the Y market.

In an interview with Jörgen Andersson, former global brand director of H&M, the main reason for this success in his opinion is H&M's diversity of styles. 'Other brands like Diesel, Esprit or Jack & Jones have a more specific style. Or certain competitors have a specific heritage. For instance, Zara has a Spanish style, which makes the retailer successful in the south of Europe, but at the same time it's a barrier to conquer the Nordics. H&M, as a global brand, offers a

TABLE 2.1   Most favourite Gen Y clothing brands

most favourite brand (one single choice)	
H&M	9%
Esprit	4%
Nike	4%
G-Star	3%
Adidas	3%
TopShop	3%
Zara	3%
Jack & Jones	3%
Only	2%
Diesel	2%
Tommy Hilfiger	2%
Levi's	2%
Puma	1%

buffet, you pick whatever you want.' For Generation Xers brands said a lot about who was wearing them. Andersson is convinced that today's fashion is much more about creating your own unique style by mixing vintage with Gucci and… H&M. Generation Y is rather expressing its own personality and moods through style surfing. Since there's no logo on H&M clothes, youngsters can freely combine that expensive Marc Jacobs bag they have been saving for with a G-Star jacket and a Cheap Monday (the denim brand bought by H&M) jeans. Next to the wide variety, another key success factor is the democratic price point that enables young people to buy what they like. 'We are bound to deliver the best prices', says Andersson, 'if leather pants are in fashion we will bring affordable ones. This democratic approach is our Swedish heritage.' H&M has 20–30 per cent price variations depending on the fabrics used and quality. 'The fashion designer collection for instance is made in a higher textile quality and of course it has the brand name, but still we keep the prices low, so that the collection is not just a dream for youth', says Jörgen Andersson. 'While years ago our customers would put their

H&M shopping bags in another one of a more expensive shop, they now feel proud of making a good deal.' The third reason for H&M's success is the flow of new things happening all the time with the brand. Just think of the Fashion against Aids campaign, or the yearly collaboration with fashion designers. 'It's important that youngsters are talking about H&M. We offer them enough triggers to start the conversation', says Andersson. 'We don't just work together with one fashion icon but every year it's another one. We are exploring the entire diversity and global coverage of the fashion landscape with very differing and international designers like Karl Lagerfeld, Stella McCartney, Viktor & Rolf, Roberto Cavalli, Sonia Rykiel, Jimmy Choo.... Hopefully, we have gained some respect in the fashion industry and designers too will be talking about H&M. In our stores, we also create a flow of new things happening all the time. We move around the merchandise to reinforce the impression of a complete new collection and have to renew our assortment continuously. Our young customers like the excitement of finding something new. They do have more time than the elderly and this process of searching and finding something is an important part of the H&M experience.' The global presence of H&M is important for the brand's success too. 'Youngsters read about new shops opening in the USA or Asia. It's a source of brand authenticity. If youth in Tokyo is buying H&M and celebrities are wearing our clothes on the red carpet, it's a guarantee to youngsters all over the world that H&M is truly cool.'[9]

Results for cell phone brands

In the **mobile device category** the 14- to 29-year-olds spontaneously reported 34 different brands. Compared to the 30+ market where Nokia is the dominant favourite brand (43 per cent versus 17 per cent for number two Sony Ericsson), the important Gen Y market seems more challenging for the appliance manufacturers. In this age group, competition is head on between the top three players: Sony Ericsson (28 per cent favourite brand), Nokia (25 per cent) and Samsung (19 per cent). Apple, which relatively recently entered this new market, was already able to beat LG (6 per cent) with its popular – but, for many youngsters in unsubsidized markets, expensive – iPhone (11 per cent).

Results for sweet snacks

In Table 2.2, you can see the top results for the favoured **sweet snacks** (chocolate and sweets). In total 309 different brands were cited.

TABLE 2.2   Most favourite Gen Y sweet snacks

most favourite brand (one single choice)	
Milka	10%
Haribo	6%
Kinder	5%
Snickers	5%
Cadbury	4%
Mars	4%
Galaxy	3%
Lindt	3%
Twix	3%
M&Ms	2%
Kit Kat	2%
Nestlé	2%
Ferrero	2%
Marabou	2%

Again, local markets have their local preferences: Cadbury in the UK, Milka in Germany, Marabou in Sweden.[10]

The five success factors of Gen Y brands

When examining over 5,000 stories in these categories, the five most common denominators of favourite brands that we had experienced in our years of research and practice with Generation Y were confirmed: brand coolness, realness (authenticity), uniqueness, self-identification with the brand and happiness. These five aspects of a youth brand will enhance its success in the Generation Y market. For mnemonic purposes, we have coined the acronym 'CRUSH' to describe what's important to Gen Y. Each of the subsequent chapters of this book is dedicated to one of the CRUSH elements – the basic building blocks of successful youth brands:

- Coolness: What does it mean to be a cool brand for this generation? How do you achieve a cool status and why should you bother?

- Realness: Brand authenticity is a key aspect that discerns long-term winning brands from fads. With Generation Y, authenticity is attained in another way than the traditional approach of claiming origin, heritage or history.

- Uniqueness: A clear positioning based on a sustainable brand DNA will increase impact among youngsters. This generation is craving for anchor brands in a fragmented world. But how do you assert uniqueness when most innovations are copied within only a couple of months' time?

- Self-identification with the brand: Gen Yers will only feel emotionally connected with your brand when it feels like a friend to them. This implies that your brand should reflect their diverse lifestyles. A better understanding of their identity construction will make your brand fit in with youths' lives while embracing diversity.

- Happiness: Almost 80 per cent of the 5,000 brand stories were severely coloured by emotions, with happiness being the most uttered one. Popular youth brands know how to leverage from positive emotions and avoid arousing negative ones.

Brand leverage: one step beyond brand equity

In our study, we linked the individual CRUSH scores of each favourite as well as non-favourite brand to the brand strength to measure the impact of each CRUSH component. More information on how we executed these analyses can be found in Appendix 1 at the end of this book. Traditional models measuring the strength of a brand are often too much focused on brand equity or brand image. They mostly take brand awareness, image and loyalty into account. More recently, the degree to which someone would recommend a brand to others (also called the Net Promoter Score or NPS) was added as a key brand metric. InSites Consulting participated with Houston University to develop its brand leverage model. As a result of the study, a clear relation was found between the extent to which consumers talk about brands and brand leverage. Brand leverage is defined as a combination of brand satisfaction, recommendation and closeness to ideal.[11] Brand leverage is the guarantee that your brand will sustain throughout time and remain hot year after year.

Figure 2.1 gives an overview of how the CRUSH elements contribute to this brand leverage among youth. The detailed impact of each CRUSH component derived from our study is shown in Appendix 1.

FIGURE 2.1   The CRUSH components

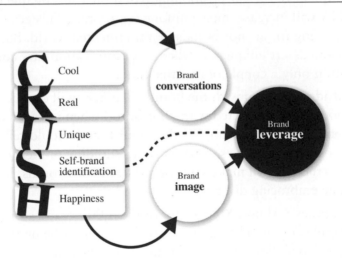

If Gen Yers highly rate your brand on each of the CRUSH elements, your brand's image will improve and they will talk about your brand. Both brand image and brand conversations will have a substantial positive effect on your brand strength (brand leverage), ensuring that your brand will stay hot with this fickle consumer generation for a long time. We also found a very strong direct relationship between youth's self-identification with the brand and brand leverage as indicated by the dotted arrow in Figure 2.1.

Two case studies on branding to Generation Y

Let's illustrate the CRUSH model with a couple of cases.

Jack & Jones: creating leverage through brand uniqueness and self-identification

In the **clothing category**, Jack & Jones, part of the Bestseller group, was one of the runners-up in our brand research with an impressive brand leverage rate of 8.38 on a 10-point scale. The drivers for this high brand leverage score seem to be a high self-identification with the brand and high uniqueness rate. Bestseller is a family-owned Danish clothing company founded by Troels Holch Povlsen in 1975. Today, the company employs more than 41,000 people ands sells clothes and accessories under 10 different brand names including Jack & Jones, Vero Moda, Only and Selected in Europe, the Middle East, China and Canada. Jack & Jones is the jeans and casual lifestyle fashion brand of the group targeting men. Cool, confident and casual are the key DNA characteristics of the brand that has already celebrated its 20th birthday in 2010.

In an interview with Anders Gam, international design and purchase manager of Jack & Jones, he explains the reasons for the brand's success. They are mainly linked to years of consistently emphasizing the brand's uniqueness. 'Jack & Jones started in 1990 with mainly denim and some sweat- and T-shirts. Today, we have several sub-brands that offer a broad range of styles in line with our consumers' evolving demands and lifestyles', he explains. 'There's the "Jeans Intelligence" line for casual moments, the "Premium tech" sports line for active and sportive occasions and our "Premium" sub-brand for the more sophisticated moments when going out.'

Gen Yers are more individualist fashion buyers today compared with 10 years ago. 'Today's youngsters are influenced by so many media and different stimuli, they change their mind very quickly and want their own personal look. Jack & Jones needs to follow this trend', says Dennis Birk Jorgensen, international sales manager. 'Ten years ago, guys also wanted fashion but back then if a few wanted a certain style or brand, everyone wanted the same. That has definitely changed.

They want their own look, and they regularly want something new. Before, guys came to our shop to buy their clothes two to four times a year, now they drop in nearly every week to check what's new.'

This has of course influenced the way the collections are organized. Jack & Jones is currently providing up to 20 collections a year, whereas it used to work with four to six in the past. 'We have to give Gen Yers an opportunity to buy the latest stuff', says Gam. 'We could easily repeat certain successful styles for a few years and that would work for several seasons. But soon the youngsters would in notice that we are not bringing in any novelties and they would judge us to be a boring brand.'

To be able to react swiftly to Gen Y's changing needs, one of the core strengths of Jack & Jones is that designers are able to deliver new items, colours or styles within only two weeks. The company works with a team of young designers (average age of 26) who are still very much part of the Jack & Jones target group and who get inspired by watching their peers and travelling the globe for new ideas all the time. This approach explains why the Danish brand is so successful in achieving a high self-identification with Gen Yers. The core philosophy of the brand is to offer very high quality for a good price. Jack & Jones denim is made in Italy for instance, with Italian quality fabrics, and they are striving for long-term collaborations with suppliers. 'We want to let our products speak for themselves', says Jorgensen. 'Other brands have, for instance, a series of expensive ads in magazines. The consumer is paying for these costs of massive branding. We prefer to invest that money in our new designs and quality and are still able to use honest price levels. We have been working with some suppliers for 20 years now. They understand our brand, we know their steady quality. It allows us to offer great value for money.'

Another key competitive edge for Jack & Jones is the chain's A+-located stores. 'Generation Y men won't come back just for the brand, but because they found what they were looking for at a fair price and in a shop that succeeds in arousing their interest', adds Jorgensen (see Figure 2.2).

'Our shops have to be a cool place with the right smell and music and a great atmosphere.' Jack & Jones shops have a central music system broadcasting the same music at the same volume level in every store at the same time. During the afternoon, the music is turned up, for example. They are also using store scents that are linked to the season of the year: the store will smell of grandma's cookies during

FIGURE 2.2 Jack & Jones shop interior in Rome (Italy)

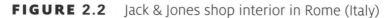

Christmas, and the sea in summer. 'We want the guys to feel comfortable and secure in our shops', says Anders Gam. 'We work with materials and racks that don't look cheap to avoid a supermarket look. Our personnel is thoroughly trained at the Jack & Jones Academy to match with our brand's spirit. No-one will give you that "didn't you walk into the wrong shop" gaze.' The fashion brand is putting a lot of effort into changing the stores every day to keep the youth generation stimulated. 'We have a daily look at the weather forecasts', says Jorgensen. 'We want to put the right articles in front of the shop where there's the most traffic, and that's related to the weather, to holidays, to certain regions or even to national days.'

To fuel the traffic to the stores, Jack & Jones want to be local heroes in every city. Local PR events are fostered. For instance, in Spain, the brand endorses the Antonio Banderas motor biking team. It's more than just sponsoring, a clothes line was developed together with some of the racers of the team. Jack & Jones has supported the tour of the Swedish rock band Takida who played unplugged in the stores in Sweden. In every country, local initiatives are set up. They are always linked to the main interests of young guys, such as sport teams or athletes, bands, etc.

The most critical success factor for Jack & Jones is that they are constantly listening to what their consumers want and not telling them what they have to wear. 'We are a humble brand. It's our client who decides where the brand will go tomorrow', says Dennis Birk Jorgensen. 'If we don't follow him in his habits, we won't exist tomorrow.' Designers often work in the Jack & Jones shop during the weekends. They are observing and talking to guys visiting the stores, who direct them to design the trendy styles of tomorrow. The brand has 4,000 independent distributors and is one of the main suppliers of Peek & Cloppenburg. 'We're also listening carefully to the feedback of these multi-brand customers. Sometimes we might get blinded in our own Jack & Jones universe, but these customers experience why youngsters are choosing Jack & Jones in their stores instead of competing brands that are lying next to our articles.'

Jack & Jones is sensitive to corporate responsibility and the social dimensions of business as well. The 'JJ-Eco' label offers fair trade certified organic jeans-wear at a very affordable price. In 2010, the brand donated €500,000 to the national Danish fund-raising for the earthquake victims in Haiti together with five other Bestseller brands, and it has launched a collection of T-shirts of which the entire profit went to the children's rights organization 'Save the Children'.[12]

Nokia: brand leverage through sustaining authenticity (realness)

In the **mobile device category** the rates of Nokia, Sony Ericsson and Samsung on the CRUSH components and on brand leverage are very close to each other, although the last two brands are scoring slightly better than Nokia on coolness among Gen Y consumers. Samsung is better in brand self-identification and happiness and Nokia is the most authentic mobile brand. Still there's one big challenge for the top three brands: the Apple iPhone. The brand is outperforming the other three on simply all CRUSH components, which results in a brand leverage rate that is much higher (8.75 on a 10-point-scale compared to 8.23 for Nokia and Sony Ericsson and 8.27 for the Samsung brand).

In an interview with Satu Kalliokulju, global director of opportunity identification at Nokia, she acknowledges that the Finnish brand has managed to build a solid and sustainable identity of quality and continuity. 'Generation Y has much bigger expectations of authenticity and transparency', says Kalliokulju. 'Generation Yers are much more savvy and more mature consumers. They use parallel ways to stay up-to-date and look behind the scenes to feel it, see it, and experience it. By using social software, Gen Yers are curators of information for each other and they are much more conscious about the forces behind corporations. In this demanding environment, Nokia has stayed consistent and true to itself throughout the years. On top of this solid foundation, we need to innovate in a much faster pace than ever before in order to stay hot. Not for the sake of innovativeness but to offer improvements that are relevant for people every day.' The director of opportunity identification says youngsters want something they can rely on, but at the same time they are looking for constant renewal. 'It's in Gen Yers' human nature', says Kalliokulju, 'they have this sense of discovery and surprise. Although they are constantly looking for similarities with their own view of life, once they have found things in common with a brand, they are stimulated to discover new aspects.'

Instead of buying more and more, youth is looking for meaningful things to do and ways of self-development. 'Today, content is what brings young people together', says Satu Kalliokulju. 'Whether it is content on social media, in real life events or on mobile apps, it gives them something to talk about and engage in meaningful social connections. They are not buying technology for technology's sake anymore. Nokia is in the "daily relationship" business. Our DNA is connecting people socially and our brand facilitates and empowers whatever type of connections they find meaningful. The tonality of different relationships varies and we have to cater for these different needs and moments in daily life as well.'

Gen Y want to feel each other's presence. To know friends' whereabouts and what they are up to has become a new way of spending time together. Nokia taps into this feeling of closeness in its brand imagery and communication. 'This life casting is almost like a form of daily social entertainment. In the stories we tell, we want to illustrate how Nokia is bringing value to the different types and aspects of people's relationships', explains Kalliokulju. 'The best way to achieve that with this conscious generation is by letting them experience our brand in their daily life moments as well as face-to-face through local live events.' Nokia is encouraging people to find meaningful connections and engage in collaborations that lever each other's creativeness. 'Participation in live events such as a Rihanna concert and sharing these moments either live or recorded are examples of how youth collaborate and bring joy to their everyday', says Satu Kalliokulju. 'Our solutions allow youngsters to spot people who have things in common with them or share locations and points of interests.' Some other examples of social events include the Nokia design contests or the Trends Labs in which leading-edge participants were using Nokia phones to co-create music and video clips with local celebrity bands.[13]

To launch the Xpress Music series in Sweden, Norway and Denmark, Nokia cooperated with MTV to create 'MTV Selected', Scandinavia's largest DJ competition. 'To deliver on the "connecting people" brand promise of Nokia, we didn't want to adapt the same strategy as Sony Ericsson that was using the big arena stars of their Sony Music catalogue to endorse their mobile brand', says Patrik Söder, business director of DDB Stockholm and former Nordic marketing director for Nokia. 'We made it more personal and engaging by allowing everyone to upload their own DJ mix and collect votes or just to vote on other amateur DJ work.' A Facebook application embedding the mixes on the walls of involved youngsters made the contest a viral hit resulting in more than 300,000 votes. Finalists were selected by a jury consisting of some of the most renowned DJs such as Axwell and Steve Angello. The feedback from youngsters was extremely positive. The interest around the new XpressMusic portfolio increased, and the Nokia 5310 was the best-selling device in the lower price segment.[14]

Conclusion

From listening to over 5,000 Gen Y stories of favourite brands, we learned that the brands with which this critical generation become engaged share five basic elements. We created the 'CRUSH' acronym to anchor these components of successful youth brands in your mind. In the subsequent chapters of this book we will explain to you in-depth how each of the CRUSH components can contribute to a better connection between your brand and the new consumer generation. Both research insights and case illustrations will give you inspiration to create cool brands. Although developing a cool brand is a first important step to being relevant for the youth market, it takes more to stay hot for a long time with this fickle consumer generation. The chapters will each highlight the steps to keep your cool brand hot for Generation Y.

Hot takeaways for cool brand builders

Gen Y's most favourite brands all share five key elements:

- **C**oolness;
- **R**ealness;
- **U**niqueness;
- **S**elf-identification;
- **H**appiness.

These CRUSH components have an impact on brand image as well as brand conversations that will result in a substantial leverage for your brand.

To keep your cool brand hot for this fickle generation, the CRUSH model offers a proven branding approach.

Chapter Three
What cool means to brands

> *Be just like the Fonz... and what is the Fonz? He's cool... that's right... just be cool...*

That's what Samuel L Jackson's character tells the robber at a diner in the final scene of Tarantino's *Pulp Fiction*, without any doubt one of the coolest crime films ever made. Arthur Herbert Fonzarelli or 'Fonzie', 'The Fonz' was the lead character of the US sitcom *Happy Days* (1974–84) played by Henry Winkler.

The Fonz's coolness is not only originating from the way he is dressed: his inevitable black leather jacket, the white T-shirt underneath and blue jeans, not forgetting his hair regularly combed and greased into style. It is also in the way he walks and talks. Fonzie is an Italian-American high school dropout driving a motorcycle. He's notorious for his romantic experiences with all attractive women in his surroundings. But the womanizing car mechanic has some other skills too. He's able to fix the jukebox at Arnold's restaurant with a single punch of his fist. And he solves most of his friends' problems in 'his office', the Gents in Arnold's restaurant. Both acts usually end in The Fonz's iconic finger snapping, double thumbs up and the inevitable catch phrase 'Aaaaay'!

This combination of jukebox music, looks, skills, movements and language certainly contributes to the cool image of The Fonz. In fact, sociologists would immediately recognize the resemblance of these traits with the symbolic codes teenagers use to identify with peers during adolescence. In this awkward period, teenagers are extremely concerned about how they look and believe everyone is constantly observing their appearance and behaviour. The drastic physical changes they have to struggle through and the emotional crashes involved simply make symbolic codes and behaviour vital to them. To them 'cool' equals a set of discernible body movements, postures, facial expressions and voice modulations that gives them a strategic social value within the peer context.[1] Marcel Danesi, Professor of Semiotics at the University of Toronto, focused his book *Cool. The Signs and Meanings of Adolescence* on dress codes, hairstyles, language, musical tastes and other symbolic systems used to identify with peers.

In this chapter, we will question what 'being cool' means for today's youth and how brands can tap into this cool world and develop a cool identity. This is the first step of the CRUSH model that will leverage your brand's connection with Generation Y.

Gen Y's definition of 'cool'

Because of the fragmentation of media and styles, today it is harder than ever before to find one single definition of 'cool'. Although the meaning of 'cool' is subjective, it certainly signifies some sign of admiration or at least approval. Still, when MTV Networks asked us three years ago to study which brands where the coolest among youth, we were not so sure we were on the same wavelength. The one thing that worried us the most was the way Generation Y describes something cool. Could we just ask which brands were cool to them, or perhaps 'cool' wasn't the right word to track 'coolness' anymore. In fact youth slang is continuously changing and generations tend to linguistically differentiate themselves from their ancestors. There are indeed plenty of synonyms for cool: hip, in, trendy, wicked, sick, chill, dope, hot, dry... Some of them are typical products of the zeitgeist, as you can see in Figure 3.1.

To all, seeming 'cool' has enduringly managed to resist this genera-tional changing of the guards. At the end of 2007, we asked 500 Gen Yers to help us understand which words were in fashion to express someone or something to be cool.[2] As a first conclusion of the study, we saw that everyone was capable of explaining the concept of 'cool' in their own words. Youngsters spontaneously came up with 39 dif-ferent meanings. To the majority (29 per cent) 'cool' is just a synonym for appealing or fun. Others mentioned connotations such as 'in' (15 per cent), renewing and innovative (10 per cent), hip (6 per cent),

FIGURE 3.1   Synonyms for 'cool' throughout time

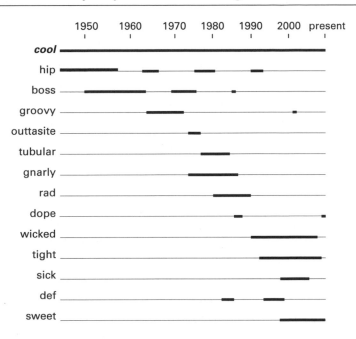

original and unique (6 per cent), pleasant (4 per cent) and trendy (3 per cent). If you look at these descriptions, most are related to products, brands or events: must haves or trendsetting stuff. Six out of 10 even agreed that advertising determines what's cool and what's not. Yet 12 per cent referred to the other sense of cool: a relaxed state or personality, which is more linked to persons and role models. In aided associations, we found that three key dimensions of 'coolness' were confirmed. Gen Y perceives a brand as cool when it is attractive to them (51 per cent) and when it has an air of novelty and originality (55 per cent). Denotations that were the least connected with coolness were: arrogant (4 per cent), luxurious (8 per cent) and alternative (13 per cent). The last one was particularly interesting to us, since the original use of 'cool' attitudes was clearly more edgy and alternative than Gen Y's contemporary definition. Only 11 per cent of the surveyed young people, mostly boys aged 13–19, found it a necessity to break rules or be a rebel in order to attain coolness.

These findings reassured us that 'cool' was still a good word to use to discuss cool brands with this generation. In 2010, Ypulse endorsed our European results with similar research in the United States. More than 4 out of 10 teens and collegians, regardless of gender, are regular users of the word 'cool' to describe something they like or are excited about. More than half of them see it as an appearance, attitude or style. One-third considers cool to be integral to a product. Most Millennials feel coolness is a personal and subjective item and therefore only mildly influenced by others. Ypulse also polled for current alternatives to the word cool. While youth came up with more than 50 synonyms, including neat, epic, badass, tight and rad, highlights included: awesome, sweet, nice and amazing.[3]

Cool barometers

To be cool as a person, wearing the right clothes, adopting the latest trends and looking great might help. Yet you can't learn to be cool, it's more a personality trait. The top sources that set the youth standard for coolness are: their own friends (61 per cent), television broadcasts (32 per cent), magazines (29 per cent), advertising in general (26 per cent) and music festivals (23 per cent). For teenagers, aged 13–19, advertising, musicians and music videos are a more valuable source of cool. The least imperative cool barometers are professional sports stars and sports events. When asked unaided to name the persons they believe were the most cool, friends (23 per cent) won by a nose from music artists (20 per cent) who appear to be much cooler than actors (11 per cent). Merely 2 per cent of youngsters (most of them above the age of 20) would call themselves cool. Athletes, politicians and freedom fighters were barely mentioned. The bulk of respondents also condemned teachers and parents to the uncool league. The latter should not worry too much though. In the list of people considered as role models they are the absolute sovereign with only close friends reaching near their position. Below the age of 20, international celebrities are also recognized as role models.[4]

Cool archetypes

From the brand stories we have received from more than 5,000 European Gen Yers we could derive 14 archetypical characteristics predicting the coolness of a brand. In order of importance, these cool ingredients were:

- trendy;
- high status;
- clean reputation;
- successful;
- creative
- fun;
- cheerful;
- own style;
- changes a lot;
- luxurious;
- clearly stands for X (X = specific claim or positioning);
- contemporary;
- honest;
- retro.

When brands were linked to items such as cheap and impatient, they had significantly lower coolness rates.[5] This all comes back to having a clear and consistent brand vision or DNA, a unique cheerful style and constantly creating exciting and creative innovations confirming that vision. This is what Steve Jobs embodies for Apple with personal passion and charisma. It is about reinventing yourself but not by looking at what others are doing but by developing from within the heart of the company or brand. This grassroots building has nothing to do with chasing coolness but with creating and maintaining relevance for the stimulus-addicted Generation Y.

Quiksilver, Inc: grassroots marketing in practice

A good example of grassroots marketing can be found at Quiksilver, Inc, founded in the early 1970s by Australian Alan Green. It is now one of the largest manufacturers of board sport (surf, skate and snowboard) equipment and clothes.[6] 'We sometimes get credited with designing the first "technical" boardshort, but the truth is, we used snaps and Velcro instead of flies because I'd bought a supply of them when I started making Rip Curl wetsuits', says Alan Green on the corporate website, 'and, although Carol (one of the co-founders) was a bloody good sewer, maybe she didn't know how to do flies!

The yoke waist, which was higher at the back than the front, was the other difference; they hugged your back and still hung low on your hips. They were distinctive, functional, comfortable boardshorts, and two-toned yokes made them different from the rest. Surfers seemed to like them.'

The company now owns more than 600 stores in Australia, New Zealand, Europe, America, Asia and Africa. Quiksilver's brands are also sold worldwide in other retail outlets, mainly skate and surf shops. In 1990 the firm launched a new brand for young women, Roxy, that has grown to be the biggest action sport fashion brand for girls in own branded stores.[7] Other outdoor sport brands DC and Hawk are also a part of the Quiksilver corporation.

In 2005 The Quiksilver Foundation was initiated. The Foundation is a charity organization aimed at providing environmental, health, educational and youth-related projects to board-riding communities around the world. Since 1978 Quiksilver has been involved in sponsoring rider teams. They are now endorsing more than 500 amateur and professional surfers, skiers, snowboarders and skateboarders including celebrities such as surfer Kelly Slater and skateboarder Tony Hawk. The brand also organizes the Quiksilver Pro surfing tournament for men and Roxy Pro tournament for women in Australia and France. Quiksilver partnered with MTV to create *Surf Girls* together with competitors Volcom, Billabong and Rip Curl. The TV show featured 14 babes with a board in search of a world championship and was an industry-wide initiative that resulted in a women's surf market growth of 12 per cent while introducing the surf culture to 54 million viewers. Making a category cooler to certain Gen Y groups, like Roxy and other board brands did towards girls, can really grow your businesses. Co-founder Matt Jacobson, today head of market development for Facebook, commented the brand was a big fish in a medium-sized pond. Enlarging the pond would definitely support the brand in an authentic way. The strategy allowed Quiksilver to grow from a $400 million brand to a $2 billion brand at the end of 2009.[8]

The magic cool formula

Some of the Coolest Brands[9]

Coolest mobile phone brand

1 iPhone (Apple)   8.3/10
2 Samsung
3 Nokia

Coolest soft drink brand

1 Coca-Cola   7.7/10
2 Fanta
3 Ice Tea

Coolest energy drink brand

1 Red Bull   7.1/10
2 Burn
3 Nalu

Coolest make-up brand

1 Nivea   7.0/10
2 L'Oréal
3 Maybelline

Coolest shoe brand

1 Nike   7.4/10
2 Converse All Stars
3 Puma

Coolest denim brand

1 Diesel   7.9/10
2 Replay
3 Levi's

Continued...

Some of the Coolest Brands   *Continued*

Coolest game consoles

1 Wii   7.8/10

2 Playstation 3

3 X Box 360

We have learned that using the word 'cool' to investigate which brands are capable of touching the hearts of Generation Y, is indeed a good option. But what is really determining coolness? Is it the attractiveness of a brand, the edginess, or originality? Is there a difference in how youth perceives the coolness of persons and brands? Is brand coolness dependent on product categories? We asked 300 leading-edge youngsters, aged 18–24 to track their cool experiences on a daily basis for an entire week. In the 'cool sneaker journal' they could classify three types of experiences themselves: a 'hit': something or someone who wants to be cool and succeeds well; a 'fail': something or someone who is desperately trying to be cool, but fails miserably; an 'accident': something or someone who unintentionally and unexpectedly comes across as 'cool'.

Then we asked them to tag the experiences (people, music, sports, TV, brands, products, etc.), explain why these experiences were cool or not cool to them and upload some pictures, videos or music. For us to develop metrics for a cool experience DNA, the young adults in this project had to rate their experiences on coolness, effort (the perceived intention to be cool), and five dimensions:

- originality;
- popularity (appealing to peer group);
- edginess;
- appeal (personal likeability);
- buzz value (is it something they would talk about to others).

In total about 500 experiences were logged: 42 per cent hits, 30 per cent fails and 28 per cent accidents. In Figure 3.2 you will notice that the 18- to 24-year-olds predominantly reported on people (specifically people trying too hard to be cool).

FIGURE 3.2   Type of cool hits, fails and accidents

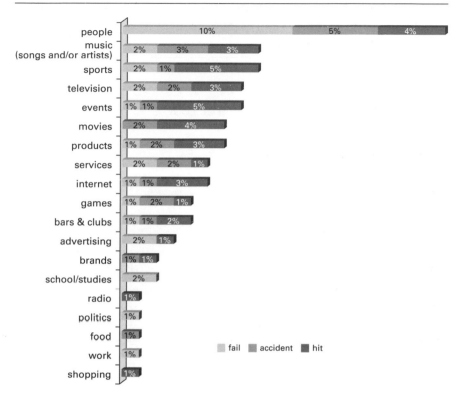

Eighteen-year-old Laura, for instance, shared with us the following 'fail' and 'hit' in the people category. FAIL: 'My mother and I, we are very close, a bit like sisters. But she has the habit of joining me for shopping. That's okay to me, but what I find annoying is that she tends to pick exactly the same clothes as me. It's like she's stealing my own identity. That's totally uncool and I think it's not for her age anymore.' HIT: 'I've been watching a broadcast on the life of Brigitte Bardot on the telly. She's really cool. All she has done to save and protect the animals.'

To develop an overall coolness formula, we made an estimation of coolness based on the attributed scores of the 500 reported experiences. Three out of the six variables had an impact on the coolness score and explained nearly 80 per cent of the cool perception.

As shown in Figure 3.3, we distilled the overall cool formula for Gen Y into 22% original + 23% popular + 55% appeal.[10] Since this formula was an estimate for a mix of different observations such as the coolness of people, music, events, products, brands and many more, we had to validate it for products and brands. In a large-scale follow-up survey more than 1,500 teenagers and young adults (13–29) had to judge brands they knew in 35 categories on the three determining aspects of cool.

FIGURE 3.3   The magic formula of 'cool'

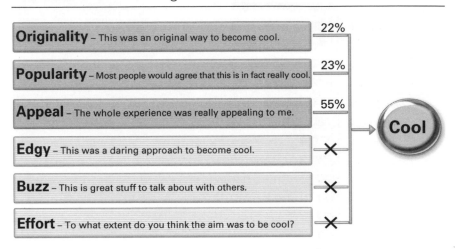

For the 375 products and brands involved, the cool formula is slightly different: popularity remains equally important (23 per cent), but the impact of originality (38 per cent) on coolness increases, while the importance of attractiveness (43 per cent) decreases slightly. The cool formula teaches us that uncool brands with lower scores on appeal or popularity can start to strengthen their brand by first working on originality, for instance in product innovation or communication. A higher perceived originality will positively affect a brand's coolness.

Not all categories are equally cool

Depending on the product category, differences were also found between the cool formula dimensions.

For example, it is clear from Table 3.1 that in categories that have a shared usage with peers (game consoles, mints, chewing gum, beer, spirits) the weight of popularity within the coolness formula is higher.

The ones that are for private usage – whether it's refreshments (soft drinks, fast food, crisps), TV stations or fashion (jeans, sports and fashion brands) – derive their coolness more from a personal appeal. Product features such as taste, style or content are often the drivers of this personal appeal.

TABLE 3.1 Cool formula for different categories

	Appeal	Popularity	Originality
Overall average	43%	20%	38%
Game consoles	37%	29%	34%
Mints	41%	26%	33%
Chewing gum	40%	25%	35%
Beer	43%	25%	32%
Spirits	43%	23%	34%
Soft drinks	49%	22%	29%
Fast food	51%	9%	40%
Crisps	47%	18%	35%
TV stations	48%	19%	33%
Jeans	48%	14%	38%
Sports brands	45%	12%	43%
Fashion brands	45%	14%	41%

Some categories have a tougher job in creating cool brands

If you are not working in the fashion industry you will probably ask: isn't it extremely difficult for my category to be considered cool by young people? It depends. We have asked them which things (products) or people will have a more or less easy job to be cool. The results could be classified into five divisions. The figures in Table 3.2 represent the Cool Handicap Index (CHI), or the number of Gen Yers who said it is easy to be cool in this category minus the number that said it is hard to be cool. A negative CHI means that more youngsters think it is hard to be cool in a category than it is an easy job. Sometimes something is 'cool' without working at it. For example, friends, music and musical artists, actors and actresses are 'cool' immediately. Just like people, some sectors naturally have more 'cool potential' than others. Mobile telephones, jeans, game consoles and shoes are products that have a significant cool status with young people. In contrast, banks, temp agencies, tour operators and coffee and tea brands hardly appeal to young people's imagination. The brands that populate these industries, however, are not as easily classified. Cool brands are not just found in cool product categories. Take mints. This sector has a negative cool potential index of −15 per cent. Yet, Tic Tac, Ferrero's brand of mints, gets a fantastic individual rate of 7.5 out of 10 for coolness. On the other hand, there are brands that profit little from the coolness status their sector has built up among youth. New Balance and Fila for instance are brands in a cool category (sports brands) but not succeeding in transferring this coolness to their brands. A category like coffee or tea and ready-made meals however, which has more difficulty being cool with young people, can increase its score by focusing on originality, as can be inferred from Table 3.1. This refutes the preconceived notion that it is much easier to be cool as a brand of jeans or a game than as a bank or breakfast cereal brand. For categories at the bottom of Table 3.2, it is quite a difficult job to make products cool for Generation Y. For the ones at the top, it is much easier because the total category radiates 'coolness'.

TABLE 3.2   The Cool Handicap Index for different categories

Mobile phones (device)	65%
Jeans	56%
Game consoles	51%
Shoes	51%
Soft drinks	47%
TV programmes	44%
Fashion brands	41%
Sports brands	40%
TV channels	38%

TABLE 3.2   *Continued*

Fashion chains	36%
Cameras	35%
Crisps	20%
Deodorant	19%
Spirits	16%
Beer	12%
Fast food chain	12%
Energy drinks	11%
Sports drinks	10%
Chocolate bars	5%
Healthy food chain	3%
Shoe chains	2%
Chewing gum	2%
Make-up	−1%
Mobile phone operator	−5%
Haircare products	−11%
Fruit juice	−12%
Mints	−15%
Breakfast cereals	−18%
Water	−22%
Shavers, razors, razor blades	−23%
Ready-made meals	−25%
Tour operators	−33%
Coffee/tea	−37%
Temporary employment agency	−48%
Banks	−53%

FIGURE 3.4 One of the cool mailings of the SAF

Injecting coolness in an uncool category

Cooling your brand is important and a possible option for every product or service category no matter what the handicap index is. Let's take the army as a challenging example. In Spring 2007, the mandatory military service in Sweden was under investigation. The number of recruits trained each year was rapidly declining from 20,000 in the past to 4,000 in 2007. In summer 2010, Sweden made the decision to shift to a fully recruited armed force for the first time in history. Although the Swedish clearly want to have a national defence force, the perception in 2007 was that the armed forces were a bit of a playground for boys. The best you got out of it was that boys learned to make their bed and pick up their socks from the floor. DDB Stockholm, elected by *Advertising Age* as one of the top five agencies in the world, created a campaign for the Swedish Armed Forces (SAF) to make the army a cooler (employer) brand. The theme message of 'Do you have what it takes' expresses that the SAF is looking for people that can make good decisions under pressure. Several consecutive campaigns have used tests to engage the youth audience. The hub of the campaign is always a website with tests or games demanding both intellectual and motor skills. The tests, puzzles and games were inspired by actual tests for pilots and were created together with the SAF psychologists. All executions in all channels (TV, radio, banners, social media) contained interactivity and a pressure to solve a challenge under time stress. Different direct mailings with puzzles, code words and USB sticks with tasks (see Figure 3.4) were sent to youngsters and the response rates were always impressively high, between 37 and 73 per cent. In summer 2009, a real live test machine (see Figure 3.5) was built that travelled within a radio station tour and attracted youngsters to test their skills and register their results online. The latter not only built a database but also allowed benchmarks with peers in other cities etc. In an interview with Thomas Brenemark, strategy and business director of DDB Stockholm, he says that this Gen Y target group can be treated very intelligently and gets involved when you reward them with the chance to share their smartness with their friends. 'We never joke about the army subject and the games are simulating the hard demands of the SAF reality', says Brenemark. 'It is serious stuff and we are transparent about it. I think this honesty is the key success factor of our campaigns.' For youngsters it is hard to resist a challenge.

FIGURE 3.5   The test machine

After one month of the first campaign, the number of recruits was already higher than in the entire year before. The SAF campaign is in its fourth year now and has won several national and international awards, including silver in Cannes. It succeeded in giving the SAF a voice and a platform to reach the younger crowd. Only a few years ago, the Swedish Armed Forces were considered boring, today they are a cool brand.[11]

How to make your brand cool

Ingredients of cool are heavily dependent on product category. For alcoholic drinks, for instance, cool brand ingredients include authenticity, rituals, exclusivity and understated marketing. Jack Daniels' coolness for instance is harnessed by the strong US icon heritage and authentic connotations such as masculine values, blues and cult. Absolut Vodka, without heritage, has a strong minimalist and exclusive image backed by low-key marketing, sponsorship of art events and limited edition packaging design (eg in black leather or mirror glass). Not forgetting that it is distributed in select venues. Absinthe, apart from its illegal opium-based hallucinogenic origin, has its ritual involving sugar, a spoon and a flame. Tequila has its salt and lime ritual.[12] To freeze your brand, common techniques include: creating exclusivity and scarcity, regular surprises, novelties and innovations and advertising and selective media usage.

Exclusivity and scarcity

Being a cool brand equals consumers fervently wanting to buy your brand. In InSites Consulting's 'Meaning of Cool' survey, we asked 13- to 29-year-olds what possibilities they could see to up the coolness of a product or service. Fifty-six per cent mentioned the fact that only a very few others have the same product. Only 12 per cent said the opposite: if everyone else has a certain item, it becomes cooler. The latter was higher among the 13- to 19-year-olds, affirming that in this life stage the need to belong to a peer group and for common brand usage is bigger. Forty-five per cent said the store where you buy something affects its coolness. One of the most successful ways of boosting desire is by creating exclusivity in retail channels or scarcity, for instance when launching a new product such as the X-box 360. Depending on your sector it can be a good option to have a more trendy upscale range with a smaller scale distribution to maintain brand appeal for the innovative cool people. Diesel, the well-known Italian jeans brand launched 'StyleLab' at the end of the 1990s, a laboratory of young designers' ideas sold as an upscale line in flagship stores and contributing to its image of stylistic and creative freedom. In 2008 the StyleLab offer was replaced by Diesel Black Gold, an exclusive casual-luxury label only available in the upscale boutiques of the brand.

Innovation and novelty

But although this exclusivity and scarcity can increase the cool factor for a while, it will also ruin sales revenues in the long term. Unless you have a niche strategy, in most cases substantial profits will only come in when your product is widely bought and not only adopted by innovators or early adopters. This breaking out of the product life cycle's introduction phase has been named 'crossing the chasm' by Geoffrey Moore. Brands addressing youth are often facing this balance exercise: moving into the big league and still retaining credibility. When a product or brand is more mainstream, the trend-setters – cool people – tend to leave it and move to the next thing, which will potentially lead to the brand's loss of 'cool'. To keep these innovators on board your brand simply has to be... innovative. Consistent and constant improvements, developments and variations will maintain the innovator's interest.[13]

Although Apple's iPod was a big hit from its first original design back in October 2001, the brand has introduced a range offering six different versions of its popular portable media player in only six years. The hard-drive based Classic (already in its sixth update in six years), the touch-screen Touch (three updates in just two years), the video-capable Nano (five updates in four years) and the Shuffle (three updates in four years). The iPod Mini and Photo have already left the scene. Innovation is the key to freeze your brand.

In a US study of 524 brands in 100 consumer categories correlating annual growth rates of revenues between 1997 and 2001 with dozens of market factors, Blasberg and Vishwanath of Bain & Company came to a remarkable conclusion. Winning brands with growth rates that tripled the average rate were found in both high and low growth categories, among new and mature products, big and small, premium and value, market leaders and followers... Only two things made them stand out from the pack: innovativeness and aggressive advertising. Winning brands drew at least 10 per cent of their sales from products introduced during the study period and were 60 per cent more likely to have a share of voice that was significantly higher than the category average. Innovations varied between ranges of attributes, new product formulas, new positioning or packaging. Nabisco's Oreo cookies were one of the winners. Since its introduction in 1912 there had been only one Oreo cookie, the regular chocolate biscuit sandwich with vanilla cream filling, for more than 60 years. Between 1974 and 1996 Nabisco only introduced a few variations. But from 1997 to 2001 the company launched a never-ending follow-up of innovations including seasonal cookies, single-serve packs, etc. Nabisco heavily promoted each new launch. The result? From 1995 to 2002 Oreo sales grew at an average annual rate of 7.5 per cent, more than four times the industry's average.[14]

Advertising and media selection

Thirty-six per cent of youngsters believe good advertising has the power to cool a brand. Only 17 per cent stated endorsing celebrities as a source of cool and a very high price would only work for 12 per cent. Another noteworthy result was that just as the retailer influences cool perception, the media containing a brand's advertisements also shape the perceived cool image. Commercials on music channels such as MTV were twice as much (29 per cent) linked with cool than the ones on general youth stations (13 per cent) and five times more than on general population TV channels.[15]

The Coca-Cola Company refreshed its second-largest global brand Sprite in 2010 after a period of slowing growth. The theme of the global ad campaign, produced by Bartle Bogle Hegarty, was 'The Spark', using the brand's logo and authenticity as an inspiration. It refers to a spark of fresh thinking as well as the spark on your tongue when drinking Sprite. The first TV commercial features the young urban singer Drake who is looking foiled during a studio recording session. 'I'm just not feelin' it', he utters, until he drinks a bottle of Sprite. Special effects show the liquid transforming his body, after which he suddenly starts singing a new tune. In China and India local popular music and film stars will replace Drake. 'Given that there will be 800 million teens in the world by 2020, with 300 million in China and India alone, we see this as a great time to be launching a global campaign for Sprite', said Joseph V Tripodi, chief marketing and commercial officer at the Coca-Cola Company, in an interview with The New York Times. 'Whether a teen is based in the United States, India or China', Tripodi said, 'he or she shares a passion for creativity and a love of music and films.' Coca-Cola used considerable digital and mobile elements including content on **sprite.com** as well as an iPhone application.[16]

Mad as a Hatter

Today, teenage girls start using make-up at an increasingly early age. Compared to the puberty years of their mums, there is now a much wider range. The new cool trend in cosmetics is linking make-up lines with blockbuster movies. With the release of the massively popular vampire movie *Twilight* in 2009, DuWop, a manufacturer of qualitative make-up, introduced 'plumping' Twilight Venom lipstick with a tingling effect, and 'metallic' sparkling mascara. Adding fantasy texts that are related to the movie storyline heightens the appeal of the products for the teenage-girl market. For instance, the following advice is printed on the packaging of Twilight Venom: 'this product should be shaken before use to represent the blending of the human and vampire worlds'. Twilight make-up is only selectively put on the market through exclusive retailers. It sold out after one week.... The release of Tim Burton's new movie *Alice in Wonderland* also inspired nail polish brand OPI to launch a limited edition of four products on 11 March 2010, the day after the movie's world premiere. Again they only use a few exclusive points of sale and linked product names: 'Off with Her Red', 'Thanks so Muchness', 'Absolutely Alice' and 'Mad as a Hatter'.[17]

Is Gen Y loyal to cool brands?

A comment we often hear among brand managers when giving workshops on youth marketing is that young people and specifically Generation Y members are fickle and probably not the most brand-loyal population. So why should you bother putting your money and efforts into this target group? Why should you freeze your brands until they are cool, if tomorrow this coolness will rapidly melt? Because it is clearly an important way to build and strengthen your brand's competitive advantage to this youth generation. And, as we have demonstrated in this chapter, coolness equals youth choosing and buying your product now and in the future, even at premium price levels. In the second chapter we saw that coolness is an important part of the CRUSH brand model that will leverage brand image, conversations and brand strength. As you have read in the first chapter, it is true they were raised in a world full of choice and experiences. These stimulus junkies aren't easily impressed and attaining their fidelity is not an easy job. But it's your job as a marketer. They are your next generation of consumers and for most marketers they are your current consumers. You should grab every chance today to make them stick with your brand. We do think the disloyalty among youth has been overemphasized and the lack of loyalty among other age groups is underestimated. Gen Y is moulded by the age we're living in today, just like you. When we give speeches on this topic, we tend to ask the audience who is still in a relationship with their very first love. In a company of 100 listeners, there's generally only one... Not only young adults like to experience new things. This is the age of the experience economy. Although there are regular articles stating that Gen Y is less loyal than other generations, there is hardly any empirical proof for this statement.

Being loyal to one

In the summer of 2009 we interviewed 3,000 13- to 29-year-olds to get a better view on their brand loyalty.[18] The first thing we wanted to learn was for which products or services they were spontaneously convinced to choose the same single brand over and over again. The highest mono-amory (brand loyalty to one single brand) was found for the following products and top brands:

- mobile phone devices: Nokia, Samsung, iPhone, Sony Ericcson;
- soft drinks: Coca-Cola;
- fashion and sports: Nike, Adidas, G-Star, Bjorn Borg;
- computers and electronics: Apple, Sony;
- personal care: Gillette, Nivea.

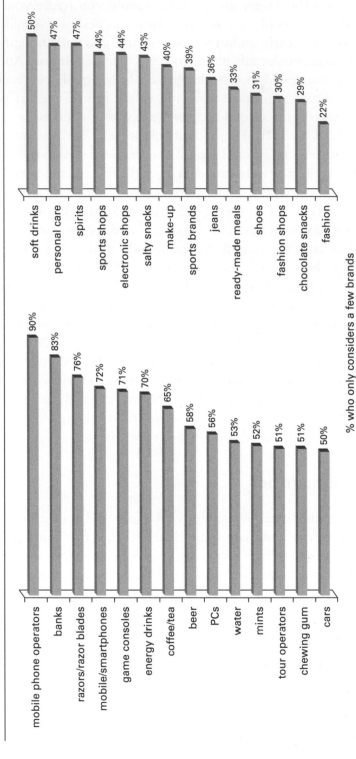

FIGURE 3.6 Number of considered brands per category

% who only considers a few brands

mobile phone operators 90%
banks 83%
razors/razor blades 76%
mobile/smartphones 72%
game consoles 71%
energy drinks 70%
coffee/tea 65%
beer 58%
PCs 56%
water 53%
mints 52%
tour operators 51%
chewing gum 51%
cars 50%

soft drinks 50%
personal care 47%
spirits 47%
sports shops 44%
electronic shops 44%
salty snacks 43%
make-up 40%
sports brands 39%
jeans 36%
ready-made meals 33%
shoes 31%
fashion shops 30%
chocolate snacks 29%
fashion 22%

You could conclude that for those sectors that are important to them, this fickle generation is capable of sticking to one favourite brand. But still we have to see this in the right perspective. Even Coca-Cola, the brand with the highest loyalty, only has 10 per cent of youngsters consuming their brand as the only soft drink. The final conclusion here seems that brand mono-amory is a too rigid way of examining youth's loyalty.

Being loyal to a few

As a result, we looked at it from another angle and asked for the number of brands they take into consideration when making a choice in each category.

Gen Y undoubtedly form a serial monogamous target group. They switch between a limited set of trusted and cool brands for many categories, as shown in Figure 3.6. In customer-bonding literature this is called attitudinal loyalty, which has replaced pure behavioural loyalty among consumers of all ages. When you look at the scheme in Figure 3.7, showing the relation between the average coolness scores of the brands in each sector and the importance Gen Y attaches to coolness, some conclusions can be drawn.

In the upper right quadrant of Figure 3.7, badge item products (categories that the youth use to project their identity to peers) have certainly understood the importance of being cool. One sector may be an unexpected member of this cell: electronics. With its loudly approved design and latest innovative additions such as the iPad (a multi-touch screen tablet computer), the MacBook Air (an ultra-thin laptop) and the iPhone, Apple is the brand that has pushed the expectations of this category. Apple's brand coolness rate is 7.2/10 and the highest within its industry. Other sectors such as non-alcoholic drinks and deodorants are still neglecting the power of coolness. In spite of this, brands such as Coke (7.9 score) and Axe/Lynx (7.1) have illustrated for years that it is possible to successfully adopt coolness in their marketing and branding strategy.

In the automotive industry there's only a few brands actively targeting youth, such as the Mini. Nevertheless, turning 18 and getting a driver's licence means so much in the lives of adolescents. It is a magic moment that allows for specific marketing campaigns. Fortunately, things are changing in the sector. In the UK Mercedes is offering driving courses for kids who are at least 1.5 m tall. In the Netherlands

FIGURE 3.7 Average category coolness and importance of coolness

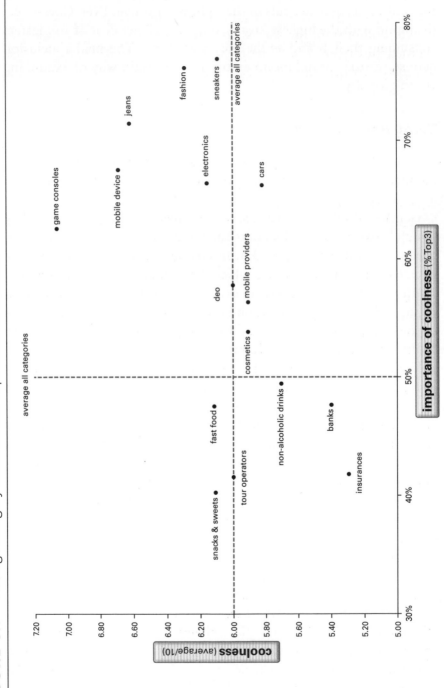

VW created a branded TV programme *License to Liberty* together with music and youth TV channel TMF. It was part of a new 2009 branding strategy of Volkswagen in which they launched relevant concepts linked to important life-stages. To rejuvenate VW's image, the brand claimed the driver's licence moment in the life of youth. In the *License to Liberty* TV programme, five candidates competed in driving course challenges. All five could attain their licence but only one of the candidates could win the VW Polo. Eighty per cent of the target group 16–24 saw this TV format on TMF. More than 430 driving schools joined in and 5,200 youngsters applied for the programme. The show received massive free publicity coverage. In the Cool Brands survey in the Netherlands, VW was the only volume make capable of reaching coolness levels across Gen Y comparable to BMW and Ferrari.

From the findings of our study, we can also demonstrate the importance of creating and sustaining cool brands. The graph in Figure 3.8 shows the relation between the individual coolness score of 540 brands in 30 different categories and whether that specific brand was picked as first choice or not. The bond (73 per cent) seems to be very strong, which is illustrated by the linear curve predicting the relation between both variables.

Cool brands (with a minimum score of 7.5/10) in the study were purchased twice as much as uncool brands (rates of 6.5 or less). When we asked the 13- to 29-year-olds whether they would buy those same brands in 3, 5 and 10 years from now, we discovered that their projected loyalty for cool brands was also more stable than for the uncool brands. This resulted in a self-reported projection of long-term preference that was three times higher than for uncool brands. Cool brands are also able to ask for a higher price, resulting in higher margins.

Four ways coolness affects brand loyalty

The 'Cool' factor can make or break your brand as consumers increasingly use brands to define themselves and use their own perception of what's cool to differentiate products and brands and to pick the most attractive ones within the massive market choice. The role that coolness can play for your brands depends on the sector you're working in.

The mapping in Figure 3.9 combining category fidelity and the significance of coolness shows four patent situations.

FIGURE 3.8 Relationship between coolness and brand preference

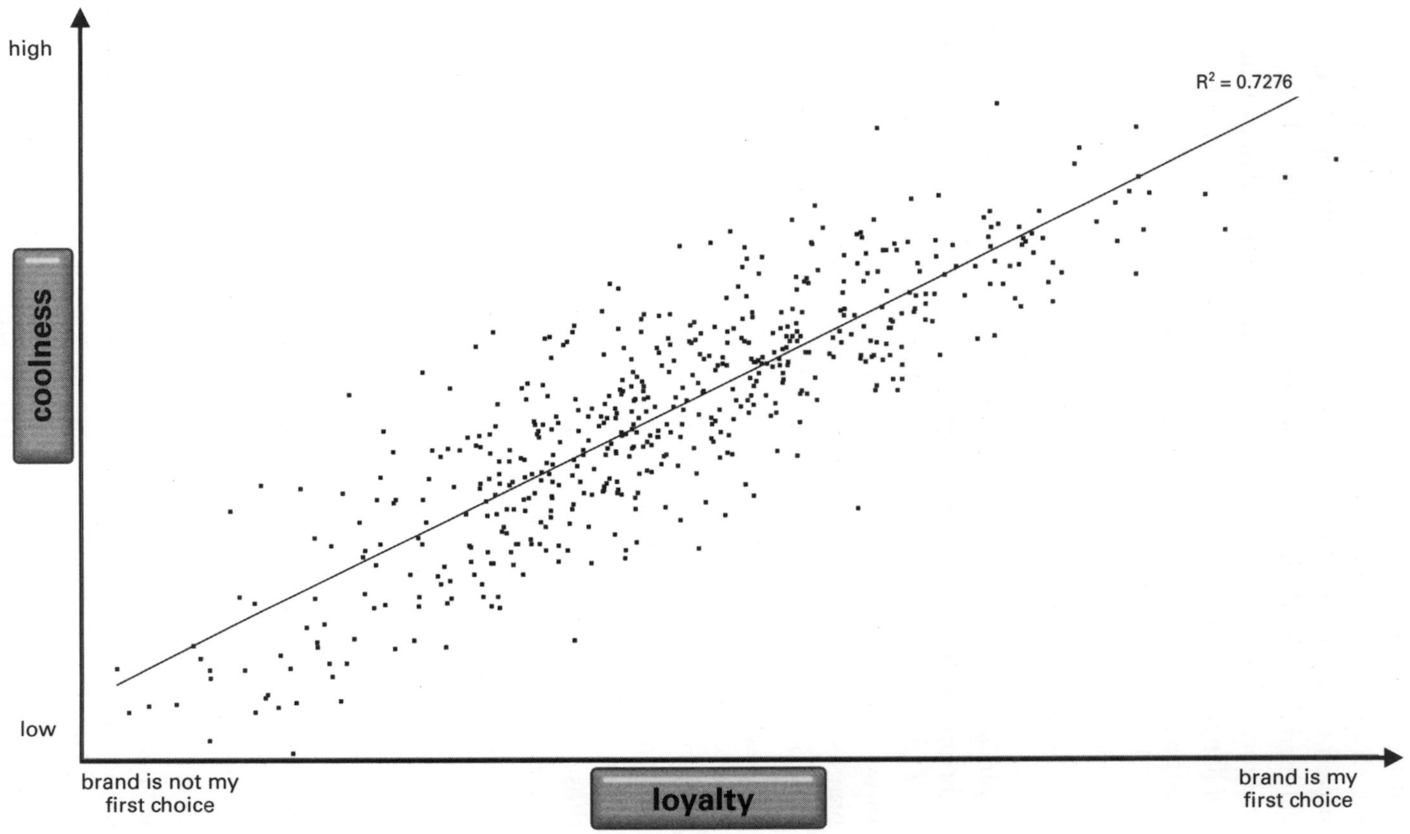

FIGURE 3.9 The role coolness can play

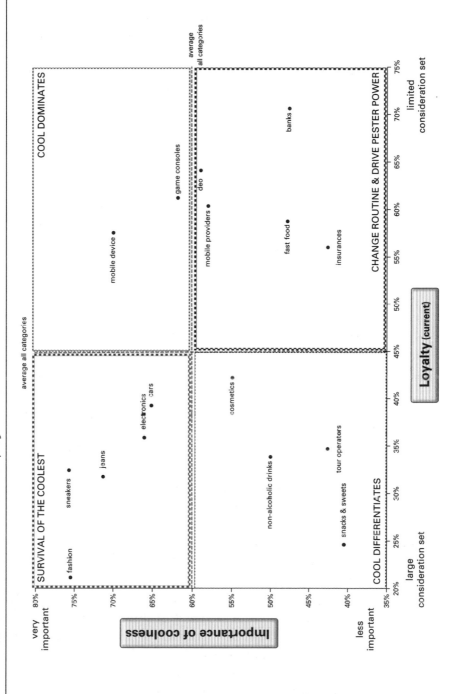

1 Survival of the coolest

In the upper left quadrant, there's fierce competition between a large set of acceptable and interchangeable brands. Youngsters choose a brand based on price/quality relationship and availability but also on marketing campaigns that appeal to them. If your brands file under this situation, being a cool brand is a must to survive. Cooling your brands will aid you to make the less brand loyal customers more faithful. For instance, if you take a look at the jeans industry, Levi Strauss was the almost single brand choice of youth until the 1990s. But the sector moved from the upper right corner of the scheme to the left when other brands like Diesel, Replay and G-Star Raw entered the market. It became even harder to keep the market share and loyalty when designer brands such as Dolce & Gabbana, Gucci, Armani and many others saw the point of joining the denim market.

2 Cool differentiates

In the bottom left corner of the mapping, fast moving and low ticket items are situated. Since these are easier to buy and often based on impulsive choices, youth's loyalty is quite low. It's just easy and not so risky to experiment. Yes, they are stimulus junkies. This doesn't mean they don't have favourite brands for these categories. In these circumstances, cooling your brand differentiates you from competitors. It is crucial to offer cool and unordinary, unexpected impulses, such as new flavours or varieties, new impulses. You have to catch their attention. In the chewing gum market Stimorol launched the 'Senses' product line, using black and silver as the main packaging colour codes together with fancy variety names like watermelon sunrise and rainforest mint. The brand also has the fusion-line combining two tastes (eg vanilla goes mint, strawberry goes lemon, etc). Competitor Mentos introduced the Aquakiss with a similar stylish aura as the Senses line. Mentos also launched the cubes, an attention-grabbing new chewing gum packaging and the Blast series, gums with a liquid centre. In the salty snack industry, PepsiCo owns a cool brand too. Doritos has been out-cooling competitors with campaigns that are in line with Gen Y's interests and desires. Just think of the user-generated commercials during the Superbowl, or the 'design your Xbox computer game' contest. Doritos and PepsiCo's sister brand Lays understood that keeping your cool equals keeping your Gen Y customers loyal. Both brands frequently introduce new flavours; the best trick to keep things fresh is to launch varieties that will only be available for a limited time. Doritos, for example, introduced the Late Night Taco range (including flavours called Last Call Jalapeno Popper, Midnight and Cheeseburger) with an online event for which a special marker on the bag of crisps was the entrance ticket. The event, virtually popping out of the bag had 3D performances of bands such as *Blink182* using augmented reality technology to mix live video footage within a 3D interactive environment. The technology allowed users to alter the video performances experienced by simply changing the way they held or moved the snack bag in front of their webcam. Participants could also enter a contest to win tickets to a live *Blink182* show in the city of their choice. The online events – described by PepsiCo as 'concerts in the palm of your hand' – were completely in line with the series of innovative efforts focused on involving and giving control to the Gen Y fans of the Doritos brand.[19]

3 Cool dominates

In the top right corner of the diagram, we find products and services for which being cool is important and here youngsters show a substantial loyalty to the brands they are used to. If you're working in this business, your challenge is to break the fidelity of the prospects that are loyal to one of your competitors. In this area of the scheme, being the pioneering brand gives you a clear first movers' advantage. Understanding the age entry points of your products is important. If you were not the innovator, the only way to steal a massive market share from your competitor is by changing the rules of the category. This implies either changing the target group, occasion of use or market standards. A good example is the game console market. Microsoft released the first version of Xbox to compete with Sony's PlayStation 2, Sega's Dreamcast and Nintendo's Gamecube at the end of 2001. It had superior graphics support, Dolby Interactive Content-Encoding Technology and a hard drive. The main success factor proved to be the *Halo* game, an exclusive to Xbox FPS (First Person Shooter). It meant the end of Sega and the Gamecube was not able to compete with Sony or Microsoft. But Xbox's battle with Sony was clearly more difficult. Early Xbox games weren't using the powerful hardware. This decreased the competitive advantage of the Xbox. Sony countered the attack of Microsoft by securing exclusives for highly popular games such as *Grand Theft Auto* for a while. Nintendo struck back at the end of 2006 by launching the Nintendo Wii console. The Wii's main distinguishing feature is the wireless hand-held controller – the Wii remote – which detects movement in three dimensions. The technology was based on hard-disk saving techno-logy (sensing movements of a portable device to save the hard disk from crashing). In an interview Nintendo's game designer Shigeru Miyamoto said: 'The consensus was that power isn't everything for a console. Too many powerful consoles can't co-exist.' In December 2006, Satoru Iwata, CEO of Nintendo added: 'We're not thinking about fighting Sony, but about how many people we can get to play games. The thing we're thinking about is not portable systems, consoles, and so forth, but that we want to get new people playing games.'[20] As of February 2010, the Wii leads over the PlayStation 3 and Xbox 360 in worldwide sales. Clearly inspired by this market development, Microsoft announced their Project Natal on 1 June 2009. Project Natal is the code name for a depth sensor that allows users to control and interact with the Xbox 360 without the need to touch a game controller at all. Microsoft hopes to broaden their audience beyond the typical gamer base too. It is scheduled for release in time for Christmas 2010. Apple entered the mobile phone market with the same innovation approach turning the multi-touch screen into the new market standard.

4 Coolness to change routines and drive pester power

In this bottom right part of the scheme, the brand loyalty of youth is strong but coolness is relatively less important to them. The products in this quadrant are either routine purchases or even stuff that is bought by parents for their adolescents. Cooling the brand will push up the brand in the chart, making it more appealing than competi-tors. Another effect brand coolness may produce is putting the brand on the youth's shopping list (pester power). Procter & Gamble wanted to grow the market share of its Braun brand by targeting the Braun CruZer, a male grooming (shaving) device, to the youth segment. In the winter of 2008–09 Procter & Gamble joined efforts with TMF, a youth music channel in Belgium and the Netherlands and part of MTV Networks. The brand solutions division of MTV created a branded TV format named *King of Snow*. During eight weeks young-sters participated in a snowboarder contest filled with tests, stunts and challenges to become the King of Snow. The Belgian champion freestyle snowboarder assisted the candidates in achieving the most spectacular results. More than 60 per cent of the youngsters that had been watching the broadcast evaluated it as original, entertaining and interesting. One third of the viewers had talked about the programme to others. Aided brand attribution of Braun CruZer with the show was 41 per cent. By supporting the TV programme, Procter & Gamble has improved the creative, young and local image of its Braun brand. Youngsters who had seen the show significantly rated those brand personality items higher. *King of Snow* viewers also had higher brand awareness and net promoter scores. Procter & Gamble also noticed an immediate consumer sales effect after the broadcast.[21] The 2009 *King of Snow* edition resulted in an ongoing growth to 6.2 per cent value share (coming from 5.0 per cent) or 16 per cent of total Braun shavers business.[22]

How to find out what's cool

The main point of the previous part is that young consumers aren't leaving your brand because they have a good reason to do so. They will switch to another brand because yours isn't giving them compelling reasons to stay with it. It happened to Reebok. It has happened to Converse and Levi's. And to many other brands that once were the coolest of their industry. And chances are that at a certain point in time, it will happen to your brand too. The biggest challenge of youth marketers is to keep their products and brands funky. The trick is to keep your marketing campaigns up to date without losing your brand's authenticity. Staying true to your own brand identity and DNA might seem patently obvious but our daily practice teaches us that it is the one golden rule that is often ignored in targeting young consumers. Marketers are easily blinded by the glamour of sponsoring cool events or creating links with celebrities. Gen Y is more aware of marketing spin than previous generations. If they don't see a clear fit with their perception of your brand personality, they will interpret this is as a fake buying of coolness. Youngsters will find your brand isn't cool because if it were, your brand wouldn't need this image stealing. It takes a subtle approach to stay a cool and relevant brand without losing your real identity. The trainer collection of Nike introduces new styles every season. The lead times of clothing designers has decreased from 18 months to a year or even six months to be able to react faster to street trends.[23] Often, marketers feel they have to continuously demonstrate their knowledge about people, looks and music.

Coolhunters

In this urge to catch the new vibes a whole new industry of 'cool-hunters' appeared in the late 1990s.[24] Sociologist Malcolm Gladwell, later famous for his books *The Tipping Point* and *Blink*, coined the term 'coolhunter' in an article in *The New Yorker* magazine in 1997. In this piece he interviews DeeDee Gordon and Baysie Wightman while they are discovering trends in the streets for trainer brand Reebok. The key to do this coolhunting is to find the cool people and not cool things. Because only cool people recognize what is cool. And because cool things are always changing, you can't look for them yourself. In fact you would only think back to what was cool before and then extrapolate this, which is of course the wrong idea. Cool people on the other hand are more constant. In Gladwell's editorial DeeDee says she is looking for individuals who don't look like peers but are setting themselves apart from everybody else. To them 'cool' is doing something distinctive. These young hipsters are often recruited in fashionable city areas and/or occupied in certain kinds of job, for instance fashion, art, photography, media, music, film-making, design, etc. It is important to employ young and trendy recruiters and moderators who can relate to this type of research participant. Cool people want to remain ahead of the herd and disdain the uncool, especially uncool researchers.

Gladwell also comments on the circularity of coolhunting. The more hunters are bringing cutting-edge trends to the mainstream, the faster innovators move on to the next thing. Eventually, to follow these high-paced trends, companies need coolhunters.[25] Because cool-hunters are constantly protecting the necessity of their work, they have received substantial critique in the past. They were the objects of contempt among anti-globalists such as Naomi Klein. Klein argues that coolhunting is a euphemism for black-culture hunting. When young black innovators are influencing white Americans then cool-hunting ensures that profits will keep flowing where they always have done. Serious researchers, both academic and in agencies, dis-approved of the 'high priests of cool' too. In particular, the fuzzy nature of what defines cool and the recruitment process of cool people depending on instinct, sixth sense or gut feelings made them quite nervous. Not to mention the commercial success, status and cooler image of coolhunters. Still, we do agree with the critics on one point: it is better for your brand to find new ways that help your Gen Y consumers to express themselves than to merely copy the stuff that cool people are expressing.[26]

Cool networks

Nowadays, word-of-mouse through social network sites, blogs, e-mail and instant messaging is boosting the viral tempo of trend diffusion. The rise of these networks has made Rogers' standard work on the diffusion of innovations obsolete.[27] Other authors such as Bob Metcalfe, founder of 3Com Corporation and co-inventor of Ethernet found that a good or service increases in value to potential users depending on an increasing number of users. Think of fax machines, mobile phones, e-mail, instant messaging, chat.... This finding became known as Metcalfe's Law.[28] David Reed commented on this law in saying that it underestimates the value of adding connections to a network. This became clear with the appearance of social network sites such as LinkedIn or Facebook. When you connect to a user in a network, you also connect to a significant number of subnetworks. This phenomenon exponentially increases the value of each connection as opposed to simply summing up the two connections. Reed's Law is an improved way of looking at the diffusion of ideas, innovation and cool products and brands.[29]

Reed's ideas have also dramatically changed the business of coolhunters. Instead of talking with a few cool people in the streets of the fashionable city districts back in the 1990s, they now connect with leading-edge consumers, cultural reporters or style runners all over the world. Rather than asking them questions about products and brands they are now observing social networks, communities and blogs where cool people are already spontaneously discussing the cool stuff.

In an interview Carolijn Domensino, ex-coolhunter of Carl Rohde's agency Signs of the Time, says:

> In the early days you travelled a lot but the problem is that you can't be everywhere at the same time. Nowadays it's important that you are in close contact with people who run their own fashion blogs. Actually, they replace you, because they give you all the information you need. A coolhunter

nowadays needs a strong digital network with online coolhunters who share their information with you (and you with them). It's not that the way of analysing has changed but the information flow is growing bigger and bigger and is increasingly powered by the internet. The point is that everyone can be a coolhunter now.[30]

Cool mining

Since more than 71 per cent of Europeans in the 15–24 age bracket and 64 per cent of 25- to 35-year-olds are sharing their own private lives on social network sites such as Facebook,[31] these sites have a wealth of information for youth watchers.

Diageo tapped into these rich data to improve the Christmas campaigns for its Whisky brand Johnnie Walker to the 21+ market. Through this Christmas campaign, the brand is targeting a specific group of young men (aged 21 and older) who are ambassadors of the Johnnie Walker values. Diageo wanted deeper insights into the behaviour and lifestyles of its target group to endorse the marketing campaigns. What were their interests, attitudes and ambitions? InSites Consulting recruited 24 participants, aged 21–30, who met the target group criteria and asked them to become friends with us in all the online social networks they were actively engaged in. We followed our new friends for a week and with the aid of web scraping software, we extracted all the information available online including conversations with other social network members, pictures, group memberships, status posts, profile information, etc. We then analysed the available data with the aid of text analytics. We were able to extract:

- role models (stand-up comedians, film-makers such as Quentin Tarantino);
- favourite music;
- preferred holiday destinations;
- the sports and games they liked;
- their online behaviour (visited websites and blogs: many newspaper sites and music sites such as last.fm for instance, but also gaming environments);
- favourite TV formats and programmes: eg *Pimp my ride*, *Jackass*, *South Park*, *Weeds*.

We finally found that for the Johnnie Walker target group life is not always easy and they try to escape from trouble now and then. This escapism translates in partying all night long, immersing themselves in other worlds such as movies, games or online social networks or e-commerce. They also de-stress by driving fast cars and motors, relaxing on holidays or watching many hours of TV feeds. They are quite confident about their own skills and value intelligence and knowledge.[32] The insights from following the Johnnie Walker target group online in their social networks were used for Diageo's Game Plan, a yearly strategic plan. In an interview, An Martel, senior brand manager for Johnnie Walker, explains:

> What consumers tell you in usual surveys is never 100 per cent the truth. Studying and observing them in their own environment without really asking questions is much more valuable. We have used these insights to adapt our media plans. As a result of the online qualitative research, we have integrated local role models into our approach. Our classic PR plan was switched to an online plan involving local bloggers. We had observed that our target group is keen on certain blogs. By following our consumers online, we were able to find new insights and confirm existing trends.[33]

Coolfarming or co-creation

Peter Gloor and Scott Cooper discern a second type of using collective wisdom in their book *Coolhunting*. They call it 'coolfarming' and it implies getting involved with creating new trends. Where traditional coolhunters would have rejected this idea and named it impossible, these authors claim the coolest ideas come from a collective mindset. Innovation is a result of the collaboration of people who share interests but not necessarily jobs or disciplines. They quite ironically coined this process as Collaborative Innovation Networks, abbreviated by the acronym... COIN. This idea is backed by MIT Professor Erich Von Hippel who found that the new products proposed by end-users to 3M produced eight times more revenues than those exclusively developed by 3M's internal R&D department.[34]

In the summer of 2009 *De Standaard*, the leading Belgian quality newspaper, asked InSites Consulting to help them increase their appeal to the Gen Y population. For one month we opened an online community engaging both *De Standaard* readers and non-readers in two age groups: 18–24 and 25–34. Everyone received a free subscription to *De Standaard* during this month and was invited to share their daily thoughts on the newspaper: the front page, layout, photography, content, writing style, topics covered, etc. They could also give their own ideas on creating the ideal newspaper. A multidisciplinary team consisting of editorial, marketing and sales staff at Corelio (publisher of *De Standaard* newspaper) then implemented the results of this co-creation project. On the editorial level, new openers to the paper's articles were integrated, such as 'three questions'. Journalists now use more quotes, summarize longer articles in three bullets and use more pictures. Longer texts are divided into smaller 'snack news' content. Front pages are built on a large size picture with a few quotes from the person in the picture. For the marketing and sales division one of the attention points was the lack of experience youth had with the newspaper. Although *De Standaard* suffered from an old-fashioned image, this was not the case once youngsters had the chance to read the paper. To tackle this situation, the newspaper launched an e-mail campaign to students that led to 5,000 students requesting a free monthly subscription. Secondly, *De Standaard* did a summer camp action allowing scouts and other youth movements to receive the paper for free on their camp destination. As a result, 9,152 youngsters participated and the newspaper was delivered to 3,622 different youth camps. Thirdly, the paper sampled 36,000 copies in student cities with a specific wrapper offering local student-city content. Since the co-creation research had shown that students were fond of the newspaper's celebrity photographers (Michiel Hendrickx and Carl De Keyzer), this competitive advantage was put in the spotlight. Michiel Hendrickx went on a photography tour in student cities using the *De Standaard* Photobox for shootings of students. Carl De Keyzer, a Magnum photographer, created a Magnum edition of the newspaper. *De Standaard* also offered free numbered lithos of famous pictures in five Saturday editions. At the start of the academic year, *De Standaard* provided a free ticket for a concert in the rock venue AB and they regularly streamed live concerts from that venue on their website. More than three times the capacity of the venue watched the gigs of Placebo and Moby on *De Standaard*'s website. The newspaper also created a new student subscription offering a good deal for domiciling students. In a tracking among the higher educated Gen Yers target group (18- to 34-year-olds) *De Standaard* achieved the highest satisfaction rates of all newspapers.[35] In the last media tracking, the newspaper increased its circulation by 1.6 per cent.[36]

Peter Pandemonium: adults' desire to stay young and cool

Contrary to popular belief among marketers, coolness is relevant to consumers of all ages. A youthful outlook is no longer the sole preserve of the young and the essential meaning and traditional definition of 'youth' has changed. You don't have to be named Peter Pan or Michael Jackson to file under this trend. The older consumer wants to stay in touch with younger generations and is more eager than ever to stay young for as long as possible. Some brands, think of Apple as the ultimate example, allow them to keep a cooler image while not affecting their maturity. It may come as a surprise that in Europe 62 per cent and in Asia 61 per cent of the MTV viewers are older than 25 years old. In the United States and Latin America the percentage is lower but still about 49 per cent.

Viacom Brand Solutions International, MTV Networks International's advertising and marketing sales division, conducted a large-scale study named 'The Golden Age of Youth' in 18 countries worldwide among more than 25,000 26- to 46-year olds. Findings indicated that globally people are staying younger longer and are connected to contemporary youth pursuits for a more extensive period of time. The fact that people are having longer lives is one major contributing factor along with the 'youthification' of culture. It has now become more acceptable for older people to indulge in youthful behaviour. While teenage youth are highly focused on material gain and employ brands to define their identity, 'Golden Youth' (25+) own and enjoy premium and luxurious brands in order to affirm their identity. Fifty-two per cent of them agree with the statement that they still have a lot of growing up to do. Twenty-three per cent would even love to be a teenager again. Contemporary youth can now be defined more accurately as 'the absence of functional and/or emotional maturity'. This requires a completely new marketing approach. Traditional adult brands need to adopt a more youthful tone to avoid being seen as irrelevant or 'for older people than me'.[37] In 2006, Christopher Noxon wrote a brilliant book on the youth-celebrating consumer culture and coined a word for the phenomenon: 'Rejuvenile'. 'They constitute a new breed of adult identified by a determination to remain playful, energetic and flexible in the face of adult responsibilities', Noxon says. For the boomer generation, brand

and youth nostalgia may be the drivers, for Generation X it is merely suspending adolescence. The book is loaded with examples, such as the trend for colourful cupcakes; 'Disnoids', obsessive adult fans (with no children) of Disney theme parks; AFOLs, adult fans of LEGO; or 'grays on trays', ski slope slang for elder, sometimes arthritic snowboarders.[38] According to ESA, the US entertainment software association, the average computer and video game player is now 39 years old. More than 25 per cent of Americans over the age of 50 play video games. In 1999, this was only 9 per cent.[39]

Flip-flop generations

In his article 'Old is the New Young' in *Adweek* of 17 March 2010, William Higham, author of *The Next Big Thing*, calls this phenomenon Flip-flop Generations. The New Old are still pursuing the sex, drugs and rock 'n' roll lifestyle of their youth. According to The National Council on Aging 61 per cent of all 60-somethings today are still sexually active. The fastest-growing group of online daters consists of singles aged 55 and older. The number of 50-somethings using drugs rose more than 70 per cent in the period 2002–08. There are more marijuana consumers among them than in any other age group. The average age of a motorcyclist is now 47. On the other hand researchers notice a growing trend of adolescents moving away from the typical hedonism and liberalism. They claim this is a result of paranoid parenting and the recent economic downturn. Today's conserva-teens are more concerned about their financial future and security than ever before. Only 10 per cent of teens want to be ahead of everybody else in buying the latest technologies as soon as they become available. There is a growing emphasis on morality and family in their set of values.[40]

In our research we found that the impact of the coolness rates of favourite brands on brand image and conversations was even slightly higher for respondents older than 30 than for those below the age of 30. These findings confirm the 'adultescent' trend of the past 10 years. 'Adultescent' was accepted into the *Oxford Dictionary of English* and is defined as 'a middle-aged person whose clothes, interests, and activities are typically associated with youth culture'. Jay Leno reacted in his show, saying: 'Have you heard this word? It's an adult who lives and acts like a child. Or as women call that – men.'[41]

Conclusion

The first step in sustainable brand building to the Generation Y is 'cooling' your brand. Coolness today means much more than the semantic strategic value of the movements, postures, facial expressions and voice modulations made famous by The Fonz. Coolness has also surpassed its historic links with resistance or rebel attitudes. For this youth generation, cool brands are attractive and appealing brands that are popular in their immediate social circle and bring a sense of novelty, surprise or originality. The main sources that set the standards of coolness are friends, TV, magazines, advertising and music festivals. Music artists are much cooler than movie actors. Although some product categories have a cool handicap, cool brands are found in all categories. Even in uncool sectors, brands can become cool leaders by adapting the most determining drivers of coolness in the coolness formula. Often, originality and innovation (in communication, events, packaging, varieties) are the keys to cool your brand. Other ways of freezing your brand include exclusive retailing or volume scarcity, and advertising on cool channels.

After reading this chapter, you shouldn't doubt cooling your brand anymore, it is necessary to keep your products or services relevant for the future generation of consumers, Gen Y, and it won't harm your brand in appealing to the older generations. One thing you should keep in mind is that you can't fake being cool or copy cool stuff from others. Old school coolhunting or trendwatching doesn't make sense. You need to cool your brand while at the same time staying true to your own identity. This Gen Y need for authenticity will be elaborated in the next chapter. Coolmining and coolfarming, both involving youth, are better routes to improve your brand's connection with this generation.

Hot takeaways for cool brand builders

- If your brand is perceived as cool, the positive impact on your image and brand conversations will leverage it to stay hot for the long term.

- Cool brands don't only have a higher short-term preference; they also protect brands in the long-term and are a guarantee of loyalty even for the fickle youth generation.

- The most important sources to know what's cool: social media, peers, TV, magazines, advertising and music festivals.

- Being cool does not equal being rebellious, edgy or alternative, at least not to the mainstream and biggest part of the youth population.

- In different consumer categories, coolness can help your brand in a different way.

- Cooling your brand includes constant innovation, exclusive offerings and advertising and promotion on cool channels or in cool environments.

- Hunting coolness doesn't make sense, it's better to use the collective wisdom of youth through coolmining of communities or coolfarming (co-creation).

Chapter Four
The real thing:
brand authenticity

Nostalgia. It's delicate but potent. Teddy told me that in Greek, nostalgia literally means, 'the pain from an old wound'. It's a twinge in your heart, far more powerful than memory alone.

In the final episode of the first season of the US drama series *Mad Men*, Don Draper, creative director of ad agency Sterling Cooper uses the nostalgic value of the Kodak projector to increase its market potential. Although Kodak's new slide projector is named 'The Wheel', Don advocates a different name 'The Carousel' in his client presentation built around slides of his own children, his wedding and other nostalgic family moments.[1] *Mad Men*, created and produced by Matthew Weiner, who also worked as a writer for *The Sopranos*, has won many awards including eleven Emmys and four Golden Globes. The show, set in the 1960s, follows Draper's life in and outside the Madison Avenue advertising industry. It is particularly praised for its historic authenticity. The writers are notorious for spending much time on research to include the most accurate set designs, costumes and props.[2] Viewership for the premiere on 19 July 2007 was much higher than any other AMC series to date and the third season's premiere in 2009 had 2.8 million viewers.[3] Don Draper's performance of the Frank O'Hara poem 'Mayakovsky' from *Meditations in an Emergency* in the second season of *Mad Men* has even led to the poet's work entering Amazon's top 50 sales chart.[4]

Fifty years after the *Mad Men* era, marketers are still fond of using the nostalgic values of their brands and products to appeal to Gen Y's desire for authenticity. Advertisers understood that their brands should have a purpose and point of view that is bigger than just selling stuff to the kids. The example of *Mad Men*, produced in the 21st century, also proves that you don't need an old brand to be perceived as authentic.

Authenticity is generally defined as 'the quality of being of an established authority or being genuine, not corrupted from the original, or truthfulness of origins'.[5] Many brands tell consumers when they were established. For instance, on Levi's jeans the logo (see Figure 4.1) shows us that the use of copper rivets to strengthen the stitched pockets of the denim working pants was patented on 20 May 1873. This was the day blue jeans were invented. Kronenbourg, the brewery founded by Geronimus Hatt, is also communicating its year of birth, 1664. It is also the name of the main lager brand of the firm. The label on a Heinz tomato ketchup bottle says 'since 1869', not only indicating its date of birth but also suggesting Heinz was the first brand in the ketchup category. In 2008, The Coca-Cola Company launched a global marketing campaign under the 'secret formula' flag. It consisted of a TV commercial, a website and packaging referring to John Pemberton's invention of the secret formula for Coca-Cola in 1886. The main message of the campaign was the authentic and honest Coke recipe, containing neither preservatives nor artificial flavourings.

Academic research has demonstrated that this type of information may increase a brand's likeability by inducing a perception of originality. If you are a marketing professional, there's a big chance that the thought of using labels such as 'original', 'classic' or 'the real thing', has at least crossed your mind once. They are probably more widely

FIGURE 4.1   Levi's back pocket label shows date of origin

used than the date of origin and have the power to convey the message that competitors are merely weak imitations.[6]

The classic view on brand authenticity, which uses an objective definition linked to origin, history, heritage, people or places, has been challenged in the last decade. Research revealed that people's perception of authenticity is of course highly subjective and socially constructed. It is derived from ongoing interactions between the brand manager or marketer, consumers and society. Studies have identified that brand authenticity is a good predictor of buying intention.[7] Authentic brands are more likely to attract bigger spenders and they are a good driver for word-of-mouth support.

In this chapter, we will explore the dos and don'ts of brand authenticity as a marketing strategy aimed at Generation Y. In our first chapter on the characteristics and behaviour of this generation, we amply demonstrated how they are critical and marketing-savvy consumers. They often consider the purely image-based strategies of brands that 'are' instead of 'do', once so successful in targeting Generation X, to be utterly inauthentic.

When a certain brand identity or campaign proves to be successful in the market, copycats awake. *Mad Men*'s success evoked some parodies too. In 2008, Jon Hamm (the actor playing Don Draper) was the host on *Saturday Night Live* and parodied his constantly drinking, smoking and womanizing character. In *The Simpsons*' episode 'Treehouse of Horror XIX' there's a scene in which *Mad Men*'s animated title sequence is adapted, using the theme song of the series on the soundtrack.[8] Even the children's television show *Sesame Street* ran a parody of *Mad Men* in 2009 with muppet versions of Don Draper and two other advertising guys.[9] The issue of brand identity theft will obviously have to be addressed in this chapter too.

The roots of real: why brand authenticity is the in thing

In 2007 James Gilmore and B Joseph Pine II dedicated an entire management book to the topic of authenticity. They claim the search for authenticity has become more prominent in the last years. The authors link this evolution to the rise of the experience economy. More people than before are looking for experiences, not only in travel and entertainment but also in important life moments such as their birthday, wedding, matchmaking, dating, etc. But service providers are automating customer interaction jobs; take online banking and voice recognition automated call centres as examples. In response, on the website GetHuman.com people are posting short cuts (immediately hitting the '0' or '#' or weird keypad combinations) to go directly to a human being working at the customer service division of hundreds of companies. Consumers are forced to interact more with machines and hence place greater value on person-to-person conversations.[10] This is unquestionably also the case for Generation Y consumers. In our authenticity survey for Levi's, we asked 13- to 29-year-olds which sources they would consult for advice when buying clothes. The number one response (75 per cent of answers) was 'my best friends' and at number two 'someone of the shop personnel' (54 per cent). Brochures, websites, review sites and magazines were chosen by less than 30 per cent.[11]

Authenticity as a driver of brand choice

In our postmodern society, we are all looking for less materialistic buying motivations. Choosing a nostalgic or authentic product or brand enables us to reduce the feeling of guilt. Instead of 'consuming', we discover new sensations and enjoy a forgotten or seemingly lost past. Generation Y is constantly looking for new experiences or thrilling events that engage them personally and will be remembered forever. This might give the impression that 'old' or 'nostalgic' attributes aren't appealing to them. But that's not the case. The market is not only flooded with an abundance of goods and services, but also increasingly filled with deliberately staged live experiences. The distinctions between real and unreal or fake are blurring for youngsters. This has affected the choice criteria young consumers are using today. Their perception of how real, genuine or sincere a company or brand is, has become essential in doing business with them. When lacking time, trust and attention, brand authenticity plays an important role in choosing between equal alternatives. Youth seems to value authenticity in a world that is characterized by mass production and marketing. The popularity of reality shows on TV, for instance, can be seen as a quest for authenticity within the traditionally fiction-oriented entertainment industry. The vintage trend in fashion and design is a reaction to mass production and a consequence of youth's need to differentiate and stand out from others.[12] In the postmodern market, nostalgia for the 'good old one' appeals to Gen Y's demand for simplicity. Converse All Star basketball shoes for example, haven't changed the overall design since Charles 'Chuck' Taylor created it in the 1920s. The style consistency and its rock and art heritage made the brand a popular choice for an alternative and creative groups of youngsters.[13] The key to creating brand authenticity is providing opportunities for self-expression and self-fulfilment. Consumption of products often functions as a marker of identity. We will discuss this in Chapter 6.

An ancient marketing strategy

Although authenticity gets a lot of attention in postmodern marketing books, there's nothing new under the sun. Back in the 14th century Bordeaux winemakers felt severe competition from the lower-priced Bergerac *terroirs* along the Dordogne river in the interior east. In their first reaction, the merchants convinced the English controlling the port of Bordeaux to impose heavy taxes on wine from the interior. When Italian, Spanish and Portuguese wine-growing expanded and the French couldn't cope with the lower prices anymore, Bordeaux winemakers focused on the authenticity of their products. This allowed them to charge a premium price. They unified the small *grands crus* into a few larger holdings and associated them with neighbouring country houses or chateaux such as Pétrus, Margaux, Latour and Mouton-Rothschild.[14] This marketing technique, positioning luxury wines as a natural product as opposed to industrial and mass-produced, is still employed today. French winemakers stress the historic style specific to the particular chateau, or *terroir* and create a brand aura. Michael B Beverland examined the strategies of 26 French wineries and discovered they are outwardly downplaying their real scientific and business expertise to appear different from commercial competitors. Instead, they project their sincerity by telling a story of commitment to tradition, production excellence and passion for the daily craft.[15]

Authenticity in the music industry

Authenticity has traditionally been of high importance within cultural sectors such as the arts and music. Think of the German music project

Milli Vanilli in the late 1980s, early 1990s. When producer Frank Farian confessed the recording didn't contain the voices of Fab Morvan and Rob Pilatus, their Grammy Award for Best New Artist 1990 was withdrawn. The Beatles were famous for singing their own compositions as opposed to The Monkees who sang professionally written songs. Today many pop music artists are still using their own personal roots as a sales message. It is not only often projected in rap (50 Cent, Eminem) but also in pop music. For instance in her 2003 hit *Jenny from the Block*, Jennifer Lopez stresses her authenticity singing: 'no matter where I go, I know where I came from (the Bronx).'[16]

It started as a joke

In October 2008, Dustin McLean, an LA-based film-maker/musician came up with an inside joke with his colleagues working at *Current TV*. They found that music videos often didn't really authentically portray what the song lyrics were saying. 'Wouldn't it be funny if we sang very literally what was happening in music videos and replace the lyrics and audio with describing lyrics?' McLean produced a literal dubbed video of a-ha's 'Take on Me' and posted it on YouTube. A new trend, 'literal music videos' was born.[17] In March 2010 over 7,100 literal music videos could be found on the online video channel. David A Scott, a commercial producer in upstate New York, posted the most successful one so far on 25 May 2009. His literal version of Bonnie Tyler's 'Total Eclipse of the Heart' reached more than 2 million views in the first three weeks. At the time of writing the video had reached more than 6.7 million viewers and *TIME* magazine's website listed the video as the number six top viral video of 2009. Due to copyright claims of Warner music and EMI, both mentioned videos were banned for a while but then suddenly restored without any explanation. Less than two weeks after Dustin McLean's literal version of Beck's 'Loser' music video was posted, Beck himself featured the dubbed version in his own official website.

Authenticity in advertising

In advertising, the use of authenticity is prevalent too. Although the authentic stereotypes such as Marlboro cowboys, genius artists and outlaws had been parodied a lot by the end of the 20th century and hence lost their mythical aura, the underlying values of freedom, autonomy and individuality are still relevant in youth marketing today. In an extensive study 1,000 print and television advertisements for trainer and jeans brands directed at 18- to 25-year-olds between 1999 and 2005, were analysed. Only 15 per cent of the ads had no link with authenticity at all. The jeans sample was especially striking. Escape, challenge and relaxation from formal rules were depicted in scenes straight from the desert, a rooftop, the edge of town, the street or the everyday. Quite often the ads ended with an open road representing a path of authentic self-discovery. Models were travelling across wide landscapes on dirty motorcycles or in worn and dusty vintage cars. Designer jeans were modelled on the street, not a catwalk, and showed people engaged in ordinary, mundane acts (eg drinking coffee, eating yoghurt). Interior locations in the ad scenes were mostly downmarket, dirty places. Long-haired, bohemian characters frequently appeared in music studios or were involved in creative arts such as painting or sculpting. Creative people are often regarded as being authentic because they are authors of their properly created art. The trainer advertisements often related to the hip-hop street culture including creative acts such as break-dancing, graffiti and dj-ing. Adidas ads were referring to nostalgic footage of Muhammad Ali, combining the artistry of Reebok with the athleticism and achievement appeals that Nike has been claiming consistently throughout the years.[18]

True tales and crafted cult: how brands portray authenticity

Michael B Beverland, an Australian Professor of Marketing, has dedicated much of his academic career to the subject of authenticity. According to his work published in the 2009 book *Building Brand Authenticity*, iconic brands can portray their 'realness' through seven habits. We have used his structured knowledge to illustrate how youth brands can tap into authenticity too.

Authentic habit 1: storytelling

Authentic brands are collections of stories that provide an emotional connection with the consumers. They create stories from the consumers' circumstances, take advantage of lucky events and allow and stimulate others (both ordinary consumers and celebrities) to tell their own stories about the brand for them. Even if the stories aren't true, they are relevant to consumers. Beverland suggested multiple possible story themes that authentic brands can use. Often they are connecting companies and brands to real people. Some examples of themes include:

- Creation and creativity: brands that lack creativity are usually me-too or follower brands. Authentic brands are obsessed with innovating. Think of Quiksilver continuously investing in wetsuit and board technology. These stories reinforce the perception of the brand's sincerity because the people behind the brand are viewed as lovers of their craft and merely motivated by the pursuit of perfection rather than money.

- History: many brands are linked to history. Vans and Quiksilver, for instance, originate from the early days of surf and skateboarding.

- Community: consumers forming offline and online communities around brands. For instance: Coca-Cola has more than 26,000 groups on Facebook, one fan page even counts more than 13 million fans today and was started by two friends who had no relationship at all with the company.

- Place: links to geographical locations are often used by food and beverage brands but are also common in the fashion (Italy), hi-tech (Japan) and car (Germany) industries.

- Consumers: own stories of consumers showing their affection and commitment and expressing their own identity, for instance the Mentos and Coke fountain experiment.

Authentic habit 2: appearing as artisanal amateurs

Mainstream brands will often emphasize quality and production efficiency. Authentic brands often stress their craft traditions combining the passion of the amateur with the skill of an artisan. They will downplay behind-the-scenes and state-of-the-art R&D and production processes, as well as market research and marketing budgets. Common techniques include illustrating the lack of training of the founders. Remember how Ben & Jerry, two hippies who weren't able to get into medical school, followed a $5 correspondence course on ice cream making? Or the young founders of Innocent Drinks whose future depended on the two trash bins at a music festival labelled 'yes, we want you to start a company' or 'no, we don't'? Ralph Lauren never had any fashion training and Steve Jobs can't write code.

Authentic habit 3: sticking to your roots

This is not the same as simply repeating past practices. Although authentic brands have to evolve and be creative, the novelties always have to reflect the roots of the brand and the original spirit of the founders.[19] We think the story of Vans is a good illustration of this.

The roots of the US manufacturer of trainers that primarily targets boarders and surfers, go back to 16 March 1966. Paul Van Doren and his three partners started The Van Doren Rubber Company to produce shoes and start selling them directly to the public. The sticky soles and rugged colourful designs made the Vans popular among skateboarders and BMX riders in the 1970s. In an effort to compete with large athletic shoe companies at the start of the 1980s, Vans made the decision to produce more mainstream football, baseball, basketball and even wrestling and skydiving shoes. Although Sean Penn made Vans Slip-Ons internationally popular when wearing them in the youth movie *Fast Times at Ridgemont High*, the core action sports lovers turned their back on their once beloved brand. The wide range of products had drained the companies' resources and when Vans didn't manage to overcome its debt, it had to file for bankruptcy in 1984.

In 2004, Vans was acquired for $396 million by VF Corp, home of brands such as Eastpak, North Face, Lee and Wrangler. Vans then learned its lesson to stay true to its authentic roots when addressing their core target group of 10- to 25-year-olds. According to the VP of Marketing, Doug Palladini, the four pillars of Vans culture are: action sports, music, street culture and art. Since 1995 Vans has been the primary sponsor of the Warped Tour music festivals. The brand is also co-sponsor of Mountain Dew's action sports tour. In an interview with *Brandweek*, Palladini said: 'The biggest challenge now is to maintain the energy that we have. We want this to last for the long term, not ride the trend while it's hot and then figure out what the next cool thing is. It's about continually reinforcing who we are as a company, always going back to our action sports heritage and DNA to find new opportunities instead of trying to blow something out for the moment.' To keep their cool, Vans shifted to a segmented offering. The high-end assortment, named Vault by Vans, is only sold in limited editions through boutiques with higher pricing. The Classics line, targeting a core group of boarding youth, is sold at skate- and snowboard shops. Another line for the masses is sold at bigger retail outlets. Vans sells different styles that appeal to different personalities, ages and gender.[20]

Authentic habit 4: love for the craft

The people behind authentic brands radiate their love for their craft. This reflects the desire of consumers to get paid for doing what they love. It involves product-orientation with an eye for detail, involvement of senior management in the core activities, and a never-ending quest for excellence or perfection. Authentic brands are often design-led and they let consumers experience the production, their own craft, as opposed to co-creation and co-design approaches.

Authentic habit 5: consumer immersion

Authentic brands absorb their surroundings to inspire breakthrough innovations. Companies such as Nike hire staff that are engaged in amateur or professional sports and are in fact Nike customers. The Chinese sports brand Li Ning developed inner soles uniquely adapted to Chinese feet after its staff immersed themselves in running and found that most global brands did not comfortably fit Chinese feet. Playmobil's distinctive head was developed after observing how children draw faces and figures. The *World of Warcraft* development team is encouraged to play around with the game and recast characters. The introduction of blood elves and recasting the draenei as heroic has increased the mystique of the game and resulted in a new one 'The Burning Crusade', of which more than 2.4 million copies were sold on the first day of release.

Authentic habit 6: be at one with the community

Apart from stressing their national and regional roots, authentic brands also play a significant role in the development of their industry, not only by introducing innovations but also in a broader perspective. For example, Chuck Taylor, the originator of Converse All Stars basketball shoes, wrote books on basketball strategy. Authentic brands are also sensitive to culture and gaining legitimacy in sub-cultures. Levi's made sincere commitments to gay rights. It was one of the first brands to advertise in gay publications and the Levis Strauss Company extended its employee benefits to same-sex couples. It even ended its relationship with the American Boy Scouts because the organization banned gay scout leaders.

Authentic habit 7: indoctrinate staff into the brand cult

Authentic brands are backed by fanatical and devoted staff that share the same brand values and are both passionate about the company's cause as well as open to new ways of thinking and doing. This requires a specific HR approach. Applicants at Virgin were requested to perform, sing, mime or dance. It's a way of recruiting people who will want to go the extra mile to satisfy customers.[21]

To conclude, Gilmore and Pine have formulated a simple but interesting set of 'axioms of authenticity' in their book *Authenticity. What Consumers Really Want*:

- If you are authentic, then you don't have to say you're authentic.
- If you say you're authentic, then you'd better be authentic.
- It's easier to be authentic, if you don't say you're authentic.[22]

The first, the last, my everything: using indicators of origin

Have you ever wondered what happens to the sales revenues of an original song when a cover song hits the charts? What do you expect? In 2009, Lisa Hordijk won the TV format *X Factor* in the Netherlands with a cover of the song 'Hallelujah'. One week later, her version of the song was leading the Dutch Singles Top 100. It was in that first position for 10 consecutive weeks. Jeff Buckley's interpretation, released back in 1993, entered the charts immediately at number three. The original version by Leonard Cohen, a song from 1984, also managed to get into the top 100 of 2009, in the 27th spot.

A similar phenomenon had happened six months earlier in the UK when Alexandra Burke won the same talent scouting TV show... with the same song. Now, you might think it's the 'Hallelujah' that incites a spiritual mysterious effect on people, but there's no sixth sense involved in these statistics. Apparently, whenever a cover song enters the charts, in 60 per cent of cases it will cause an immediate positive effect on the revenues of the song it originates from. The original song climbs on average 240 places in the sales charts compared to the year before. It is only a temporary effect because one year later the original song will drop 190 spots in the list.

Of course, this is partly linked to a mere reactivation in people's memory. Experiments have shown that the top five preferred songs of people are susceptible to recent exposure. For instance, if you let them evaluate a number of ABBA songs, and then ask them what their all-time favourite tunes are, the chance the list will contain at least one ABBA song is significantly higher.[23]

The first = better intuition

On the other hand, it's not just a mere exposure effect. People favour stimuli they encounter first. When they were asked to listen to similar fragments of an original and its corresponding cover song, without knowing the songs nor which one was the original, 96 per cent preferred the version that was heard first, no matter if it was the original one or the cover song. If the songs used in the experiment were known to them, they preferred the one that they indicated to have heard first, prior to the study, and which was released before their birth. This phenomenon seems analogous to the process of 'imprinting'. A young animal develops an attachment for the first object it encounters. It is somehow stamped upon the nervous system. Although this imprinting only occurs once in a critical life period, it seems that the first exposure effect can happen time after time. People believe that being first has many advantages. After all, we live in a society where the winner (sports, school, etc) is celebrated with a gold medal, flowers and champagne.[24]

When we translate this human trait to a business context, the phenomenon is also known as the 'first mover's advantage'. Customers attach meanings of innovativeness and superior quality to the (perceived) first company in an industry. The positive effects of perceived originality on attractiveness and consumer choice for pioneers have been confirmed in various researches. In experiments with youngsters, participants preferred the song version labelled 1964 to the 1967 version when the third version they heard was labelled 1969 but not when the third version was labelled 1962.

Indicators of origin

Since Gen Y customers are mostly not able to distinguish the original first brand on the market from copycats, the potential power of originality indicators is huge. However, if your brand is not the pioneer in the market it would be the wrong strategy to try posing as the original one. This could undermine your credibility when the truth becomes clear and then it would only stress your dependence on the real innovator. Non-comparative indicators such as 'since 1869' on the other hand can influence Gen Y's perception but still have the danger of the pioneer competitor's reaction with explicit expressions such as 'first on the market'.[25] We will show you later in this chapter that although dates of origin do appeal to a nostalgic feeling with Gen Y, it will not be the most successful way to adopt authenticity in this market.

These labels of being 'the original', 'the first', 'the creator', are obviously tightly related to the concept of brand authenticity. Young consumers, with limited product and brand buying experiences, are looking for cues that decrease purchase risks and indicate that a brand offers good value for money. Origin, history and heritage of a brand are cues that support this brand positioning and can be seen as the traditional definition of brand authenticity.

The 'origin', as illustrated in the examples of Levi's and Kronenbourg, is the invention, the starting point or beginning of a company or brand. 'History' is what happened since the origin of a brand until now, such as new product launches, new identities, advertising campaigns, etc. In the case of the Levi's brand, this is a bucketful of iconic advertising memories. Nick Kamen undressing in the laundrette commercial of the 1980s. The motorcyclist who enters an office building in his cool 'The Fonz' style to the tune of 'The Joker' in the early

1990s. The ADHD-style head-banging yellow puppet Flat Eric used for Levi's Sta-Prest at the end of the 1990s. The difference with 'heritage' is that the latter is also a collection or collective memory of things that happened with a brand without the involved company or brand having a deliberate influence on this. Examples of heritage are: celebrities who consume or use a certain product or brand in public, for instance movie stars such as Ben Stiller and Cameron Diaz wearing Puma sneakers in the box-office hit *There's Something About Mary*. It could also be leading edge or even mainstream consumers that pick up brands and make them fashionable or cool.[26]

How Stéphane became Flat Eric

It was the famous techno deejay Laurent Garnier who discovered the 24-year-old Frenchman Mr Oizo (aka Quentin Dupieux) when he was buying a car from Dupieux's dad. He promptly asked Dupieux to produce a music video for his 1997 hit 'Crispy Bacon'.[27] Mr Oizo, a young, talented music-maker/director, had been making some short films in which Stéphane, a fluffy yellow creature similar to Flat Eric but with ears appeared. The movies had a small cult following in the UK and France when in 1999 Levi's decided to build a television commercial campaign starring the puppet. They asked Mr Oizo to direct the series of commercials and produce music for them. The yellow character was renamed Eric to allow a more international career compared to the original French name Stéphane. The initial idea for the commercial pictured a car running over the head of the puppet and flattening it. This storyline would support the Sta-Prest One Crease Denim Clothing of Levi's. Although the concept wasn't kept for the actual series of commercials, the name 'Flat Eric' stuck. Stéphane was recreated by Jim Henson's Creature Shop in the UK. Mr Oizo commented on the collaboration with Henson: 'When they first made him, he looked too much like Kermit. He had a rounded body, which Flat Eric isn't supposed to have. It took 15 days to make him but the second puppet was too tall – he was like a small child and he wasn't funny. Flat Eric has to be little and small to be laughable, so I said no to number two. The third or fourth time he was just about right. He had to be redesigned several times before he created the same mood and feeling that I had with my first, original puppet Stéphane.' Flat Eric also featured in the music video for 'Flat Beat', one of the songs Mr Oizo had used in the soundtrack of the commercials. He even appeared as a prop in the BBC Comedy *The Office*. The yellow creature became so popular at a certain point that people were desperate to get hold of merchandise such as T-shirts, puppets or anything carrying Eric's/Stéphane's image.[28]

Irony killed authenticity: Gen Y's perception of authentic claims

Little is known about how the critical Generation Y perceive and value brand strategies based on authentic claims. Therefore, we collaborated with the Levi Strauss Company to verify youth's perception of authenticity. The classic way of looking at the concept of 'brand authenticity' is defined by components such as origin, history and heritage of a brand. Levi Strauss & Co are known as the inventor of the denim jeans with its Levi's 501 jeans model positioned as the ultimate original jeans. They were interested in finding out what the modern interpretations of authenticity for youth are today.[29]

Origin and history

Youngsters are seldom aware of the origin of their favourite brands. For instance, in the beer category where the date of origin is often an integral part of the brand logo (eg Kronenbourg, Stella Artois) the recognition and recall of these packaging or logo items is very low. Although they believe Levi's is an authentic brand, less than 25 per cent really know the origin of the brand. Despite the label on the back of each pair of jeans clearly mentioning the date of origin, youngsters have never noticed it. When the age or history of a product or brand is concerned, youngsters tend to think more in relative and comparative terms. A brand such as Apple seems to have the same association of quality and 'being around for a while' even if it is in fact a rather recent brand. In their limited years of being conscious consumers, youngsters have always known the presence of Apple. The fact that parents or grandparents are using a certain brand is also a proof to youngsters that the brand is 'old'. They tend to think that if a product has been on the market for a long time, this is a secure proof of good quality. They also associate dates of origin with feelings of cheerfulness and nostalgia. 'Cool! My grandmother may have used it too.' But again, they don't tend to go too far back in time when considering brand history. When a brand has existed for ten years or longer, it truly is an aged brand.

Concerning the country of origin, the critical Generation Y makes a distinction between the real origin and the country in which a brand or product is produced. Most youngsters don't know the country of origin of their favourite brands, but the awareness of where it is manu-factured is higher since this is often indicated in a label 'made in...'. For certain product categories the country of origin can evoke good as well as bad quality associations. Some countries spontaneously evoke connotations of labour mistreatments or animal abuse. Japanese brands nowadays seem to have the halo of being techno-logically advanced, for instance as opposed to Chinese, which equals crap for them. Gilmore and Pine have correctly emphasized that some regions that were once known for junk, like Japan, are today symbols of quality. China is currently possessing the image of 'ManuFAKEture', a term coined by Ted Fishman in the *New York Times*,[30] but may one day be known for its authenticity. Country of origin plays a more important role for the quality perception among young target groups in certain industries such as food, health and beauty, technology (durables), cars and clothing. In contrast to what we had expected from these savvy consumers, youngsters don't mind too much when brands fake a certain origin. For instance, they automatically link Häagen-Dazs ice cream to Switzerland or a Scandinavian country. When confronted with the fact that it is actually a US brand using foreign branding as a marketing technique, and the digraphs 'äa' and 'zs' are actually invalid in all Scandinavian languages, they consider this to be funny and cunning.

Authentic Bronx Ice Cream sold with an Umlaut

Häagen-Dazs is a brand of super-premium (dense, high butterfat) ice cream that was created by Polish immigrants Reuben and Rose Mattus in the Bronx, New York in 1961. The first retail store was opened in Brooklyn in 1976. Today Häagen-Dazs is sold in 55 countries around the world. The brand name was meant to look Scandinavian for Americans. The Häagen-Dazs name gives European cachet and radiates craftsmanship and tradition, justifying the premium retail price. On early labels Mattus used an outline of Denmark, although the umlaut is never used in Danish. He also added some Scandinavian capitals on the packaging: Oslo, Copenhagen and Stockholm. The font type of the logo was set in bold Futura, adding a muscular Germanic effect to the name.

This marketing technique is named 'foreign branding'. It implies the use of foreign-sounding or foreign names to create a superior or authentic image. Many cosmetics and fashion brands for example use French or Italian names to make the connection with the fashion shows and designers of Paris and

Continued...

Authentic Bronx Ice Cream sold with an Umlaut   *Continued*

Milan. Other product categories have discovered foreign branding techniques too. Although the Mars' brand Dolmio sounds Italian, the pasta sauce is not made or sold in Italy. The Chinese retailer of home appliances Haier uses the German-sounding brand Liebherr to convey a message of quality. The UK manufacturer of Moben Kitchens trademarked 'Möben' in 1977 to use the German and Scandinavian quality image. The oldest known usage of foreign branding goes back to the 1910s. The day 'Soup Vichyssoise' was invented... at the Ritz-Carlton Hotel in New York.[31] The umlaut also became popular in the heavy metal and punk rock music scene to stress their toughness and macho image. In 1972, the American rock band Blue Öyster Cult set the scene. Since then, rock groups like Motörhead, Mötley Crüe, Hüsker Dü and Queensrÿche have followed the example. There's even a Finnish punk rock band called Umlaut.

The success of Häagen-Dazs invited copycat companies to implement the same strategy on the ice cream market. Richard Smith, an American, created Frusen Glädjé, using an almost Swedish name to position his products. Without the accent on the final e, frusen glädje means 'frozen joy' or 'frozen delight' in Swedish. Häagen-Dazs was quite unhappy with this copycat and sued the company unsuccessfully in 1980 to stop them from using a Scandinavian marketing theme. In 1985 Smith sold the brand to Kraft General Foods. What has happened to the brand since then is a marketing mystery. Kraft states that Frusen Glädjé was sold to Unilever in 1993, but a spokesman for Unilever denied this. The association of frozen milk with Scandinavia hasn't disappeared though. Canada has its very successful Yogen Früz, a frozen yoghurt brand, and there's also Freshëns frozen yoghurt selling Smoöthies.[32]

Heritage

Youngsters are not aware of the heritage of brands and it is not something they are really interested in. The history of a brand and how it was affected by acts of external people have very little importance to them. Although they seem to have respect for brands with a heritage, they are hard to convince that certain stories are true. When we confronted Gen Y with a global TV commercial of Adidas picturing the brand origin (Adi Dassler), history and heritage (including Muhammed Ali), 93 per cent of the 13- to 29-year-olds thought the story was invented. It just sounded too good to be true. Being bombarded by many made-up brand stories, adolescents generally consider these types of story to be fake and marketing tricks. Advertisers that want to claim brand heritage such as Adidas face a difficult challenge to persuade the Generation Y consumers that their brand stories are genuine and real. It is a bad idea to use large advertising and marketing campaigns to convey messages of authenticity. Their mass media connotations undermine the authentic claims. Advertising strategies to Gen Y have been using a lot of humour and irony. Typical youth advertising strategies included stressing the fact that 'it's only advertising, baby', and 'yes, we ARE trying to sell you something and you know it!' As a consequence, using heritage or authenticity claims in advertising will be considered to be 'only another advertising trick'. Brand origin, history and heritage should be whispered when you use them.

Only seven monastery brew houses in the world are authorized to produce authentic Trappist beer. Trappist monks are part of the order of the Cistercians. Armand de Rancé founded one of the two great Cistercian orders in 1662 in the French Normandy town of La Trappe. The name 'Trappist' was derived from this abbey. The Trappist monks originally brewed their beer to cater for the needs of the community. Nowadays they are allowed to sell their production in order to fund their works and good causes. When Trappist breweries expanded their market to an international level, commercial breweries such as AB InBev (using the Leffe brand) saw potential in mass-producing a copycat alternative: Abbey beers. During the 1980s and 1990s the difference between Trappist and Abbey beers became less clear to consumers. Commercial breweries used names from abbeys that no longer existed, such as Grimbergen, an Abbey beer produced by Alken-Maes, part of the Heineken Group. This gave them the chance to use images of monks and abbeys in packaging, merchandise and advertising. In 1997, the International Trappist Association created a label 'Authentic Trappist Product' that can only be used by the seven authentic Trappist abbeys.

Michael B Beverland researched the perception of 40 marketing visuals (advertisements, bottle labels and packaging) from both Abbey and authentic Trappist brewers. His conclusion: advertising may reinforce an image of authenticity but only in an indirect way. Generation Y in particular seemed to have trouble distinguishing the real thing from the copy. When youngsters looked at the bottle label saying 'Authentic Trappist Product', they considered it proof that the beer was probably not really the authentic one. The clever abbey advertising however, using indirect cues such as historical font types and colours (brown, yellow), simple packaging and images of monks, abbeys and cellars, supported the authentic image of the commercial copycats.[33]

If you want to use your brand's origin, history or heritage, to connect with youth, you should not do this with 'in your face' labels or campaigns literally telling the stories behind your brand. The critical Gen Y will not believe the story is true. Instead, you can either use indirect subtle cues of authenticity or, if you really want to stand out from the copycat inauthentic competitors, let your consumers experience first-hand how authentic your products are. If your brand authenticity is linked to the production process or location, you can achieve this with guided or behind-the-scenes tours. If your brand heritage is linked to leading-edge consumers or celebrities (eg athletes or musicians) this is often done by sponsoring certain events or people.

Celebrity endorsements

Using celebrity endorsements for branding to Gen Y isn't without its complications. Youngsters are very critical about this marketing strategy. To them, celebrity endorsement implies that a brand is not confident enough to have an image of its own and hence it is interpreted as a weak moment of a brand. It shows that a brand has no real personality on its own and needs to buy coolness by using cool persons. Therefore celebrity endorsement only pays off in certain circumstances, for instance if the product sector is related to the natural environment and the skills of the celebrity. Real athletes such as Michael Jordan or Tiger Woods supporting the Nike brand or a real designer, Philippe Starck designing the bottle, glass and can for the 1664 beer brand do create an added value for the brand. On the other hand Gordon Ramsay, the Michelin-starred celebrity chef, endorsing Gordon's gin – only based on the similarity with his famous first name – is not linked to the gin brand's heritage. The date of origin of Gordon's gin goes back 200 years before Ramsay was born. Youngsters will reject this kind of celebrity endorsement. The fact that Gordon Ramsay is simultaneously supporting about 400 other products is of course also undermining the credibility of this celebrity endorsement.[34]

In a survey by InSites Consulting among 900 13- to 29-year-olds, their new definition of authenticity was confirmed. Items such as 'years of presence on the market' and 'like in the past' were only mentioned by less than 2 per cent of youth, indicating that these connotations are less relevant to them. For almost 6 out of 10 young people authenticity is primarily detected by the brand values – social responsibility, what the brand propagates and what it stands for. Thirty per cent link authenticity with the history of a brand and only 2 out of 10 make the link with the brand's origin or heritage.[35]

How Gen Y values honesty

Honesty as a concept is much more diverse and complex for youth than the upfront interpretation of just avoiding telling lies. It is also about being respectful to youngsters, to society, to the environment, to children, animals, etc. Honesty to Gen Y includes being open and transparent. It is about not being afraid to listen to youngsters, to discuss topics with them and to stay constructive when receiving negative comments. Youngsters want to feel respected and valued in their opinion. Generation Y was raised by Baby Boomer parents, who gave birth at an older age (average age of having first child was 30). This resulted in a more mature and democratic way of taking up the role of educator, coach or teacher. As a result Generation Y seems to value authenticity in many more aspects of life than only in the products they buy. They would be unwilling to take a pill that would enhance their traits but at the same time fundamentally change who they are. Sometimes Gen Y might even prefer an inferior but authentic product to another that is superior but not authentic.[36] During the Opening Ceremony of the 2008 Olympic Games in Beijing the nine-year-old Lin Miaoke 'sang' the *Hymn to the Motherland*. Although the performance was perceived as perfect, youngsters were shocked when it turned out that the girl actually performed a playback and the real singer was not allowed to perform in front of the cameras because she was not beautiful enough.

Interestingly enough, lying is not a definite no-no for this generation. People can admit their mistakes, explain everything and win back their credibility. Bill Clinton and the Oval Room confession concerning his relationship with Monica Lewinsky is a good illustration of this. The Bill Clinton 'brand' actually became suddenly more like them: accessible, human, fragile, imperfect and thus forgivable. For youngsters it is quite difficult to recognize honesty in people when they do not really know them. When discussing honest people with them, they will refer to people in their close neighbourhood (parents, friends, teachers) because they have known them for a longer period and have experienced whether they are honest or not.

Brand honesty

The same conclusion can be made with relation to the honesty of brands. It is quite difficult for a brand to claim honesty with youngsters today. Although they want to believe that some brands are honest, they feel they are never really sure. Being 'honest' as a brand means that you are worth the youngsters' money, and you never disappoint them. This reliability is detected by 'trial and error' choice strategies.

Apart from reliability, brand honesty also means staying true to your own identity. It is the typical youth market paradox of focusing on the authentic core businesses on one hand while also being innovative enough to stay interesting, thrilling, not boring and relevant to this fickle generation of 'stimulus junkies' on the other. Strong brands should balance their actions reinterpreting their symbolic brand stories in response to changing tastes.[37] Considering this paradox, line extensions are often more credible than brand extensions. McDonald's can easily start serving breakfast, salads or ice cream but mobile phone cards would be too far-fetched.

In the older age group, the 18- to 29-year-olds and specifically above the age of 25, honesty is closely linked to Corporate Social Responsibility programmes of companies and their position towards child labour, animal testing, ecology (carbon footprint) and charity. In March 2009, InSites Consulting organized online group discussions in 12 time zones across the world. The discussions focused on CSR programmes. More than 80 consumers in 63 countries took part. As a result, we defined the critical success factors of CSR programmes:

- Recognizable: Gen Y feels involved and recognizes situations covered in the CSR programme.

- Close: local programmes and actions have more chance of success.

- Credible: use and maximize your own sector's competence and expertise, do what you're good at. For example, Philips has the 'a simple switch' green programme reducing the environmental impact of their products by energy-saving developments, clearly part of the brand's expertise.

- Transparency: youngsters should understand what the CSR programme is about and understand how it works.

The Mexican beer brand Corona's Save The Beach programme, a campaign the brand started in 2008 to preserve endangered European beaches isn't really in line with what Gen Y expect from a CSR programme. The fit between the target group of Corona Extra (upscale ego-centric youth) and care for the environment is low. So is the match with the company's expertise. How Corona will save the beaches is not really clear to youth. Compare this to Unilever's 'Dirt is Good' CSR campaign. It started from the insight that childhood space is shrinking because of lack of spaces to play, lack of time among working parents and increasing fears of physical safety. The Omo/Persil detergent brand sponsored the creation of safe playgrounds across the world, in all relevant countries. Children that play become dirty and that's a clear link with Omo's product. Omo's CSR programme was backed by research, scientific whitepapers and an emotional TV spot – 'Roboboy' – showing how a robot transfers to a boy when playing outside in the rain and getting dirty in the mud.

Corporate honesty

Youth link an honest brand to certain people working or representing that company or brand; for instance, celebrity CEOs Steve Jobs, Richard Branson, Ben Cohen and Jerry Greenfield.

For multinationals like Coca-Cola or Nike it is much more difficult to be honest according to youngsters. The reasoning behind this is that multinationals employ more people, and the more people involved with businesses, the bigger the chance that someone within the organization could do something dishonest and ruin the company's image. In this digital age where consumers have more power using social networks, blogs or discussion boards to discuss brands, advertising or customer experiences, they have all the tools at their disposal to detect what is real, honest and true. This new reality of transparency has put an even higher premium on authenticity, making it an import driver of brand credibility.[38] This does not automatically imply that a company or brand that gets negative comments on the internet is immediately perceived as inauthentic since 'authenticity' is a combination of several dimensions and 'honesty' is just one of them. In general, the favourite brands of this generation of youngsters need to be more human, more honest and more real than brands used to be. Especially in image-oriented product categories such as clothing, fashion and jeans a brand should be like a real friend to youngsters.

The more your products concentrate on honesty as a core brand value, the more media will be closely watching your moves. Innocent Smoothies was accused of misleading claims about its environmental credentials in the summer of 2008. The *Daily Telegraph* revealed that although the Innocent website stated that their fruit always travels by boat or rail to reduce the use of fossil fuel, the drinks are blended in Rotterdam and then transported by trucks across Europe before they are bottled in the UK. Founder Richard Reed had to admit that the website had not been updated on the new production situation. 'We are attempting to get the best quality drinks to our customers while generating the least amount of carbon', Reed commented to the *Telegraph*. 'Rotterdam is the port which all the fruit comes into, so it makes sense to blend our drinks there. It had been our policy not to talk about where our drinks are made for commercial reasons but we now seek to tell our customers everything about the drinks and be completely open with them'.[39] Innocent Drinks tries balancing ethics and business. Its products are sold in 11 countries. The company sources fruit from ethically aware farms, uses 100 per cent recyclable bottles and donates 10 per cent of its profits to charity. The Innocent Foundation gives grants to NGOs and other charities through three-year partnerships. The company has faced some other criticisms in its past.[40] In 2007 a deal with McDonald's inserting Innocent drinks into kids' Happy Meals was heavily criticized. More recently, the sales of a small stake of the company to Coca-Cola in Spring 2009 led to a tsunami of unhappy website and social networking messages.[41]

Levi's translates authenticity to Gen Y

In the last decades of the previous Millennium, Levi Strauss & Co positioned their 501 jeans model in what can be seen as the classic way of defining 'brand authenticity'. Levi Strauss & Co uses the term 'original authenticity' to describe the fact that they are the oldest brand. In fact, Levi's is probably the youngest oldest brand in the world. The 501 is the first and genuine, the classic, the original, 100 per cent American iconic jeans brand. The fact that movie stars such as James Dean made the blue jeans popular as a fashion item to youth subcultures as opposed to a worker's-class pants is also an essential part of the brand's heritage. For years Levi's was also one of the only global jeans brands available. By the end of the 1990s, new entrants in the market such as Diesel, Replay, Pepe Jeans and G-Star Raw challenged the American classic by adding a rather edgy aspect of brand personality and introducing more extreme jeans models and ways of washing to the market. Other luxury fashion brands such as Armani, Dolce & Gabbana, Gucci, etc also acknowledged the value of the denim market and entered the category with their own luxury line of expensive jeans. Both strategies were well received among young target groups, especially with the status-seeking part of the market whose main concern is to look cool in front of others to gain social success and belong to a group of popular kids. While most Baby Boomer parents were wearing the Levi's brand, it became more challenging for the brand to connect with the youngest generation and fight against a whole new range of competitive brands. Although origin, history and heritage serves as a means-to-the-end perception of good quality and reliability, it was worth exploring whether generation Y consumers were still enough involved with the traditional 'brand authenticity' attributes. To develop the marketing campaign of the 501 jeans model in summer 2008, Levi Strauss & Co decided to investigate their own 'original' and 'authentic' brand DNA and examine whether a modern, more attitudinal and emotional interpretation of brand authenticity would equally secure their appeal among today's generation of youngsters.

Levi's honesty to itself

By propagating the idea that Levi's is honest to itself and not pretending to be what it is not, the brand modernized the brand value proposition to the market of Generation Y youngsters. In the marketing campaign of the 501 jeans, Levi Strauss & Co wanted to stress that it believes everybody has the freedom to express their own individuality and creativity without being judged by others. The campaign idea 'Live Unbuttoned' is related to being completely yourself. To live unbuttoned is to be uninhibited, unrestrained, unembarrassed. It's about throwing off the restraints of convention and doing what comes naturally. The campaign (see Figure 4.2) started with the 'live unbuttoned' websites showing movies with local heroes (for instance emerging music or artists) demonstrating the revelation of 'personal secrets'. The 'hero' answered five intimate questions and invited the visiting audience to do the same and be honest and open. The audio-visual ad campaign showed a flirting couple revealing personal stuff to each other stepwise – while literally unbuttoning the 501 jeans.

FIGURE 4.2　The 'live unbuttoned' website

By integrating this modern or attitudinal interpretation of 'authenticity' into the 501 jeans campaign, Levi Strauss & Co managed to come up with another interpretation of its brand values proposition that would match with the Generation Y youngsters.

Levi's honesty to society

Levi Strauss & Co is also honest to society in several corporate social responsibility programmes. In 1985 the Levi Strauss Foundation was

FIGURE 4.3   The back pocket auction

Photographer: Franky Claeys
Artists: Bas Chrispijn; Sabine Pascale; Naad; Nouch; Fons Schiedon; Lon; Royal Steez;
Out of Order; Yowie; Voicst; Bastian; Michael Owen Dale

the first US corporate foundation to address the HIV/AIDS epidemic,
and it has since contributed more than $40 million in grants to HIV/
AIDS service organizations in more than 40 countries. The foundation and company-supported programmes help to prevent the spread

of HIV/AIDS, specifically in communities with extreme need and scarce resources. The Levi Strauss Foundation funds programmes that challenge the stigma and discrimination surrounding HIV/AIDS, support disproportionately affected and underserved communities (for instance by research activities that contribute to the development of strategies for HIV control) and increase the availability of clean syringes to prevent the spread of HIV through needle sharing. In a recent brand activity, linked to the work of the Foundation, Levi Strauss Benelux and Nordic Countries invited artists from the most diverse disciplines – but all breathing the spirit of the brand – to add their personal touch to the classic back pocket. This resulted in valuable little works of art by artists including fashion designers, TV hosts, actresses and 'must see' artists and bands. The back pockets were then sold as collectables through internet auctions and the proceeds donated to the Foundation (see Figure 4.3).[42]

Conclusion

In the experience economy, the authenticity of brands becomes more important. Not only because its uniqueness helps them to differentiate from the many alternatives but also because consumers value 'reality' in a world flooded with imitations and staged experiences. To the new Generation Y consumers the old interpretation of authenticity (origin, history and heritage) is less appealing and less relevant. Often they are not aware of these brand claims and it is not the most enticing strategy to win their hearts. The concept of 'perceived authenticity' seems to be quite interesting for advertisers. Considering the limited time frame and brand context of youngsters as well as their consumer cynicism, subtle cues suggesting authenticity (for instance in advertising or packaging) will often connect much better with them than stressing the old authenticity claims through mass advertising or labels of origin. The latter will evoke doubts of their truthfulness, while the former support an image of reliability and credibility. The modern interpretation of authenticity: being honest to yourself (the brand DNA), to youngsters (transparency) and to society (CSR) relates better to the current consumer climate as well as to specific Generation Y expectations fed by their education.

Being honest as a brand (or 'authenticity new style', if you want) truly differentiates your brand from its competitors. In this digital age, honesty, as opposed to the old definition of authenticity, cannot be faked and is therefore of much bigger value to the young generation.[43] In the next chapter, we will discuss creating unique brand assets.

Generation Y consumers make purchase choices based on how well they reflect their own self-image – who they are and who they aspire to be. For instance, for many Apple lovers the brand reflects a sense of creativity and design-led innovativeness that equals their own desired personality. This will affect the degree to which they see brands as authentic. We will address this topic in the sixth chapter.

Hot takeways for cool brand builders

- The second step in keeping your cool brand hot is keeping it real.
- Brand authenticity drives Gen Y's choice.
- Don't underestimate the power of face-to-face personal contact with Gen Y.
- Brand origin, history and heritage are often not relevant or even not credible for the critical youth.
- This classic interpretation of authenticity should never be shouted (no mass media) but only be whispered and even better: be experienced.
- Authenticity is all about staying true to yourself; not imitating, not faking.
- Keep your brand's vision central but reinterpret the meaning of your brand following changes in tastes, interests or values.
- Honesty means more for a brand than CSR programmes or 'not lying', it's about being respectful to youth and youth's life, about listening and discussing with them on the same level, and about sticking to your own ideas.
- Real brands are transparent, open and human: like a friend.

Chapter Five
We all want unique brands

When we say 'Moonwalk', what are you thinking of?
Perhaps the Apollo 11 will immediately flash through your mind, or Neil Armstrong or even the Grand Marnier cocktail that Joe Gilmore invented to celebrate the event. But there's a good chance that most of you will rather think of Michael Jackson. Ever since Jackson performed the popping dance technique during the *Motown 25* TV special in 1983, it became his signature move for his song *Billie Jean*. Michael Jackson's 1988 autobiography was titled *Moonwalk* and he starred in the movie *Moonwalker*. Michael claimed the dance move and made it popular around the world, but he certainly did not invent the 'moonwalk'. He was inspired by David Bowie's strange moves after attending Bowie's Los Angeles show during the 1974 Diamond Dogs Tour. Bowie had studied mime under Etienne Decroux, Marcel Marceau's teacher. The latter, one of the most famous French mime artists, had been using the 'backslide' (later called 'moonwalk') throughout his career from the 1940s to the 1980s. In his famous 'Walking Against the Wind' routine, Marceau pretended to be pushed backwards by the wind.[1] In spite of all these predecessors, most people deem the moonwalk to be Michael's uniquely distinctive move.

How unique is your unique selling proposition?

The 'USP', or 'Unique Selling Proposition' must be one of the oldest core marketing principles. Rosser Reeves, a very successful US advertising executive and chairman of the Ted Bates agency, is the father of the concept and coined 'USP' in his 1961 book *Reality in Advertising*. His three principles were:

- each advertisement must make a benefit proposition to the consumer;
- the proposition must be a unique one that the competition either cannot, or does not, offer;
- the proposition must be so strong that it can move the mass millions.[2]

Reeves' views led to dozens of strong slogans, many of which, like M&M's 'melt in your mouth, not in your hand' are still known today. But already in the 1960s, the claim-based differentiation strategy became obsolete when consumers got more marketing-savvy and were saturated with ad claims. The more creative and image-based campaigns proved to be more successful and Reeves retired. Today, the critical youth generation is not so easily wowed with image-driven campaigns either.

Perception of uniqueness

Michael Jackson's moonwalk illustrates that there's much wisdom in the words of Ecclesiastes in the Old Testament:

> The thing that hath been, it is that which shall be; and that which is done is that which shall be done: and there is no new thing under the Sun.
>
> (Ecclesiastes 1: 9–10)[3]

We do believe however that even in connecting with the extremely marketing-wise Generation Y, a brand's unique positioning is still one of the drivers of choice. But brand image definitely lies in the eye of the beholder. In other words, it is youth's perception of a brand's uniqueness that is more important than reality. For Gen Yers, and for most of us, moonwalk equals Michael Jackson. The extent to which Gen Y *perceives* your brand as unique therefore matters. After all, a brand's main function is to express its difference from its competitors. Due to the overload of choice that Generation Y is confronted with, they are more sceptical of new products than ever. More than 6 out of 10 think new products are not really different. In the chapter on brand coolness, we have stressed that in high frequency categories with more competition, youth brands need to build on coolness, novelty and uniqueness to create interest and preference. In our research for this book, the perceived uniqueness of a brand improved brand image and stimulated brand conversations or buzz among Gen Y. This word-of-mouth is crucial since a quarter of 16- to 24-year-olds will only buy a product if someone recommends it to them.[4]

The uniqueness of H&M

'The uniqueness of H&M is not about what we do, it's how we do it', says Jörgen Andersson, former global brand director of H&M, in an interview with us:

> The products in our category are more or less the same. They could even be made from the same fabrics or in the same factory. And today, thanks to internet and cheap airlines, everything around the world is accessible to youth. My 14-year-old daughter often asks me to bring her stuff from the regions I visit for my work. Abercrombie & Fitch used to be exclusive for Europeans but now you can buy it online. It is difficult to find something unique nowadays. So, it's more about branding and positioning. H&M wants to be the 'fun of fashion'. We don't dictate styles and we don't exclude anyone. We want to be inviting as opposed to excluding and exciting as opposed to dull.

Excitement is built up through H&M's collection but also through its marketing actions. The 'inviting' aspect involves pricing, store staff and retail locations. 'Our stores are very important for our brand', says Andersson:

> In discussion groups when consumers talk about H&M they always talk about the store. That's different for other brands, they can talk about the Nike brand, for instance, for 15 minutes without even mentioning the products. Our creative director always uses the 'bus stop' paradigm. If you have 10 minutes to wait for a bus in Oxford Street, where do you jump in? We want our stores to have enough positive vibe, excitement and things happening to be the 10-minute favourite of youth. This also means that H&M needs to claim the best locations in the city centre. We want our stores to be the new meeting points of youngsters.

So when pricing, products and stores of fashion retailers increasingly look the same, what is really making the difference? Jörgen Andersson says it's about injecting the brand with vitamin pills in the form of events, marketing, temporary collaborations and offering more reasons to connect with the H&M brand. It makes your brand less vulnerable for things that are out of a marketer's control such as the weather or the economy. 'You want your brand to become a friend', Andersson says. 'You will always defend your good friends, no matter what happens. This kind of feeling of affection protects a brand. For instance, if a certain seasonal collection of H&M is not completely your own taste, you will still want to buy it, because it's H&M.' This emotional connection with brands became more important because products and services are increasingly equal. There's also much more competition than 25 years ago when there were only small expensive boutiques and department stores. For Jörgen Andersson the relevance of what a brand is doing has become more crucial in connecting with the marketing-savvy youth generation. 'Doing relevant things is the key to authenticity', says the former global brand director:

> If Britney Spears is endorsing Pepsi, I'm sure Gen Yers are thinking: 'How much has Pepsi paid for this?' So when we discussed sponsoring Madonna's World Tour, we wanted to make it relevant for H&M by not only dressing Madonna and her dancers on stage but also the roadies and truck drivers. It's in line with our democratic DNA and with the diversity of styles. The truck driver chose black jeans and a black t-shirt from our collection. We don't pretend to be what we are not. I think Gen Yers admire that. The human aspect is something we embrace at H&M, for instance in the choice of our models in advertising or on the catwalk. Imperfection is human and it's less boring.[5]

Brands that present themselves in a sustainable, unique way will reinforce their value propositions.

A brand's perceived uniqueness is mainly the result of executing a consistent positioning strategy. For Gen Y consumers, it is only when a brand begins to merge with their own identity and becomes self-expressive, that they will feel a bond with the brand. In Chapter 6, we will dive into the topics of self-image and brand identification.

In this chapter, we will highlight several views on how a brand can differentiate itself from competitors. We will explain the concepts of brand DNA, battlefield analysis and brand distinctive assets or memes. A number of recent Gen Y case stories illustrate how a youth brand can build on uniqueness.

Brand DNA

Suppose we asserted that the iPod design (with its frontal round selection wheel and several distinctive colours such as black, white, red, olive green and pearlescent blue) is a copycat of a transistor radio invented by Dr Heinz De Koster, a Dutch PhD of physics, back in 1954. Would you believe us? Perhaps, after reading the chapter intro and Jackson's moonwalk story, you would. The point is, when we ask the same question in our discussion groups with Gen Yers, they think we are out of our mind. Nevertheless, it is a fact that the Regency TR-1, was the first commercial transistor radio sold in the United States, for $49.95, and it looked pretty much like the iPod. It was even launched using a punchy slogan 'See it! Hear it! Get it!' in November 1954 by a company based in Indianapolis named I.D.E.A.[6] So, the idea of the iPod design suspiciously descends from a 1950s transistor radio. Actually, Sony developed the iPod's long-life battery and Toshiba perfected the hard drive....[7] The fact that the iPod is from Apple Inc and is so embedded in the daily life of youngsters makes it an unbelievable story to them. Although Apple's slogan 'Think Different' hasn't been used for a few years, it is still part of the brand's deoxyribonucleic acid.

Every living organism owns unique deoxyribonucleic acid ('DNA' to friends) molecules that contain the genetic instructions of how the organism should develop and function. DNA is the basis of our own unique identity. Similarly, a brand's DNA is the unique identity that defines a brand's functioning. Apple's DNA for Generation Y includes: convenient, easy to use and innovative products, with an aesthetic, distinctive design for creative young people. If you look at Apple's last decade backtrack: the iPod with iTunes, Apple TV, the iPhone with the Appstore and lately the iPad tablet computer... it's no wonder that youngsters believe that the brand is different – that Apple is unique. And it's not only youth of course. The company has so many brand devotees and advocates that *Fortune Magazine* selected Apple as the world's most admired company in 2010, for the third year in a row. In the summer of 2010, Apple devotees created **Cupidtino.com**, a dating site exclusively for diehard fans of Apple products. The site's name is referring to Cupertino, a suburban city in California and home to the global headquarters of Apple, Inc.

Yet, Apple's design genius Jonathan Ive is heavily influenced by designs from the 1950s and 1960s. Apart from the Regency radio, bloggers found a striking resemblance between Ive's designs for Apple and the work of Dieter Rams, the German designer of Braun. Many of these designs are exhibited in New York's Museum of Modern Art.[8] Just like our own genes are partly copies of our creators, a brand's DNA can be based on earlier work. Apple definitely under-stood that the honest, simple and aesthetic designs of the 1960s would very much appeal to today's young consumer generation. By invest-ing in innovative products and staying true to its own DNA in every detail, including packaging and retail interiors, Apple succeeded in claiming a unique positioning. Like Alex Bogusky and John Winsor of Crispin Porter & Bogusky advise in *Baked In*, differences have to *look* different. The Apple iPod didn't just have a different colour from black, but it boasted the opposite of every other MP3 player cord and ear bud.[9] In the *Narcissism Epidemic*, Dr Twenge linked the increased importance of product design to our image-obsessed culture. According to her, today's desire for physical beauty springs from self-admiration. More than 7 out of 10 18- to 24-year-olds ap-prove of plastic surgery. This pursuit of beauty, illustrated for instance in the teeth-whitening trend in toothpaste, is a way to seek status and attention from others.[10]

The Axe/Lynx effect

Another great example of consistent positioning is Unilever's personal-care brand Axe targeting young men. Axe was first launched in France in 1983 and introduced in the rest of the world from 1985 onwards. In the UK Unilever had to use another name (Lynx) because of trade-mark conflicts. Ever since 2003, Axe/Lynx has been building on its simple and unique DNA: 'helping men to attract women'. Its campaigns mostly feature attractive babes chasing men who use Axe/Lynx. It is commonly referred to as 'the Axe effect'. In 2009 Craig Roberts, Professor at the University of Liverpool, actually found scientific proof that there is a certain Axe/Lynx effect. But it has nothing to do with pheromones or irresistible scents. In his experiment, women didn't have to sniff men but watched 15-second videos of men in their twenties describing themselves. The men who were given a can of Lynx-fragranced spray deodorant were found to be more attrac-tive than men wearing a deodorant without fragrance. Apparently, men in the fragranced group were feeling more self-confident, which had an effect on the women. The confidence turned out to be com-municated purely through body language, because the difference was only significant when the sound of the videos was off. The research proved that fragranced deodorant helps men to feel better, and that the increased confidence helps in the mating game.[11] The 'Axe effect' positioning is simple and powerful and it even has an effect on Gen Y's self-esteem, what more could a marketer wish for?

On YouTube many of the Axe commercials are a big success, especially the ones that were banned on commercial TV stations around the world. In 2010, the brand launched the 'Axe Detailer', a giveaway shower scrub tool, by producing a 2.45 minutes long infomercial on YouTube. In the parody of TV Home Shopping programmes, named 'Clean your balls', ex-tennis player Monica Blake demonstrates cleaning all kinds (and always a duo) of sport balls. The ad is highly suggestive with the host slowly rolling golf balls through her hands while commenting: 'Wow, I'd play with these balls all day!' and Monica Blake mentioning 'what a big ball sack'. The commercial ends with an overview of the Axe product line and a phone number to get the Axe Detailer.[12] After merely four months, the video on YouTube obtained more than 2 million viewers.

Volvo diverges from its DNA

It isn't always easy to stay close to your own brand DNA though. And sometimes, it isn't wise to implement it rigidly. If we say Volvo, what kinds of association come to your mind? We're pretty sure you will first think of safety. It's the core of Volvo's DNA. Now, if you want to target Generation Y, who's currently buying more than a quarter of all new cars, and by 2020 will account for almost half of them, stressing safety is probably not the most enticing strategy.[13]

In 2004, the brand shifted away from its conservative image for the first time to promote the S40 model. Performance and excitement were the desired different associations in positioning towards youth. One of the TV commercials was executed in video game style using the S40 in Xbox's *RalliSport Challenge* setting. The other one used a music video style featuring rap celebrity LL Cool J. The S40 was also promoted in retail environments other than the traditional car dealers, such as Virgin Megastores and Bloomingdales. Volvo created an online mock-documentary 'The Mystery of Dalaro' in which 32 people from the small Swedish town Dalaro mysteriously buy the S40 on the same day. The online movie attained 1 million visits to the website in Europe and in a few months' time the brand experienced a 105 per cent sales increase for the S40 segment.

Although the video game setting was criticized for ruining both the safety and responsibility image, Volvo attempted to stay close to its DNA by ending every commercial with the tagline 'it's still built like a Volvo'.[14] When Volvo introduced its C30 model in the United Kingdom at the end of 2008, the creative design of the model was the core aspect of the youth positioning. Volvo initiated an online contest, 'creative30', looking for young creative talent in Britain. More than 30,000 participants signed in to compete for the people's and expert panel's prizes.

What's up Doc?

Dr Martens iconic boots, aka Doc Martens, Docs or simply DMs, celebrated its 50th anniversary in 2010. Klaus Märtens was a doctor in the German army during the Second World War. On leave in 1945, he injured his ankle while skiing and found his army-issued boots uncomfortable. While recuperating, Märtens designed himself a pair with soft leather and air-cushioned soles. After the war Dr Märtens tried to sell his invention but without much luck: until he met an old university friend Dr Herbert Funck. With discarded rubber from Luftwaffe airfields the friends started to produce the shoes in Seeshaupt in 1947. The comfortable soles become a big hit among older housewives. In the first decade of production, 80 per cent of Dr Märtens sales went to women over the age of 40. In the 1950s sales had grown so much that they opened a factory in Munich. In 1959, they looked for a marketing opportunity to brand the footwear internationally. British shoe manufacturer Griggs bought the patent rights, anglicized the name, improved the heel fit and added the signature yellow welt stitching. On 1 April 1960 the first eight-eyelet Dr Martens boots in the UK were launched (hence the classic style '1460' still in production today). In the beginning, they were popular among factory workers, policemen and mail carriers. At the end of the 1960s skinheads started wearing them and in the 1970s bands such as the Clash, the Who and the Sex Pistols made Docs popular among punk fans as well as other subcultures such as New Wavers, Goths, etc. The youth movements tended to customize the upper side of the boots with spray paint and bottle caps to make each pair unique. Although Griggs wasn't exporting the shoes until the 1980s, rebel youth from all over the world visited the Dr Martens shop situated in Camden, London, to get their own pair of the unique boots. In the 1990s, the shoes were exported, sold in shopping malls and Docs went upscale. By 1999, sales globally reached $400 million and the brand was heavily investing in advertising and sponsoring. But at the start of the New Millennium sales

Continued...

What's up Doc? *Continued*

started to decline and to cut costs the UK production was shut down and moved to China and Thailand. Luckily the brand got a little help from famous fashion designers such as Jimmy Choo, Vivienne Westwood and Jean-Paul Gaultier to reinterpret and customize the original 1460. Models like Naomi Campbell were bound to wear the boots both on catwalks and in glossy magazines, which made the cool brand Dr Martens hot again.[15]

Love is a battlefield: identifying market drivers

How do you claim a certain identity in a market full of competitors? Of course, your brand's strengths, and the way you succeed in endorsing your competitive edge through product innovations or smart marketing will make the difference. However, competitors will often use the same kind of brand associations and meanings if they seem to be the most salient in a certain market.

Let's take the example of the denim category again. In Figure 5.1, you will see a 'battlefield analysis' of two brands: Levi's and Diesel. On the horizontal axis, we have plotted the number of times that Gen Yers who prefer Levi's for their next purchase have attributed certain brand image items to the Levi's brand. On the vertical axis, we did the same for the Diesel brand (items linked to Diesel by Diesel-lovers). This technique allows us to map the real battlefields in the jeans market. To be preferred, a jeans brand should be well-known, respected and associated with cool people. Both Diesel and Levi's are competing with each other on these image items. If you were to look at the results for G-Star Raw or Replay, you would notice that the same items form the real battlefield. The upper left zone of the mapping depicts those image items that are currently more associated with Diesel than with Levi's. Diesel is more progressive and radiates prestige. From Levi's point of view, these could be items they could try to focus on if they want to gain back market share from current Diesel buyers. But Levi's shouldn't try to stretch its brand DNA too far because then the brand risks losing its credibility for the critical Generation Y. When you take a look at the lower right area, you can identify the unique Levi's brand image items. Levi's fascinating history is the most important one.

FIGURE 5.1 Battlefield analysis for Levi's vs Diesel

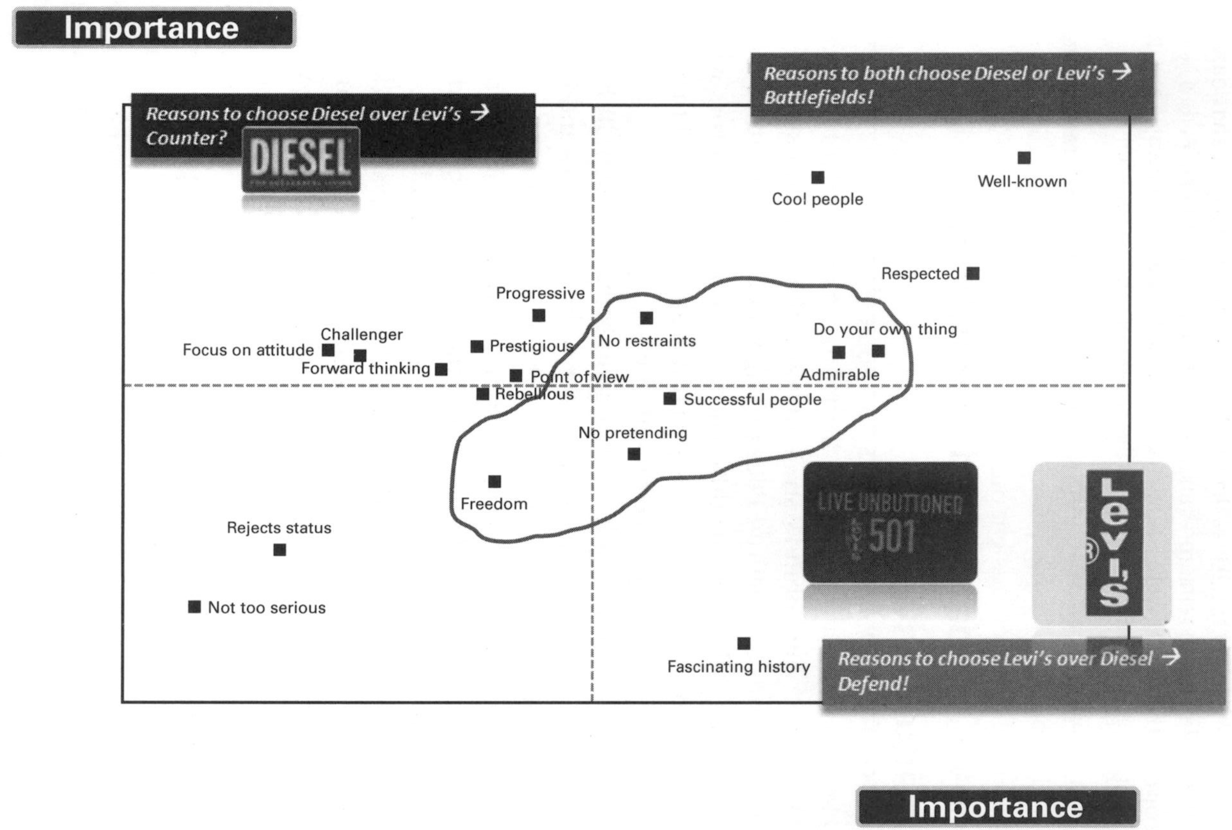

Nevertheless, in the previous chapter on brand authenticity we have learned that stressing the origin and history of a brand in advertising will have the wrong effect on this youth generation. Moreover, a regression analysis on Levi's brand coolness score revealed a negative effect of history on coolness. So, what could Levi's possibly do to cope with the Diesel competition then? They could concentrate their marketing approach on those brand items that are both associated with Levi's and equally important to Diesel buyers. Statements such as 'do your own thing', 'no restraints' and 'no pretending'. As illustrated in the previous chapter, this was exactly the main message in the 2008 'Live Unbuttoned' campaign for the Levi's 501.[16]

Choosing new battlefields for your brand

History has evidenced that David can take on Goliath. Think of brands such as Virgin, Apple or Mini. Sometimes, when the combat with your competitors is head on, it can be a good branding strategy to push yourself away from the battlefield by changing the environment you're working in. In the coolness chapter, we already gave a few examples of brands such as Nintendo Wii that have changed the category definition. Let's give another illustration from a differentiating youth brand strategy in the telecom industry.

Vodafone, an international mobile provider introduced a new subbrand named '360' at the end of 2009. In the price-sensitive youth mobile market, the battle between providers is all about tariffs and tons of free text messages. But Vodafone's DNA is not centred on price but on service and consequently the brand's premium pricing strategy made it hard to recruit young customers. With the new 360 sub-brand, Vodafone wanted to address other needs of the Gen Y target group: the ultimate interconnectedness. The 360 internet services combine and integrate phone contacts, e-mail, chat and social network accounts into one simple and always synchronized smart phone's address book. Vodafone's service was developed on the consumer insight that the price-sensitive youth target group is willing to pay more for mobile devices that simplify network communication. The '360' approach would allow parent company Vodafone to beat the price argument in the youth market. The campaign therefore had to demonstrate the ease of use of the single source approach in an entertaining and engaging way.

The brand decided to work together with MTV Networks in its most important European market, Germany, to create a branded entertainment series outside of the advertisements break: 'Joko's 360 trip'. Joko is a popular German MTV anchorman and, in the branded format, he brought the 360 ideas to life on a road-trip. Joko's tasks and destinations were completely chosen by the youth community voting on Facebook and were transmitted live to Joko's mobile phone. For this exciting journey, the MTV host had to activate various 360 apps to 'survive' Berlin, Munich, Hamburg and Dresden. User-generated challenges were supported by the TV and online formats and were perfectly embedded in the stories. Joko's 360 apps allowed him to communicate with his network and receive hints that were necessary to manage every situation along his trip. More than 8 out of 10 viewers of the programme understood the 360 benefits and found them to be relevant. The Vodafone 360 campaign achieved 61 per cent share of the planned full year sales during the campaign period, which was 20 per cent higher than the objective. Vodafone was able to recruit 11 per cent new Gen Y clients with this new service, which was more than double their projections.

Brand mascots, somatic markers and memes

In an effort to reduce complexity, Gen Yers, like any consumer, group products together in a so-called consideration set. Brand salience or uniqueness is the most important factor to be part of the consideration set. Through brand evaluation they choose between the brands evoked in their consideration set. Although brands within the consideration set are typically similar in terms of their product attributes, it will be the brand image that will ultimately create perceived differences between the competing brands. This brand image is, of course, more than the desired positioning of a brand. It is the collection of all brand associations held in consumer memory.[17]

Gen Y's brand choice is at least partially determined by representations of brands in its memory. According to associative network theories, these representations are never isolated in the brain but linked by connections that vary in strength. The stronger the association strength of brand representations the more they will influence youth's purchase behaviour. Many kinds of brand or product association might be relevant to consumer behaviour of Gen Yers. Brand representations can be product attributes, such as the shape and colour of packaging or the brand logo, but also usage situations and occasions, previous first-hand brand experiences, word-of-mouth or even marketing campaigns. The most successful youth brands focus on constant innovation, heavy advertising and promotional support, quality and a visually distinctive identity.

Sometimes iconic brand identities arise by coincidence. In 1997, Larry Page and Sergey Brin decided to dump their search engine's working name 'BackRub' for something shorter and simpler. They eventually chose 'googol' (a math term for 10 to the 100th power) but misspelled the word while checking whether that internet domain was unregistered. **Google.com** was available and **googol.com** was not.[18] Meanwhile Google is one of the world's best-known brand names, and its ever-changing homepage doodles keep the brand fresh. In the summer of 2010 Google organized its first global 'Doodle 4 Google' contest asking youth aged 4–17 to send in their 'I love football' designs. The winning one was used on 11 July, the day of the World Cup Final.

Logos that are distinctive often become memorable. Think of the Perrier, Kellogg's or Carlsberg logos. A distinctive tone-of-voice reflected in every text of, for instance, Innocent Drinks or Ben & Jerry's, contributes to the perception of brand uniqueness as well. Other tactics include claiming a colour, such as Cadbury's purple or Heineken's green. Or memorable packaging shapes such as the Heinz ketchup bottle, Toblerone's pyramids, or the Absolut and Coca-Cola bottles.[19]

Brand mascots are powerful association builders too, like the puppy to advertise how soft Andrex toilet paper is or Bacardi's bat that originally symbolized good fortune and is now associated with nightlife. In his book *Buyology*, Martin Lindstrom calls these brain short cuts 'somatic markers'. They serve to connect experiences or emotions with a reaction and help us to narrow down possibilities in a buying situation.[20] The strength of somatic markers is built by repetition and will only change slowly in time. This process, called evaluative conditioning – related to Pavlov's classical conditioning – allows our brain to link stimuli and form brand attitudes even if there's no causal or meaningful relationship between them. In other words, if Gen Yers repetitively noticed a brand at a cheerful youth happening, they would transfer the positive emotions to their attitude towards the brand.[21] The Canadian mobile telecom company Fido redesigned its flagship stores to appeal to Fido's Gen Y market. The shops display prominent pictures of people with their dogs throughout its interior to link the idea of warmth, trust and companionship to their brand. The somatic marker Fido wants to create is: 'a dog is a man's best friend, and it's always there for you, just like a mobile phone can be'.[22]

Mapping your brand's distinctive assets

To map what parts of your brand are truly unique for your consumers, brand distinctive asset research can help. The associative strength of brand representations is tested implicitly by giving respondents the online task to match visual stimuli with a target brand.[23] Let's illustrate this by a study we did in the energy drink category. We confronted 1,000 16- to 29-year-olds, all non-rejecters of the energy drink category, in five European countries (France, Spain, Sweden, Italy and Belgium) with three randomized blocks of 36 visuals. The set of visuals contained six stimuli for each energy drink brand involved in the test: Red Bull, Burn (of The Coca-Cola Company) and Rock Star (of PepsiCo). The six stimuli used were:

- a blinded can (picture of a can with brand name removed but logo kept);
- the main brand colours;
- the logo (without the brand name present);
- an advertisement;
- a picture of a brand event (sponsored or organized by the brand: Flugtag for Red Bull, a dance show in a nightclub for Burn, a mixed martial arts event for Rock Star);
- a generic activity (congruent with the brand values but not taken from the brand's website: skateboarders for both Red Bull and Rock Star/nightlife for Burn).

We first asked them to look at a set containing six blinded (unbranded) visuals of Red Bull, each shown three times throughout the randomized block, combined with 18 noise visuals of competing brands Burn and Rock Star. They then had merely 750 milliseconds to decide each time whether a displayed visual matched with Red Bull (hit space bar) or not (do nothing). The same exercise was then repeated for Burn and Rock Star.

In the analysis, we first calculated a 'unique identifier' index, a score calculating the difference between hits (correct match) and false alarm rates (perceived yet incorrect match). Each of the 1,000 youngsters had a 'unique identifier' score for each of the three brands. As you can see in Figure 5.2 Red Bull came out as the clear winner – its 'unique identifier' index is significantly higher than either Burn or Rock Star. This means that Gen Yers made more correct associations and fewer mistakes in identifying all visuals in relation to Red Bull. This result is all about Red Bull's uniqueness since the youngsters had to discriminate between images of a target brand (eg Red Bull) and images from the competitor brands (eg Burn and Rock Star). The more the visuals are uniquely attributed to a brand, the more correct responses and the fewer mistakes, resulting in a higher 'unique identifier' score for that brand.

To test this method for implicit measurement of uniqueness, we also asked Gen Y explicitly to what extent they agreed with the statement 'this is a unique brand' for each of the three energy drink brands. About 46 per cent of the 16- to 29-year-olds in the five countries found Red Bull unique, compared to 23 per cent for Burn and 12 per cent for Rock Star. This confirmed the implicit uniqueness findings.

FIGURE 5.2   Unique identifier index for three energy drinks

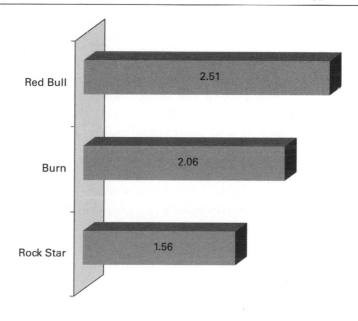

It was even more interesting to dive into the specific visual results. In Table 5.1 you will find the average percentage of correct hits per person for each image. This reveals the brand representations that are most identifiable with a brand. As they were displayed in combination with competitor images, they are a clear indication for the strength of brand assets.

TABLE 5.1   Percentage hits for specific brand assets

Brand Asset	Red Bull	Burn	Rock Star
Can (packaging)	89%	82%	66%
Colours	54%	31%	26%
Logo	78%	82%	70%
Advertising	74%	71%	64%
Brand event	27%	39%	10%
Generic activity	14%	9%	8%

The most distinctive brand asset of Red Bull seems to be the colours of the packaging since this brand representation attains the biggest difference in hits with the two competitors. The cold colours of Red Bull, blue and silver, represent the intellect or mind, while the hot ones, red and gold, symbolize emotion and the body.[24] Burn and Rock Star are both using black as their dominant brand colour, which explains the brand confusion. Both Burn and Red Bull clearly have a very strong brand logo. The bull, part of the brand name, embodies strength, courage and stamina. The flame in Burn's logo is also perfectly visualizing the brand name as well as its energizing powers. For Burn the flame logo seems to be the most distinctive brand asset together with its own nightlife brand event.

From the figures in Table 5.1 we can also deduce that Red Bull should reconsider its advertising strategy. Not that it isn't recognized by most youngsters, but the difference from Burn is rather low. When we take a look at the average reaction time, which is another indicator of association strength between a brand and its assets, we learn that the average reaction time to the Red Bull advertising visual was

589 milliseconds compared to a lower 575 milliseconds for the Burn ad. The reason for this is clear. Burn makes use of the flames in its ads whereas Red Bull visualizes the sign-off slogan of the brand ('Red Bull gives you wings') but is not endorsing it with the red bulls of the logo, nor its dominant packaging colours. From the analysis above, we could advise Red Bull to increase the use of its blue and silver colours in advertising, since that is currently their biggest distinctive brand asset. Although both Red Bull and Rock Star are endorsing skate events, the former is better at claiming the activity and associating the skate lifestyle with its brand in Gen Y's memory chunks.[25]

The lady in Special K red

One of the main distinctive assets of Kellogg's Special K brand is the slim lady in a red dress. She's there in all advertising and on every Special K package. Her presence clearly contributes to the perceived uniqueness of the Special K brand. Women were so charmed by Kellogg's summer 2010 campaign that the cereals manufacturer was swamped with questions on where the summer dress could be bought. Kellogg's made a deal with the British retailer Marks & Spencer and the dress was offered for 23 euros (£20).

A memetic approach to branding

In recent brand research, the brand representations and associations in our memory, or 'somatic markers', have been linked to 'memes'. Memes are the cultural equivalent of the biological genes. Just like genes, they are replicators and jump from brain to brain. Everything we have learned from someone else, whether it's a story, fashions, ideas, tunes, a brand or a product is a meme. Our own brand associations are constantly infected by the associations of other people and we infect the memes of others. Memes can propagate themselves and are passed on by replication or imitation.[26] In the next chapter on self-identification, we will give some examples of youth subculture lifestyles and tribal behaviour that is also influenced by spreading memes.

But let's illustrate brand memetics with an example of Coca-Cola's Vitaminwater. Coke bought the brand in 2007, but in 2009 Vitaminwater's sales volume slipped 22 per cent as a consequence of recession. Price-conscious college students and Gen Y's young professionals traded down to tap water or sodas. To respond to this market situation, Vitaminwater used the memes 'nutrients' and replenishing fluids or 'hydration' in their 2010 campaigns. The TV commercial 'Epic Night', featured a young male getting knocked in the head with a hammer, while a voice-over asks, 'Have you ever woken up on the wrong side of the bed? Your brain's throbbing and your face is in a pile of nachos?... Vitaminwater's purple "Revive" has B vitamins and potassium that will help rehydrate after epic nights.' The use of these memes will increase the differentiation and uniqueness of Vitaminwater compared to tap water or sodas. The new metallic bottle label with a nutrient matrix, an enlarged box highlighting the vitamins and minerals inside Vitaminwater, will also have a memetic effect. Competitor Gatorade (a brand of PepsiCo) is using completely different memes that are not associated with hangover relief. They focus on 'athletic performance'.[27]

In Charles Darwin's description of evolution the process of 'natural selection' indicates that the fittest species will have the most progeny and become more prominent in future generations. The idea in memetic theories is that both genes and memes have a direct relation to brands and brand management. Memes that eventually dominate will be the ones that were reproduced the most, because they express traits that are 'the fittest' for the environment. Successful brands will ensure their existence through possessing winning memes. Brands that satisfy more customers will tend to increase their presence in a competitive market. Sometimes this requires product development and differentiation. To enhance further growth in China, Sprite's biggest market in the world, the brand launched Spritea. The tea-flavoured carbonated beverage is only sold in Asian markets where both Sprite and green tea are very popular drinks. Sprite is the leading carbonated soft drink brand in China, outselling even the Coke brand. The ready-to-drink tea consumption in China has increased by more than 30 per cent annually in recent years. To fit with this environment Sprite needed to adapt the green tea meme. To support the spreading of the meme, Spritea will be sampled across China, providing 15 million free drinks to domestic consumers. Jay Chou, a popular Taiwanese musician and actor stars in the new TV commercial for Spritea.[28]

Brands targeting Gen Yers often have to adapt to a changing environment, because youth's consumer behaviour is more affected by trends. In the denim market, for instance, the premium designer jeans trend changed the environment for the more democratic labels such as Levi's. Levi Strauss & Co has recently hired executives from competing designer labels such as Ralph Lauren and 7 For All Mankind to improve its fashion credibility. In 2009, the brand created a super-premium division called 'Levi's XX'. It also offers a premium denim line with better fabrics and fit called 'Made & Crafted' which is sold through upscale retail outlets such as Saks Fifth Avenue and Barneys New York. Another premium sub-brand is Levi's Vintage clothing, offering reproductions of the brand's historical archives. Although the expensive jeans will only take up a very small part of Levi's business, investing in the premium meme is important to fit with the new denim environment and radiate a credible halo over Levi's brand name.[29]

When brands miss out on changing memes in the environment, this might lead to dramatic business results. For example, in the second half of the 1970s market leader Adidas neglected the running and jogging meme among casual users although they had a strong presence in running among athletes. Nike was more sensitive to the growing interests and needs of jogging participants and surpassed Adidas. Ten years later the highly successful brand Nike failed to recognize another meme, the fitness and aerobics craze among women. Competitor Reebok introduced comfortable athletic footwear in soft, pliable leather and a variety of fashionable colours. Style-conscious consumers suddenly switched to Reebok whose sales went up from $35 million in 1982 to $300 million in 1985.[30]

Just as errors happen during DNA replication, meme mutations can also appear during reproduction. The theory of brands acting as memes gained attention during the first decade of the new millennium following the rise of viral marketing. New technologies such as the internet and mobile phones facilitate meme reproduction at a much faster pace. But they can also create the so-called 'doppelganger image' when consumers spread off-strategy brand messages. The many spoof movies and parodies on YouTube can be seen as meme mutations.[31]

Conclusion

In this chapter we have dealt with the questions every Gen Yer will certainly ask about any brand, including yours. If it isn't made explicitly, it will happen at least implicitly:

- Who are you?
- What is your unique brand DNA; your identity that makes you stand out from competition?
- What are you?
- What 'brand meaning' do you offer me? What's your brand's vision? These brand assets are structured in youth's memory in associative networks, somatic markers or memes.

In order to make your brand really relevant to youth target groups, and to create this long-lasting CRUSH, two more Generation Y questions remain unanswered:

- What do I have in common with the brand?

Only when Gen Yers share values and interests with your brand, will they identify with it. In the next chapter, we will address this self-identification process and how brands can play a role in it.

- What do I feel about you?

The role of emotions in branding has increased in the first decade of the 2000s and youngsters especially are more emotional in their brand choice than ever before. In Chapter 7, we will explain how happiness and emotional branding contribute to bonding with Gen Y consumers.

Hot takeaways for cool brand builders

- Gen Y is sceptical about product novelty or a brand's uniqueness.
- But it's all about how youth perceives a brand's major claims as consistent.
- Youth talks about the brands they perceive as unique and buys brands on recommendation.
- The positive perception of your brand's uniqueness will thus lever your brand's preference and recommendation.
- Claiming your brand's DNA in all details (including retail, packaging and so on) will support a consistent positioning.
- Choose the right battlefields to stress in communication: those close to your DNA that are of importance to the buyers of your competitors as well.
- Brand identities act as somatic markers or memes.
- Marketing situations and environments are continuously evolving; specifically in youth markets, brands needs to adapt to changing memes.

Chapter Six
Self-identification with the brand

The word 'tattoo' is derived from the Tahitian word *tatau*, meaning 'from Tahiti'. West-European explorers in the 18th century such as Thomas Cook discovered the tribal tattoo practices among Polynesian people. This explains why tattoos in Europe were initially popular among sailors before spreading to broader society. The skin marks are much older than this discovery though. Even Ötzi, the Iceman who was found in the Ötz valley in the Alps and is believed to have lived in the fourth to fifth millennium BC, had approximately 57 carbon tattoos on his lower spine, knees and ankle. Some mummies (second millennium BC) from Ancient Egypt have tattoos too.[1]

Although many youngsters bear tattoos as a fashion style statement or to connect to their lifestyle subculture, many tattoo designs are originally related to gangs. The three dots in a triangle, illustrated in Figure 6.1, usually found between the thumb and forefinger, is such a 'generic' tattoo and is popular among Hispanic teenagers. The three dots have different meanings. It is said to have its origin in gang members affiliated with the Surenos or Sur 13. They place three dots on one wrist and a single dot on the other to indicate the number '13'. '*Tres Puntos*' refers to the 13th letter of the alphabet, 'La Eme', or 'the M' for Mexican Mafia. They also stand for '*mi vida loca*' ('my crazy life').[2]

Tattoo marks have always been used to identify with people belonging to the same culture. From the Maori tribes to the Harley-Davidson riders, the skin marks embody affiliation with other like-minded souls. Identity is always about the body, the bodily states and desires of being, becoming, belonging and behaving.[3]

In this chapter, we will zoom in on the identity construction of teenagers, the different Gen Y lifestyles and subcultures and the way

FIGURE 6.1   The three dots tattoo

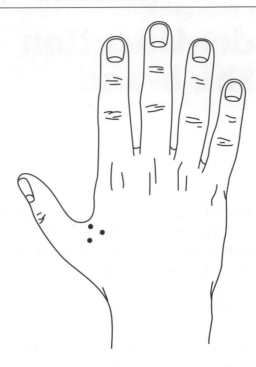

this postmodern tribal behaviour is influencing brand choice. We know that the brands and products youth buy become one of the central building blocks of their identity. This is clearly the case for what we have called 'badge items' in the chapter on coolness. Youth use product categories such as clothing, sneakers and mobiles to show they belong to certain peer groups. Youngsters choose those brands that are relevant to their individual selves and that represent those aspects of their identity they want to accentuate. Products have a symbolic value and are not solely used as a tool and means but rather as signs representing their thinking and values.

In the CRUSH brand model, youth's self-identification with the brand has a very strong direct effect on brand leverage. Next to that, identification is also influencing brand image and conversations about the brand. Together with the other CRUSH factors, self-identification is crucial to obtain a good connection with Generation Y and keep your cool brand hot for the long term.

We kick off this chapter by explaining the differences in personal, social, aspired and non-identities of youngsters. Then we will explore the concept of subculture and present a practical mapping of different youth lifestyles. Understanding what kind of lifestyles are attracted to your brand will teach you a lot about what type of brand personality your brand has to reflect to get a better connection with the Generation Y. The rise of social network websites, such as Facebook and MySpace, has supported online social interactions between adolescents. We will also discuss how youngsters are using their identities online.

Knowing me, knowing you: teens' identity construction

Scientists at Illinois University speculate that a teenage brain shrinks when going from adolescence to adulthood. In laboratory tests on rats neurons disappear from the prefrontal cortex in male and female pups undergoing puberty. Although you might anticipate a difference between a rat and an adolescent, it could make sense. Teens behaving badly, running away, smoking, slamming doors, body piercings, endless discussions... for parents of teens, it may not be the most pleasant period in their lives, but puberty is the backbone developing a youngster's personality and identity. The adolescent brain reorganizes in a very fundamental way. The questions: 'who am I', 'how do I fit in' and 'where am I going in life' are especially pertinent. While growing up, fitting in with a group on one hand and finding out your own personal values and styles on the other hand are important phases in identity development.

A period of storm and stress

Identity is only an issue when it is under development, threatened or contested. All three conditions are obviously present during adolescence. The pioneering US psychologist Stanley Hall wrote in his 1904 book *Adolescence* that it is 'a period of storm and stress'. To cope with puberty, Hall suggested a therapy combining gymnastics, muscular development and last but not least the virtues of a cold bath.[4] If you have some adolescents living at home, the idea of cold baths probably does seem appealing from time to time. Erik Erikson coined the term 'identity crisis' in 1968. He described adolescence as a period during which young people must overcome their uncertainty and become self-aware of their strengths and weaknesses. Through interaction with caregivers (such as teachers, parents, other adults) and peers, and through contact with media (video clips on MTV, fashion magazines and social network sites) they will try to solve three key questions:

- What are my values and ideals?
- What does my future look like: how will my occupations and career develop?
- What is my sexual identity?

Erikson believes that if parents allow the teenager to explore and experiment, he or she will finally become confident in his/her unique qualities and achieve an individual identity. However, if parents continually push their adolescent children to conform to their own views, teens will face identity and role confusion. So, let's forget about the cold baths.[5]

The multilayered identity

Identity is a multilayered construction consisting of four different elements:

- The personal identity: the identity a person believes he/she has.
- The social self: the identity he/she has in the eyes of others and that can only be discovered in social interactions. Since there are different social groups a person interacts with, there are actually different social identities.
- The aspired self: the 'ideal' identity or the one he/she would very much like to have.
- Non-identity: the not-wanted self or counterpart of the aspired self.[6]

It is thus clear that identity construction cannot be studied in an isolated context: it takes place while teenagers are interacting with peers. Often, the term 'collective identities' is used to refer to groups someone is affiliated with. To obtain a desired identity, youngsters will behave in accordance with the lifestyle of their social and ideal groups. In the youth marketing context, we speak of lifestyle tribes or subcultures. At the same time, adolescents want to distinguish themselves from groups they would rather not be part of. This is especially the case for collective identities that are unwanted but also to a lesser extent for groups that are different but acceptable.

In 2008, we followed teenagers (aged 13–17) during six consecutive weeks in an ethnographic study using personal blogs. We asked them to take pictures of all those aspects of their life that they believed we had to see in order to understand who they really were. They received several assignments. For every identity layer we created a set of tasks we introduced to them without mentioning the goals.

Personal identity

Central in adolescents' bedrooms, we often spotted objects symbolizing what they had achieved or reflecting how they were very 'unique' in comparison with other teens. Medals or certificates proving that they attained swimming or skiing skills, music instruments, paintings or poems they crafted themselves. A pile of school books showed how clever they were or how much they had to study. We could easily see the teen's bedroom as a 'ME-seum': a term we coined to name the would-be museum collection of stuff that reflected their own 'self'. It is a collection of what has happened in the teenager's life so far. It contains elements from childhood such as teddy bears or board games they loved when they were kids, often hidden in a corner of the room. Especially at the age of 12–14, teenagers are in transition from child to adult. Although they still like childish objects, they tend to put them out of sight. Some of them hide the childish wallpaper (containing cartoons or boats for instance) in their rooms with posters. Walls are full of references to their family relatives and people with whom they are close. Adolescents often stressed that something was made by their mother or father, or was 'very old'.

A number of youngsters literally had their own little 'shrine': a shelf central in their room containing souvenirs from holidays or events that they had collected during their lives. Especially girls around the age of 15 find the mirror in their room the most important object. The bedroom is not only a symbol of who teens are but also a collection of links to the people close to them and their ancestors, such as parents or grandparents.

When looking at brands, we learnt that two places where youngsters spend time (bedroom and outdoors) are almost brand-free spots:

youngsters did not tag any brands in these areas. There were in fact almost no brands visible in the pictures.

When we asked for pictures of objects that would typify them to others, similar themes came back. Escapism and social contact were represented in MP3 players (to cut oneself off from the daily world by listening to music), games (to be a hero in a virtual world) for boys, books (to enter the new world in the book) and mobile phones for girls (to have connections with peers anywhere, at any time). Some objects referred more to their social identity: the desire to look good for their peers was shown in make-up or perfume (for girls) and hair wax (for boys). Some participants even took pictures of objects that are typical of membership in certain groups: entrance bracelets for festivals, youth movement scarves, group entrance tickets for clubs, etc. In contrast to what happened in their most favourite locations, almost all typifying objects were branded. The pictures included food and beverage brands like Coca-Cola, Lays, Doritos or Pringles. A 15-year-old boy said: 'My friends call me Coca-Cola. Because I always drink a lot of Coke. And I drive a Dax, it's part of my image. I therefore use Dax hair products as well.'

We also noticed fashion brands such as Diesel, Adidas or Converse. Both genders also took pictures of cosmetic brands such as Wella or Axe.

Social identity

Although we had expected to receive plenty of pictures of trainers or favourite clothing items or brands when we were looking for their typical personal objects, not one single clothing picture was submitted. The specific clothing assignments revealed why. Teens are 'chameleon outfitters'. They adapt to the colours, patterns and styles from the social group to which they belong. Since being different carries a social risk, most of them therefore articulate their unique personality in smaller and safe accessories such as belts, scarves, jewels or handbags. These items can easily be removed in case one of their friends makes negative comments. The clothes they wear at home are often outfits that are also too risky to wear outside: clothes they used to like when they were younger, childish items with cartoon figures, T-shirts with very big labels and brands that could be a source of criticism for peers. We observed the chameleon behaviour mainly among 'mainstream' youngsters who did not belong to specific subcultures.

We also learnt about the social context of adolescents. Youngsters referred to their family in many cases. They reported a great deal on their parents, sisters, brothers, grandmothers, nieces, etc. The father was considered to be a particularly special person: a great number of young people do not have much contact with their father since he is out of the house more or because their parents are divorced. A girl (aged 16) in the study phrased it as follows: 'I have two bedrooms but I only have one dad.' The participants often had a special bond with the youngest family member. They loved to be the older nephew or niece and to take care of 'the young one'. In their social identity, a special role was also reserved for the 'BFF', the best friend forever. This friend is generally somebody they have known since kindergarten. In a world where parents get divorced, families split and are recomposed, and teens are in transition from primary school to high school, 'BFF's are the single stable component in their life. The BFF is in some occasions really considered as a family member. Youngsters even refer to them as brothers and sisters.

Aspired identity

Adolescents look up to older teenagers who aren't yet behaving like adults and still act crazy from time to time. The appeal of 'being older' was also reflected in the clothes they preferred to wear when going out. We observed that many girls picked very feminine clothes with low necklines, skirts or dresses. Boys often chose a more business style of clothes such as a neat and proper shirt with a collar or a blazer. Adolescents apparently start to practise their respective gender roles when going out.

In the pictures of youngsters with whom they would like to be friends, we observed a great number of groups of smiling cheerful friends. They were never pictured alone or sad. In their comments it became apparent that an aspired friend was often popular at school but also very tolerant and open towards other or unknown people. Aspired friends rarely belonged to certain subcultures and were more 'mainstream'. We also discovered that the young people who admitted belonging to a subculture systematically ignored this 'people you think much of' exercise. They were already living their aspirations. Teens that are active in certain subcultures aim to become 'better' or more representative of their own subculture.

Non-identity

Young girls (13- to 14-year-olds) often rejected boys in general or youngsters who showed tough behaviour. Authenticity appeared to be a key element in evaluating others. Teenagers of their own age who acted older by for instance wearing make-up or drinking alcohol, were often disliked. Adolescents who drew too much attention and were always negative about life were also often placed in the group of 'youngsters with whom you do not want to be friends'.[7]

All we want is just another tag on the wall

'You are what you write.' That's what graffiti writers will tell you about their 'pieces'. Their graffiti speaks for them. What they write determines who they are and what they stand for. Their tags are marks of their alter-ego, a physical extension of the writer left behind. For them it is a virtual and secret identity. Other people who see their tags don't know who they are. The names chosen by graffiti writers mostly communicate power, strength and control. They are often short and will say something about the owner. 'Acrid' for instance, a synonym for bitter, tells us something about the personality of the writer. Most graffiti lettering styles have a very strong, dominant and robust appearance. It looks a bit like a machine or armoured tank. Again, this confirms the masculine or macho part that the virtual identity of graffiti writers is playing.

Although most people will see graffiti as a dirty kind of urban wallpaper or scenery, it is actually a secret sign language for those who are in the scene. Many graffiti artists will say hello by positioning their own tags close to another one to whom they want to pay a tribute. But virtual wall fights also exist. Placing your name above rather than next to another tag is a simple way of saying I'm better or more than you. Lining or crossing out other tags is the virtual way of slapping other writers in the head. In London, a real tag war developed when 'Cred', a relatively young and unknown writer in the *RCS* crew began to line out 'Drax', a figure who had gained quite some status as a writer. For more than a year and a half, members of rivalling crews were ruining each other's pieces until a ceasefire was declared. The funny thing about this story is that Drax and Cred never actually met each other in person. They insulted, attacked and despised each other for a year and a half without actually knowing who their enemies were.

Shy and less confident adolescents often find a voice and virtual identity through graffiti. Think of this before criticizing the tags you notice in the city landscape![8] Advertisers and brands have discovered the impact of graffiti. For example, Havaianas sprayed walls full of colourful graffiti

Continued...

> **All we want is just another tag on the wall** *Continued*
>
> designs in New York to promote its line of Brazilian flip-flops. When Sony promoted its PSP portable game console with graffiti of cartoon characters in the United States, the graffiti scene reacted negatively. The world's most famous street artist Banksy criticized what he called 'brandalizing' of urban art and stickers saying 'corporate vandals not welcome' were seen on graffiti walls. Sony's Graffiti campaign was crossed out and writings read 'Get out of my city!!!'[9]

A quest called tribe: teens' search for a fitting lifestyle

Teens develop relationships with peer groups. These groups consist of similarly aged, fairly close friends. They are critical in puberty because they help teens to learn how to socially interact and become more independent from parents or other adults. Peer groups also give the necessary feedback during the search for identity and personality. They offer instrumental and emotional support.

Cliques and crowds

Basically, there are two types of peer group: cliques and crowds. Cliques are small groups with an average of five to six adolescents. Their smaller size allows teens to know each other well and appreciate each other better than others outside the clique. Cliques are the groups within which adolescents hang out and form friendships. They can be activity cliques formed by circumstance, for instance in sport clubs or music schools, or friendship cliques, which a teen chooses deliberately. In early adolescence, most cliques are single gender. Later, clique leaders start to get interested in the other sex and eventually couples will replace cliques as the new social structure. The second type of peer group is called 'a crowd'. Crowds are much bigger in size and not based on friendship but on common lifestyles, reputation and stereotypes. These reference groups contribute less to exercising social skills but are necessary to develop a sense of identity and self-concept. During early adolescence, a crowd provides self-definition before a teen is capable of creating an own self.[10]

When 'crowds' or 'tribes' are not considered mainstream, sociologists tend to call them 'subcultures'. We feel this term is a bit outdated since SUBculture implies a reaction to a mainstream culture. Large oppositions like the punk movement or the hippie culture, all reacting against a materialistic consuming world, are less prevalent today. As discussed in the first chapter on Generation Y, youngsters are not in an opposition movement against their parents either. This doesn't mean that today's crowds are all sharing the same ideas and preferences. The traditional approach of subcultures, however, is less relevant today. The French sociologist Pierre Bourdieu coined the concept of 'cultural capital'. It is defined as the knowledge that is accumulated through upbringing and education or social status. His theoretical scheme includes social capital: you don't just get your identity from what you own or know but also from who you know and who knows you.[11] In her study on club culture, Sarah Thornton elaborated on this concept and coined 'subcultural capital', emphasizing that subcultures today are more formed on the basis of music tastes, fashion styles and slang language rather than on values or as a response to the dominant mainstream culture. Haircuts, record collections and media usage are all identified as 'subcultural' capital.[12]

The Multi-vidual

Even those traditional sources of 'youth authenticity' described above have severely changed in the Gen Y society. 'Multi-vidual' youngsters like to pick and mix different fashion styles. Carrie Bradshaw, played by Sarah Jessica Parker, in *Sex and the City* for instance is depicting a postmodern reality. She wears an eclectic bohemian patchwork of trends. Yes, she's totally into Jimmy Choo shoes but she combines them with vintage dresses. *Sleazenation* and *The Face*, two style-dictating magazines both went bankrupt in 2004. One of the reasons for dissolving was that Gen Y was no longer into following the fashion police.[13]

It is not only difficult but also dangerous to find authenticity in the clothes you wear. Styles become mainstream faster than ever and brands are hijacked out of subcultures within one single year. Lonsdale, which was once a popular brand among mod revivalists such as Paul Weller, got hijacked by neo-Nazi kids in the mid-2000s. Von Dutch, an authentic US fashion label was a mainstream lower-class brand in no time. In our global village fashion designers are copied by the time their designs move from the catwalk to the shops. But this doesn't mean style differences among youngsters are non-existent. In fact, as a consequence of the 'multi-vidual' trend, there are more different lifestyle groups than ever before. Some sociologists would even claim that every youngster is a subculture on his/her own.[14] The emerging diversity and increased individuality in our postmodern society has led to microscopic mappings of youth tribes. Channel 4 in the UK for instance started tracking British youth culture in 2005. Since then, they have issued four versions of the 'Find Your Tribe' survey. The large-scale research gathering data across more than 250 brands and media found not less than 23 different tribes in the UK scene. All 23 lifestyles are based on four key groups: urban style, alternative style, leading edge and mainstream.[15]

Tribal marketing versus psychographic segmentation

A sense of belonging and differentiation among youth is still present today and will never disappear. For marketers, knowing and recognizing the different crowds in a teenage target group is vital and far more useful than sticking to motivational segmentation schemes. Brands that target youth should follow lifestyle tribes and identity construction with great attention in order to make their offering more appealing to them. Adolescents tend to adapt their consumption and concrete brand choice to a crowd's reference behaviour. They will also look for brands that reflect their self-identity. Following crowds is therefore more important than traditional psychographic segmentation methods. These methods, often based on values, seem to have lost their significance. All Gen Yers share the same core values of hedonism, freedom and friendship. Psychographic segmentation is a method to simplify reality by assigning individuals to groups of homogeneous persons who share the same characteristics. In reality, the members of segments are not connected to each other and take no collective actions.

Crowds or 'tribes' on the contrary are networks of heterogeneous people linked by a shared passion or emotion. Its members are advocates and since they meet each other both in real life and virtually, they are capable of collective actions. Tribal membership doesn't necessarily involve certain personality traits or common values. Tribal marketing is not about creating products or services for youth segments but supporting brands that keep youngsters together as a group of enthusiasts. The key to achieving this is to identify tribes that are relevant for your brand positioning. Then your brand has to reflect the passions and interests of the selected tribes in your marketing actions. Instead of limiting efforts to a mere observation, tribal marketing entices involvement with tribe members in highly emotional and ritual experiences. You should treat tribe members as partners in marketing and even involve them in co-designing your products.

The German trainer brand Adidas created a free iPhone App, Adidas Urban Art Guide, offering four different guided tours along masterpieces of street art in Berlin. With the 'find artwork nearby' tool, the mobile's GPS function locates graffiti near the user and visitors can rate each work or upload other street art they are fond of themselves. Adidas used the marketing idea of branded utilities and developed a useful tool for youngsters in an area that is in their line. In youth marketing today, successful brands don't scream who they are, but find the passions Gen Y are screaming about and then facilitate these.[16]

Tribes are fuzzy societal sparkles rather than socio-economic realities. This implies that they are not easy to determine and hard to track by traditional quantitative research methods.[17] Members of lifestyle tribes signal their membership through tangible and intangible symbolic choices. Their preferences in fashion styles (clothes, trainers and haircuts), gatherings and places, and music genres tell us who they are and what group they belong to. Explicit usage or rejection of brands and slang language are also common differentiators.

Most youngsters will see themselves (personal identity) as just normal, ordinary mainstream guys or girls. They don't want to see themselves placed in a certain typology and are of course afraid of being labelled, since this could automatically mean the disapproval of certain peer groups. This phenomenon doesn't make it easier to discern lifestyles or map them quantitatively.

A 3D mirror for everyone: mapping youth lifestyles

In the past three years, we have followed youth lifestyles in different regions, both using observational techniques as well as surveys. We have used the identity construction layers as our guideline. In Figure 6.2, you will see the result of this work. We have found the three basic dimensions that explain 74 per cent of the differences between youth lifestyle groups or tribes.

FIGURE 6.2 InSites Consulting and MTV Networks youth tribes mapping

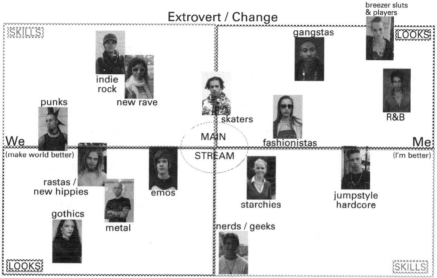

Horizontal dimension: me (right side) versus we (left)

Some youth subcultures stress the individual performance and appearance over the collective achievements of a group. These tribes are egocentric and consider themselves to be better than other youth groups. They are generally less open or tolerant towards other tribes. The more a tribe is positioned to the right of the axis, the more individual achievement and power (being the best) are important. Youngsters on this side of the scheme do not think too much ahead. They live now and don't make too many plans for the future. Life is all about the 'carpe diem' philosophy; this is the 24/7 party crowd.

At the 'we' end of this horizontal dimension, adolescents are more open and tolerant towards others. They feel it's okay to be different. Instead of making themselves better, they want to make the world a better place. At this left side of the scheme, youngsters have a more long-term vision. This is reflected in their genuine interest in politics, ecology, psychology and philosophy. We-oriented tribes value justice and equality. They will show higher engagement in society and sometimes even participate in demonstrations. At the left side of the scheme, youngsters are into reading newspapers and books. They are very much attracted by the arts (theatre, museums) and frequently go to gigs, because the artist behind the music styles they love is important.

Vertical dimension: extrovert/change (above) versus introvert/conservative (under)

A second differentiator between subcultures is the extrovert/introvert vertical axis. Above the centre line, crowds like to spend most of their time out of the home. Think of the skaters on squares, fashionistas going to nightclubs, fitness centres and shopping streets or gangstas hanging out on the streets. They are fond of exploring unknown territories and are quickly aware of novelties. They are more leading edge and trendsetting consumers than those below the mid line. Youngsters at this side of the scheme know a lot of people, have many friends and they are the more popular individuals at school. The most important source of information for these groups consists of other peer groups in the same quadrant. Compared to the crowds that are positioned below the mid line, they are much more active. This is reflected in their occupation with sports and travelling. The left upper quadrant is fascinated by exotic and adventurous backpacking in Asia, Africa or Latin-America. Youth on the upper right side is indifferent to these kinds of holidays. They prefer beach and party vacations. Tribes on the left upper side are more involved with action and extreme sports such as boarding, surfing and bungee jumping. Towards the right upper side the urban styles are into basketball, the fashionistas and breezer sluts/players into soccer, motorsports and Formula 1.

Below the centre line, adolescents are more often alone and introvert. They value spirituality and mystery and are spending more time at home or in their small cliques. Youngsters are less sportive and less interested in travelling the world. They are finding adventure in virtual and safe gaming worlds such as *World of Warcraft* or *Runescape* (the boys) and *The Sims* (girls) or in the fantasy world of books. Tribes below the centre line are often unpopular at school, and they are sometimes the victims of bullying (mostly initiated by the upper right quadrant) or jeered at because of their looks or clumsiness.

Four large groups

The combination of the horizontal and the vertical dimensions leads to four quadrants. Each of them assembles crowds or social groups that are near to each other's identities. On the other hand, quadrants that are diametrically on the other side of the scheme will be seen as unwanted identities or non-groups. This sums up five substantial social groups within Gen Y:

- The **status-seeking crowds** (upper right quadrant) want to be better than others by their appearance. This assembly consists of urban-style tribes such as the immigrant gangstas and the autochthonous copies called wangstas(with a 'w' that stands for wannabe gangsta) also named R&Bers/hiphoppers or rappers. In this quadrant, we also find fashion boys and girls or fashionistas, and their lower class copies called breezer sluts and players. The latter wear the same brands – although often a bit later than their examples – but tend to overemphasize their gender role by wearing low necklines and short skirts.

- The **social exploring crowds** (upper left quadrant) comment on what's happening in the world through their own creativity. A collection of tribes such as the indie kids, rockers, new ravers, etc.

- **Idealist crowds** (lower left) react against what's wrong in the world, for instance by the way they look. Punks, new hippies/rastas, metalheads, goths and emos belong to this group.

- **Homebody conservative crowds** (lower right) want to be better than others by having better skills: nerds, geeks, starchies, jumpstyle hardcore geezers.

- **Mainstream youngsters** (centre of the scheme) share the average youth passions of music, gaming, shopping, movies, sports and cooking. They inhabit limited reaches of every youth culture but never the extremes.

Each of these groups contains a multitude of lifestyle tribes. Some tribes, such as the skaters (above the centre line) and the nerds (below the centre line) are positioned in the middle of two quadrants, which signifies that they are in-between and will show influences of both sides. Skaters are interested in arts and creative (think of graffiti) and love (punk) rock music but they are also interested in urban music and shopping. They are fond of their own brands such as DC, Element, Ethnies, Vans. Nerds are interested in cars (and babes) but also in games.

The looks and skills dimensions

When we were studying the tribes in detail, we revealed a third dimension that corresponds with the diagonal zones in the scheme:

- **The looks-zone:** Gen Yers in the upper right or lower left parts of the diagraph in Figure 6.2 mainly differentiate from others by using their appearance. A remarkable conclusion is that although both quadrants are quite opposite in terms of values, interests and behaviour, they share an exactness for the way they look. Still, they do have a completely other way of using their appearance. The upper right quadrant for instance will actively use certain status or prestige brands such as Dolce & Gabbana, Armani, Tommy Hilfiger or Gucci to claim their identity. On the other side of the scheme they will reject all brands, avoid wearing any clearly visible labels on their outfits and use bands instead of brands. Music bands that are representative for their scenes – for instance punk bands like The Sex Pistols, metal bands such as Rammstein or emo bands such as My Chemical Romance – will be printed on their sweaters and T-shirts and replace the identity function of brands. For status-seeking tribes a fashionable and perfectly styled haircut is of the utmost importance. Idealist crowds, such as goths, punks, hippies and emos have long haircuts that seem untidy, but creating this effect requires a lot of attention too. Jewels and 'bling bling' are important differentiators in the upper right quadrant. In the lower left one, they wear jewels too, but converted into the 'darker' variant of piercings and pinned belts.
- **The skills-zone:** In the upper left zone of the scheme, many youngsters seem to play live music on stage or at least an instrument. Others design their own clothes or are creative through photography or video. In the lower right part,

youngsters use skills to differentiate from others as well. Car-tuning, mechanics and computer skills are prevalent in this area. Since these crowds are on the 'me, I'm better' part of the scheme, skills represent more the status and ego thing for these tribes. Having the most expensively tuned car, getting the highest status and top scores in computer games such as *Runescape* or *World of Warcraft* or just getting the best school results.[18]

Subcultures and music

Music, fashion style and participation in local music scenes and sports or cultural events are visible determinants of engaging in subcultures. Subcultures mostly have their favoured music styles. Listening to music is still the most dominant activity in youngsters' lives. Pop charts music is of course the most mainstream choice. In the upper right quadrant, urban styles such as hip-hop, rap and R&B are the most popular. Fashionistas and breezer sluts/players also like commercial dance and trance music. The more tribes are situated to the left, the more rock, metal and alternative music genres (punk, ska, gothic and emorock) will pop up. Skaters are in between the rock scene and the urban scene and they will like both R&B and rock. Hippies do like rock but are also into folk, world music, soundtracks and music from the 1960s and 1970s. Starchies, nerds and fashionistas also like local music in the native language.

How to speak Geek

When we were in our ethnographic research phase with 40 youngsters, one of them, Laurent, a 15-year-old, had uploaded a movie on his blog. His comment sounded like this: 'Spartacus 121 best PK. I hit something like about 27 en that is really way high, but his hits are disturbed. LOL. His sword is 140M, mine is only 10M.' We scratched our heads and were wondering what Laurent was talking about. Laurent was a metal nerd daily involved with the MMORPG (Massively Multiplayer Online Role Playing Game) *Runescape*. When we asked for an explanation, he said he had sent us a PK movie showing one of the players Spartacus 121. PK stands for player killing, an online multiplayer fight within a game between two or more live participants. Gamers tape their best PK performances to brag and show how good they are in gaming skills. They post them online on YouTube. The 'M' in his message was indicating the power of the sword.

An ever-evolving picture

As already pointed out: our tribal scheme is, like all models, a simpli-fication of reality and shows the big streams and differences. Out there, many youngsters will combine lifestyles that are close to each other. We have seen metal nerds and skate-rockers. Sometimes certain lifestyles pop up for a while and then quickly dissolve again. This was the case with Tecktonik for instance. Tecktonik started as a street-dance, typically performed with quirky arm movements on fast-paced Electro House music. It was born in the Parisian Metropolitan night-clubs in France in the 2000s. At the end of 2007 Tecktonik suddenly became a craze not only in France but also in the neighbouring coun-tries when it was showcased in the Techno Parade in Paris on 15 September. Due to a big media-hype about this subculture, the dance and music quickly became mainstream and commercial, which even-tually led to a fast vanishing of the tribe.

Why depicting lifestyle groups in ads can be dangerous

To most youngsters, the aspired crowds are those that are the most mainstream (close to the middle of the scheme) and the least extreme (not situated in the far ends of the scheme): skaters, fashionistas and starchies. The crowds at the outskirts of the scheme are often seen as unwanted identities or non-groups, especially by those sub-cultures that are positioned diagonally on the opposite side of the mapping. Befriended tribes are mostly close to their own identity and spot in the scheme. It is therefore not recommended to use music, activities or models that refer to these 'outskirt' tribes in advertising or communication for brands that want to target Gen Y. This might seem logical to you, but there are still countless commercials project-ing urban styles (hip hop) in their ads in an attempt to appeal to youth and give a fresher image to the brand. Especially when com-bined with products or services that are perceived as 'uncool' by Generation Y, such as banks or insurance companies, this kind of approach will undermine a brand's credibility and authenticity. Unilever's male grooming brand Axe/Lynx has used the urban culture in another, more ironic way in their marketing campaign to launch the Musicstar variant in Latin America during late summer 2009. The TV commercial shows a typical rapper in a luxury car together with three babes. Suddenly the Bentley breaks in two parts and the back seat of the car drifts away from the front seat where the rapper is located. The back seat surges into a home where a guy is just spraying the new deodorant. The sign-off says: 'get back what music stars have taken away from you'. The ad was accompanied by an online gaming website.[19]

No ID, no entrance: implications for brands

Consumers choose brands to develop, extend or portray their self-identity. For adolescents who are still in the process of constructing their identity this is even more prevalent than for other age groups. Brands, styles and products deliver tangible ways of meaning transference. Youngsters who seek to both fit in and express their individuality will look for brands or specific styles that reflect their self-image. Brands that are capable of representing the personal, social and aspired identity of Gen Y will find a better connection with this generation. Mapping your brand personality on the lifestyle scheme in Figure 6.2, and understanding the self your target groups wish to portray to the world is crucial to guide strategic brand positioning choices and communication strategies. Of course, brand meaning isn't just constructed in your own marketing communications. As we have highlighted in the previous chapter, it is a co-creation process in which your consumers will define your brand's identity through communication, product and event experiences.[20]

Gen Y's favoured brand personalities

The key to obtaining self-identification with your brand is to reflect the values, interests and opinions of your target group. For the critical Generation Y, this doesn't mean just saying what your brand stands for but proving it every day in the way your brand acts. The first step to do this is to understand the values and interests of your young target groups. From the previous paragraph, you know that Gen Y isn't a big homogeneous group. Youth target groups are composed of a number of different lifestyles. So, you should be aware of the brand preferences and interests of the tribes that are within your target group. Next, it is important to understand that the various

FIGURE 6.3   Brand personality items

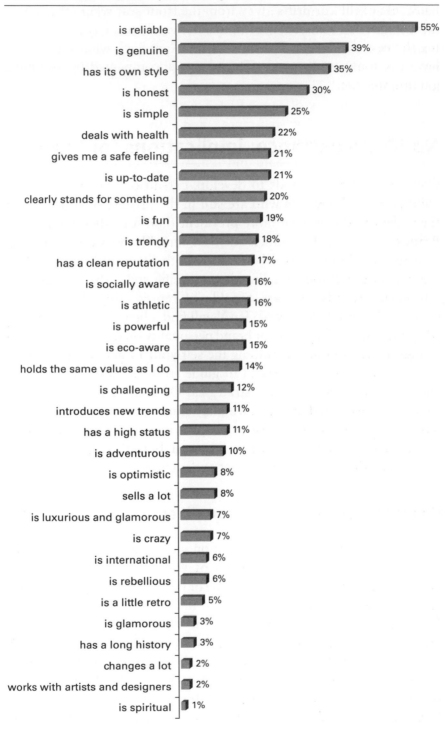

lifestyles are looking for different aspects of a brand personality before they will identify with your brands. In Figure 6.3, you will find the brand personality items that the overall Millennial population wants to see reflected. Product reliability, which means that your products always deliver the same expected quality level, is the absolute number one. The rest of the top five most-wanted personalities include components of our CRUSH brand model. Authenticity or realness, for instance, is well-represented in the need for genuine and honest brands. A youth brand should have its own unique style. It should also be up-to-date and fun. When youngsters talk about their close friends, it's striking that they use the same traits they are looking for in a brand. A friend is someone you can always count on. He or she is honest and authentic. He shares the same values and styles and is fun to have around. Gen Yers also appreciate simplicity in brands. What a brand stands for should be clear and if the product use is simple too, that's a real trump card. Apple, for instance, is a good example of a brand that combines its unique design claims with a reputation of user friendliness and simplicity.

Different brand preferences for different lifestyle groups

We analysed the desired brand personality characteristics of Gen Yers and noticed that they differ for the various lifestyles. The tribal scheme in Figure 6.2 was helpful to explain the differences.

Social groups at the me-side of the horizontal axis were in general much more brand sensitive. This is of course related to youth using certain brands to express their status and construct their social identity. To fit the personality of the Gen Yers in the upper right quadrant, hot brands radiate trendiness, status, luxury and glamour. It should always be up-to-date and international. Among urban tribes these international aspects should carry a clear US stamp. Tribes on the right side don't want a brand to be rebellious, retro or crazy.

On the we-side of the mapping, styles and values are more important than brands. A brand appealing to the left side of the mapping stresses values such as a bit edgy, rebellious and crazy. Still, brands that work for these groups are not too commercially oriented, they have an 'underground' feel and are actively involved with other broader world causes. This means brands should have consideration for health and be eco-aware. Since the left side loves live music and gigs, it is clear that a brand targeting these tribes should be present in the music scene that relates to these lifestyles. There's one big difference between brands that appeal to the upper side and the lower side of the mapping. Below the horizontal centre line, and especially in the right lower corner, brands should give a 'safe' feeling. A long history and heritage (see the classic definition of brand authenticity in Chapter 4) attributes to this perception. Above the centre line, brands should always be challenging, renewing and surprising. All these are attributes that won't work for youngsters situated at the lower side of the mapping since they value familiarity. Buying decisions are not always an individual activity of course. If we look at the main inspiration sources of youngsters to buy clothes, the vertical axis is highly influential. Peers inspire adolescents on the extrovert side. These are not only friends from their own social group; they also borrow elements from friendly groups. The more adolescents are on the bottom side of the scheme, the more their buying decisions and styles will become influenced by their home situation or relatives such as brothers, nieces or mothers.

H&M's 360° appeal to all tribes

From reading this, you will understand why it is not so easy to appeal to the entire Generation Y market with just one brand. Particularly if you are active in the 'badge item' markets, this will be hard. When certain tribes adopt your brand, others will automatically reject it. That is, if your brand is clearly labelled. Let's take a look at H&M, for instance. H&M is a retailer. The brand is not printed in a visible way on the garment. This allows H&M to appeal to a broader target group of Gen Yers. Still, the same 'shared personality' model is valuable for H&M. In the upper right quadrant, the fashionable youngsters normally want a clearly visible upscale brand on their clothes, because that's giving them status and makes them better than others. So how can H&M retain its appeal to these youngsters if they don't have this exclusive label visible on their clothes? The answer is quite simple. They have to radiate fashion, glamour and global trendiness. That's exactly what H&M does by working together with fashion designers that appeal to the upper right quadrant. The collaboration with fashion designers started in 2004 (see Figure 6.4) as a one-time initiative to survive the usually boring month of November. 'Nothing happens in November', says Jörgen Andersson, former global brand

FIGURE 6.4   Karl Lagerfeld kicked off H&M designer collaborations

director of H&M. 'We had been working with the lingerie campaigns for a while, but the trouble was that everyone was talking about the models of the campaign and not the H&M product. The buzz was mostly about who would be the next lingerie model. So we came up with this idea to do something for our customers that they could never afford to do themselves and make something exclusive for the mass.' The idea of working with designers has been copied but never in the same enduring and at the same time renewing way. 'Sometimes brands have a long-term agreement with a designer or they sell a collection for a year, but we believe the Gen Yers are easily bored with that approach', explains Andersson. 'There's a lot of hype about new Apple products before they come out, but once they are released the buzz moves on to what will be the next innovation. We release our temporary designer collection like a concert to enhance this same feeling of "did you manage to get the tickets before it was sold out".' H&M doesn't believe in selling the items for longer than three weeks because then they would lose their exclusive value. 'The worst nightmare for a girl is to go to a party and be confronted with another girl wearing exactly the same dress', concludes Andersson. The collaboration with fashion designers has certainly put H&M on the fashion map with both models and designers being proud of their connection with the brand and journalists providing much coverage in glossy magazines. The strategy has been used for six years now and was expanded with spring collections now and then. 'These are more in line with our own existing collection', says Andersson. 'We have a team of 100 designers and we want their work to be the real star of H&M.'[21]

The fact that the designer's collections are only temporarily available at certain selected selling points of course adds a taste of exclusivity, which is exactly what youngsters in the upper right quadrant of our tribal mapping are looking for. To appeal to the left side of the tribal mapping other values are more important. Apart from the Fashion Against Aids campaign, H&M sells items of which 30 per cent goes to UNICEF or other good causes. Without doubt, certain styles and colours are important to the left side. The diverse range of H&M includes items in the right styles and colours that are appealing to goths, emos, rockers, etc. Since there are no H&M labels on the clothes, they will not be rejected by the lower left anti-brand quadrant and since H&M is also appreciated by the bullying upper right fashionable quadrant, it is a safe choice for the lower right quadrant. In this quadrant, they have the competition of other safe family brands such as Mexx and Esprit (DC). This 360 degrees positioning explains the success of H&M as the number one youth apparel brand. The key to massive success does not lie in a mainstream positioning, because then you will only be attractive to 30–40 per cent of the market, the mainstream segment, which is of course big enough for many brands. The successful youth marketer finds the appropriate entrances and angles to different lifestyle groups. This strategy builds brand relevance in the entire Gen Y market, which will also inevitably translate into mainstream market demand.

Nike, Inc. uses two brands to cover the diverse youth market

In some markets, this means you will need different brands to capture the total youth market. Nike and Converse are both brands belonging to Nike, Inc. Converse has been part of the group since the 2003 acquisition, which was quite a brilliant move of Nike. If you look at the brand personality of Nike, constantly focused on athletes, performance, power and achievement, it is clear that the brand will appeal to the upper right quadrant of the tribal mapping. The notion of excellence, which is important for these tribes, will drive young consumers to value brands that perform to high standards, have a proven track record and make ongoing commitments to quality. Stressing quality-related and novelty details, functional performance and top athlete performances thanks to pioneering technology will undoubtedly support the brand's positioning.[22] Compare this specific brand personality to the other brand in the holding: Converse. The brand's positioning is more authentic and simple. The basic appearance and features of the sneaker have never changed. But the main personality traits of the brand are much more linked to the art and music scene, both interests that are in the hearts of tribes on the upper left side of the lifestyle scheme. Converse has worked with pop art pioneer Robert Indiana to create a special Red Love Pop Art collection. Incidentally, red and black are the two most successful colours to attract tribes on the left side of the scheme. Converse is also supporting many music artists and uses another key element in youth marketing: endorsing local initiatives. Sponsored artists originate from the UK, Thailand, Mexico, France, China, Argentina and more. By combining the brand personalities of Nike and Converse, the company is capable of appealing to the entire active and sportive youth market. And by not excessively focusing on the sportive aspect of the basketball Allstars, but instead stressing artists and rock musicians, the Converse brand is also attracting the lower left side of the scheme.

A brand's positioning attracts certain tribes

Let's consider some FMCG (fast-moving consumer goods) markets. In the luxury ice cream segment, you have Ben & Jerry's. The brand was founded by two self-declared hippies. Today, it is still putting a lot of effort into using fair trade ingredients while being actively involved in social programmes and ecological themes. Humour and craziness are a core part of the brand DNA and this is constantly exploited in variety names, package designs, events, etc. Ben & Jerry's is clearly a fitting brand choice for the left side of the mapping. Competitor Haägen-Dazs is using foreign branding and Scandinavian quality connotations. Advertising in black and white with packaging colours including gold, are all giving a luxury and glamorous feel to the brand. Main advertising themes concentrate on the best ingredients and seduction. These are all memes that will fit with the memeplexes of the right side of the mapping.

Or let's take personal care. The Dove brand, with its campaign for real beauty, criticizing the beauty paradigms of the fashion industry, will certainly overlap with the values of the left side of the mapping. On the other hand, the upper right quadrant will never feel shared values or self-identification with the Dove brand. Brands like L'Oréal that link themselves to fashion show, catwalks, glamour and models will immediately strike a sympathetic chord with that quadrant but on the other hand lose the left wing.

In other words, even if you are not a 'badge item' manufacturer, it still means you have to use different marketing and communication approaches to stay relevant to a broad youth audience. Let's take the example of Red Bull. The energy drink brand creates its own and participatory events. They have local events that will appeal to different lifestyles and surpass mere sponsoring. For instance, the Red Bull Racing Formula 1 team and the soccer teams in New York and Salzburg reflect the activities and interests of the right upper quadrant. Extreme sports such as boarding and BMX will appeal to the upper centre (skaters) and upper left. The Red Bull Music Academy – a talent-scouting contest for deejays, as well as rock bands – is fascinating to the upper left side of the scheme. The Red Bull Creative Contest in which they invite youngsters to create their own piece of art with a can of Red Bull, is reflecting the skills and interests of the upper and lower left side of the mapping. The scantily dressed hostesses in their polished Red Bull cars are exciting for nerds as well as other right side tribe members.[23]

From hip-hop to branded pop

Historically, hip-hop artists were the first to use brands in their shout-out lyrics as a way to define their status. The 'I grew up with nothing but now I own a Mercedes Benz' stories became more mainstream. Tommy Hilfiger grew to a $2 billion dollar company within ten years with the aid of supporting rap artists name-checking the brand in their lines. When Busta Rhymes and Puff Daddy collaborated on an ode to the cognac brand Courvoisier in 2002, it witnessed a 20 per cent jump in sales.[24] Brand strategy agency Agenda Inc. tracked all the brand mentions in the lyrics of the US

Continued...

From hip-hop to branded pop *Continued*

Billboard Top 20 singles charts in 2003 and 2004. Of the 105 songs in 2004, 42 songs (40 per cent) mentioned at least one brand. Kanye West was the king of name-dropping with no less than 19 brands in only four singles. At that time brands in music were still overwhelmingly an urban phenomenon. Only one brand of the 105 was mentioned in a non hip-hop song (Levi Strauss in Jessica Simpson's 'With You'). The tribal mapping in Figure 6.2 shows that the urban subcultures (gangstas and rappers/R&B) are in the upper right quadrant where status and brands are crucial in identity construction. If you look at the top 10 mentioned brands in the US Billboard Top 20 charts in Table 6.1, you will notice they are all prestige and status symbols: luxury expensive cars, champagne and fashion.[25] It is no coincidence that hip-hop songs are full of this type of brand.

TABLE 6.1   Brands mentioned in the 2004 US Billboard Top 20

Position	Brand	Mentions 2004
1	Cadillac	70
2	Hennessy	69
3	Mercedes	63
4	Rolls-Royce	62
5	Gucci	49
6	Jaguar	37
7	Chevrolet	28
8	Cristal	28
9	Bentley	26
10	Maybach	25

In the 1990s, hip-hop fashion brands emerged. Brands like Karl Kani and FUBU were conceived for and aimed at rap aficionados. Many hip-hop artists released their own fashion brands. Russell Simmons, co-founder of hip-hop and metal label Def Jam, was one of the first music entrepreneurs signing product placement contracts. In 1986, he invited Adidas executives to go to a gig of Def Jam's artists RUN DMC. The band had a song 'My Adidas' and prompted the audience to remove their shoes in tribute to the brand. Simmons created his own fashion brand Phat Farm that became very popular

Continued...

From hip-hop to branded pop   *Continued*

among urban tribes. Many other artists followed his example: Jay-Z (RocaWear), P Diddy (Sean John), Wu Tang Clan (Wu Wear), Eminem (Shady Clothing), 50 Cent (G-UNIT), Pharell Williams (Ice Cream) and so on.[26]

In 2008, brands' interest in linking with music artists moved to the more mainstream. Procter & Gamble formed a joint venture with Def Jam, called Tag Records. The label, named after a brand of body spray, will release hip-hop albums. Bacardi promoted the last Groove Armada album supporting 25 events of the band and acquiring online distribution rights to their new EP. Caress, a body-care line owned by Unilever asked the Pussycat Dolls singer Nicole Scherzinger to promote its Brazilian body wash on a website give-away single. Converse released a single combining the Strokes singer Julian Casablancas with Pharrell Williams and Santogold. These are just a few examples of a new reality in the music industry. It's a win/win partnership of an industry dealing with online file-sharing and advertisers struggling to reach consumers due to the same digital media diffusion.[27]

Lady Gaga's 2010 music video for Telephone (co-starring Beyoncé) was not only the talk of the town because of nudity, lesbian kissing and a mass-murder sequence. At least nine different brands including Virgin Mobile, HP and Diet Coke appeared in the clip. Most of them were unpaid extensions of Lady Gaga's marketing partnerships. The scene in which Gaga curls her hair with Diet Coke cans was meant as a homage to her mother, who used this technique back in the 1970s. Coca-Cola did not pay Lady Gaga's management to be included.[28]

From Avatar to YouTube: online identity construction

Youngsters, especially the teenagers, are increasingly living their lives in a virtual context. More than 7 out of 10 Gen Yers are active on at least one social network site, with Facebook easily reaching more than 80 per cent of the population in nations such as the UK, the United States, France and Australia.[29] 'Cyberspace' was traditionally considered a place of complete disembodiment. The anonymity of the internet makes it an ideal place for identity experimentation and exploration. Some theories claim that youngsters will have a tendency to represent themselves in an ideal way; they can pretend to be older, of a different gender, etc.[30] Other studies have found a 'stranger-on-the-train' effect: since less audio-visual information is available on the internet in comparison with real life, people are expected to reveal more information online. They will thus share more intimate details than they would in real life.[31] Finally, virtual communities are fuzzier than offline social networks, it is therefore easier to engage in deviant social behaviour without getting negative feedback.

In our ethnography study, we asked participants to become our 'friends' in their different social networks. During the course of the study, we observed their actions in their online environment. We studied their nickname, profile and their profile pictures. Social identity was also captured by looking at clan membership. In many social networks, participants have the opportunity to become a member of certain social groups or fan pages. In some cases, this clan membership also represented non-identity since different kinds of anti- or hate clans are also present on the internet. Finally, we also studied the online conversations and search terms of the participants to get a more complete picture of their social interactions and interests.

Online personal identity

In order to grasp the complete identity of the participants, we compared their offline and online profiles. In general, we observed a close fit between the online and offline identities of youngsters: all participants had the same gender, age and hobbies as in real life. We noticed that a lot of teenagers made associations to their real-life friends in their own online profile. For example, a 14-year-old boy named himself on his social network 'brother_4_life'. In the 'about yourself' section he wrote a whole description of his friends and the hobbies they shared. Friends in social networks are not just the people you know. They are also public displays to others of your connections. Teens will mostly add friends and acquaintances as 'friends' but also add people that will make them look cool or sometimes they add them just because they don't want to say no to them. Since their friends are displayed on their profile pages, they provide meaningful identity information. After all, 'you are who you know'.[32] It was also clear that the online searches of youngsters who we observed were pretty much in line with their offline interests. For instance, a 14-year-old emo girl was looking for screamo lyrics, information on piercings and henna paintings.

Online social identity

We specifically studied the overlap between their online and offline friends. In general, more friends were observed online than offline. Social network sites were used as a way to keep in contact with friends that were not seen very often anymore. Examples included friends from primary school, in divorced families, etc. Social networks were also used to connect with 'related' friends: friends and acquaintances from their friends were added to their profile. At the end of 2009, the Coca-Cola Company launched a great social campaign for Coke Zero, the Facebook Facial Profiler. Face recognition software – making use of your webcam or your profile pictures in Facebook – compares you with (unknown) others on the net to find a facial match. Once you find your match, you can immediately publish this on your Facebook profile page and connect with the other face through Facebook. The main message of this Crispin Porter + Bogusky campaign is that Coke Zero tastes exactly like the classic Coke in the same way as the tool brings you in contact with someone who looks just like you.[33]

Subcultures online

The online identity of our youngsters in social networks was evaluated in the light of the different subcultures that we had identified. Once again, we found the importance of brands for subcultures located at the 'me'-side of the mapping: in the online photo album of participants who were assigned to that side of the tribal map, we found different pictures of brands and logos. This was not at all the case for those participants on the 'we'-side of the axis. Next, the usage of online media differed depending on the subculture they were assigned to. The subcultures on the 'we'-side of the axis (goths, metalheads, hippies, emos, etc) were more active on social networks related to music (such as MySpace). They also mentioned more society-related themes such as politics and environment on their pages. Social network pages from the 'me'-groups mostly dealt with appearance and getting feedback on their profile or picture, for instance added comments such as 'Which picture is the most beautiful?' or 'What do you like most about me?'. Participants from different subcultures had a different taste in the online movies they watched on YouTube. Fashionistas were mainly looking for funny videos to have a good laugh at other people. Jumpstyle hardcore fanatics and nerds were looking for information related to their hobbies and interests, for instance cars, documentaries for school, tutorials, PK movies. The indie, rockers, new ravers, etc did not just watch online movies but also created their own movies, such as parodies or societal critiques. They were clearly the most creative segments online.

Avatars and role playing

Finally, the introvert axis appeared to have a special affinity with gaming. The nerds and starchies in particular were highly involved in online gaming and virtual worlds like *Runescape*, *World of Warcraft* and *The Sims*. They had an online avatar representing themselves in the game that had a number of physical aspects in common with their offline identity. Avatars do allow teens to experience an altered and enhanced body. Laurent, a 15-year-old geek and *Runescape* addict, created an avatar that had the same hairstyle and colour, the same eye colour and tan and had the same body shape. The only difference was that his avatar had broader shoulders, looked tougher and was wearing silver armour. The most common form of avatars for young adolescent girls is the glamorous, slightly sexualized female form. Avatars are an edited version of the self, a copy of youth's real self minus the things they don't like about themselves.[34] For some, this online game world was strongly interwoven with their day-to-day lives: they met the same youngsters online as offline. For most nerds their online achievements even determined their status among peers (also nerds) in the real world.[35]

When young people are involved with role playing they fuse their own identities into their characters, ranging from physical resemblance to complex characters that share emotional traits with their own identity. What they are doing online is quite similar to their behaviour offline: they make friends, talk about their interests, engage in hobbies and have fun. Their lives in online communities and social networks connect to their lives in the offline society. Gen Yers use online social networks to communicate their real personality. They are the mirrors of their personal and social identity. Facebook pages contain private thoughts, facial and social activity images and report on social behaviour. It would be very hard to create an idealized identity online on a social network site. Wall postings and friends will constantly provide real-time and subtle feedback on one's profile page. The majority of online friends are also their closest friends in real life. It is just another medium for engaging in genuine social interactions.[36] Virtual gaming environments with avatars, on the other hand, put adolescents in a fantasy world. They invite adolescents to present an idealized feminine (beauty) or male (tough, power) body. This mirrors the way teenagers tend to dress up and prepare for parties or social events in real life. They emphasize their gender by choosing clothes that reflect traditional gender patterns. To conclude, we can note that the online evolution led to a more rapid and easy spread of sub-cultures in the same way that other mass media such as music and youth channels have contributed. Identity construction through new media is mainly a mirror of offline identities.

Cosplay: virtual identities brought to life

Cosplay is short for 'costume play'. It refers to youth dressing up to represent specific characters from popular fiction in Japan. Inspiration sources for cosplay are found in manga comic books, anime, video games and fantasy books and movies. Cosplayers regularly interact in cosplay parties and performances based on costumed role playing. These are not to be confused with Halloween or Mardi Gras costumes because for cosplayers the real goal is to become a full copy of the selected character including body language and behaviour, just like an actor playing a role. In the last decade many cosplay cafes have shot up in Tokyo's Akihabara district. Waitresses of these cafes dress as game or anime characters too.

Outside Japan cosplay gatherings and contests often take place at manga and anime conventions. Although there are online costume shops for cosplayers, the majority of them specialize in crafting their own costumes, sculptures (props), fibreglass work and body and face painting. Cosplay is particularly popular in Japan and other Asian regions, but the scene is certainly not limited to the East. In fact, the term cosplay was coined by Nov Takahashi of the Japanese studio Studio Hard while he was attending the 1984 Science Fiction World Convention in Los Angeles. Impressed by costumed fans he then reported on the US phenomenon in Japanese science fiction magazines. The exponential growth in the number of youngsters involved with cosplay as a hobby in the last decade has affected popular culture. Apart from cosplay magazines, costume webshops and online communities, all specifically directed at cosplayers, the broader fashion industry took inspiration from the cosplay scene when they introduced the Gothic Lolita look on the catwalks.[37]

Conclusion

In this chapter we have demonstrated that Gen Y is engaging with brands that know how to reflect their self-identity. Since youth is not one big homogeneous population, this implies that youth marketers need to identify the different crowds for which their brand has relevance and salience. Next, they have to understand the (brand) personality traits that these crowds of young people are identifying with. Youth brands should never pretend or scream they have the same values or characteristics but prove this by offering valuable products, campaigns, events and utilities that support this positioning both on- and offline. Considering the diversity of Gen Yers, sometimes more than one brand is needed to fit with the entire population. At least a mix of marketing tactics and communication strategies will make sure that no one rejects the brand. Although we have stressed the differences within this generation of consumers, they do have a lot in common too of course. In the last chapter we will emphasize the most common denominator of Gen Y: the need for hedonism and escapism that is translated into the dominance of positive emotions such as happiness in brand choice.

Hot takeaways for cool brand builders

- Gen Y's self-identification with the brand is essential to lever your brand in terms of preference and recommendation.
- Youth choose those brands that both represent the identity aspects they want to accentuate and fit in with the crowd behaviour of the collective identities they aspire to.
- Differences in lifestyles can be explained on three dimensions:
  - Me versus We;
  - Extrovert versus Introvert;
  - Skills versus Looks.
- Tribal marketing is not about creating products for segments but about supporting brands that keep youngsters together as a group of enthusiasts.

Continued...

Hot takeaways for cool brand builders   *Continued*

- There are five important steps to increase self-identification:
  - identify tribes that are relevant for your brand positioning;
  - reflect the passions and interests of selected tribes;
  - consider Gen Yers as partners in your marketing and product design;
  - don't scream who you are but find the passions Gen Y is screaming about that are related to your DNA and facilitate existing passions;
  - show every day how your brand's vision is related to these passions.
- In many markets, especially badge markets, it won't be possible to appeal to the entire Gen Y population with one single brand.
- Never use tribes who are on the outskirts of the tribal scheme in your communication.
- There's a close fit between online and offline identities of youth. 'You are who you know' is not only reflected in friending but also in brand fandom on social networks.

Chapter Seven
Happiness: Gen Y's adoration for branded emotions

" _ _ _ .. _ _ _ ..

I n any type of communication that lacks the ability to convey emotions, people have always found a way to compensate. The Morse code on top of this page represents the figure 88 and was used in the 19th century to express 'love and kisses'. We could consider this code to be the ancestor of the currently widespread emoticons in texting. Generation Y in particular is seeding chat and SMS messages with these textual versions of facial and emotional expressions. Typographical emoticons, as we use today, were not invented by Gen Yers but were first published in 1881 in the US satirical magazine *Puck*.

Freelance artist Harvey Ball designed the well-known 'smiley face' in 1963. The yellow button with two black dots representing eyes and an upturned curve representing a mouth became the universal symbol of happiness. Ball created it for a large insurance company as part of a campaign to boost employee morale. Scott Fahlman was the first to propose the use of : -) 'for jokes' in e-mails and : - (for 'things that are no jokes' in a message to the Carnegie Mellon university computer science general board on 19 September 1982. Meanwhile there are probably hundreds of smiley emoticon variants. Some are more popular in certain countries because of keyboard layouts. For example, an equal sign for the eyes in place of the colon, as in =) is common in Scandinavia where the keys for = and) are placed right beside each other.

It's interesting to see that emoticons also differ between cultures. For instance, East Asians read facial expressions by looking mainly at the eyes, whereas Western cultures emote mainly with the mouth. This is reflected in East Asian-style emoticons that can be understood without tilting one's head and in which emotions are stressed by variations in the eyes and not in the mouth. For instance (*-*) depicts a neutral face, and (T-T) symbolizes crying eyes or sadness.[1]

How do you get Gen Yers to feel ☺ and not ☹ with your brand? How do you really make a difference with your brand for this target group? It's all about evoking the right emotions with your marketing strategy. In our CRUSH model, happiness seems to be the emotion that has the largest impact on brand leverage. But what makes Gen Y happy? Generation Y grew up in a world full of choice. We know from psychologists such as Barry Schwartz that although we value choice and love to put ourselves in situations of choice, it often undercuts our happiness. The more choice there is, the more we expect to find the perfect fit, but at the same time the less likely we are to pick the best item.[2] In this chapter, we will explore the role of emotions in shaping a successful Gen Y brand. We will show you examples of using positive and negative emotions and zoom in on what makes Gen Yers happy. If you make them happy, they will feel a stronger emotional attachment to your brand.

We think less than we think: the central role of emotions

Emotions are pivotal drivers of our buying behaviour. YouTube is loaded with youngsters unpacking their newly bought game console or mobile phone in an agitated way. Whenever Apple launches a new product, hundreds of people will happily spend more than 30 hours camping in front of the stores to be among the first in line to get one. And you don't have to be a fanatic to get emotional about the things you buy. Just have a look at the products that are present around you. Now think back to why you bought these products. For some of them you might find a very reasonable explanation. For a large group however, we're sure you cannot bring the exact purpose back to mind. You might remember the occasion or context in which you bought the product. Undoubtedly, you will recall how you felt at that moment.

Rational buying is increasingly replaced by emotional shopping. As stressed in the introductory chapter, for Gen Yers shopping is top entertainment, it's all about emotions and experiences.

Have a look at the story below. One of the UK boys in our story-telling research shared these lines with us when describing his favourite chocolate brand Cadbury:

> That familiar purple wrapper. It's almost like a member of my family, something which has been there since childhood. I rely on it for comfort, a treat and a motivator. Cadburys chocolate has seen me through exams, stress and heartache. It's been there when I have a celebration and hope it will be there for some time to come.

When you read this brand story, it's immediately clear that this boy is not merely talking about the functional features of Cadbury chocolates. You do notice a great deal of emotional references, such as being part of the family, helping through stressful moments and being there when celebrating. Gen Y consumers are definitely emotional consumers. When we analysed over 5,000 stories about favourite Gen Y brands, 72 per cent contained positive emotions such as happiness, surprise, excitement, peacefulness, etc. Compare that figure to the poor 29 per cent of stories that referred to functional product characteristics, and you'll understand our point.

Neuropsychology and emotions

Although the importance of emotions in consumer behaviour is certainly not a new topic, there is still a feeling that marketers have minimized them in their market approach in the past. Of course, it is easier to change the packaging of your product or add a different ingredient than to make your brand 'less sad' or more 'passionate'. However, recent neuro-research illustrates that we have been under-estimating the impact of emotions on decision making for a long time. There are three different levels in our brain[3]:

- The first layer is called the **visceral brain** or automatic brain. These are the type of brain cells we have in common with the most primitive animals. For simple animals like lizards, life is a continuing set of threats and opportunities and an animal has to learn how to react appropriately to all of them. The visceral level is fast. It compares information from the senses with pre-wired patterns of information. Based on this judgement, it swiftly gives instructions for routine deeds: running away, freezing, fighting or relaxing. This part of the brain is therefore responsible for instinctive behaviour.

- The second part is the **limbic system**. This brain adds emotions to the sensory information from the visceral brain. It is the base of the amygdale, a brain structure that is responsible for experiencing positive and negative emotions. Based on the emotional evaluation of a stimulus, the limbic system decides to continue or stop certain performances. We have this brain in common with other mammals. This limbic level is not conscious. It is responsible for so called automatic acts. Think of the way you drive your car or how a skilled piano player seems to do cerebral activities without much effort.

- The limbic system interacts closely with the brain part that was developed in the last stage of human evolution, the rational brain or **neocortex**. This is also called the 'reflective brain'. It reflects back on our acts and links sensory information to existing memory structures. Based on these reflections, it tries to alter behaviour. This leads to informed decisions and is therefore often called 'the ratio'.

The actions we undertake are the results of co-processing done by all three layers in our brain. However, research by Joseph LeDoux has shown that the impact of our limbic system is the biggest.[4] Contrary to long-held belief, it is not our rational brain that is in the driver's seat. Consumer behaviour is largely controlled by emotions and only sporadically overruled by our ratio.

Implications for branding and marketing to Gen Y

What do these neuropsychology findings teach us as marketers? It is crucial to re-evaluate the role of emotions in our marketing approach for a couple of reasons. First, they have a direct impact on consumer decision making. Emotional thinking works much faster than rational thinking. Our gut feeling directs very quick reactions.[5] The emotional brain processes sensory information in one fifth of the time our cognitive brain takes to assimilate the same input.[6]

Secondly, emotions have always had an important evolutionary meaning. Our capabilities for detecting anger, fear or disgust have served as powerful indicators for dangerous situations. Similarly, positive emotions have reassured us that we could safely engage in certain activities. Emotions are therefore important attention grabbers. We are wired to pay attention to emotions. Using emotions in communication will therefore draw your customer's attention.[7]

In the middle of our limbic system we find the hippocampus, a brain structure responsible for memory. Together with the emotion centre, the amygdale, it helps us capture new memories. Whenever a new stimulus contains emotions it will trigger the amygdale, which will then create a new memory connection in the hippocampus.[8] Every time we recall the stored information, the accompanying emotion will be revealed again. Thinking back to the exercise at the beginning of this chapter, you can now understand why it is very hard to think of the rational reasons for buying a product while we have no difficulties in recalling our feelings related to the purchase. The limbic system is therefore the seat of emotional branding. Whenever we are confronted with a brand, we will experience these emotions. We do not only consume a product, we are also emotion consumers. We eat chocolates or drink warm drinks such as coffee when we feel sad. We drink tea to relax and take away our agitation. Because of our typical memory structures, our perceptions are constantly coloured by our emotions.

What the heart thinks, the mind speaks. People who experience an emotion tend to start a communication process to share this emotion with others. Research found that only 10 per cent of the emotional experiences are kept secret and never socially shared with anyone.[9] The more disruptive the event, the sooner and more frequently it will be shared.[10] Social sharing of emotions is also positively related to the intensity of emotions. Emotions do not only appear to be an important element in stimulating word-of-mouth but also in creating online buzz. Successful viral movies trigger an emotional response in the recipients' brains.[11]

You're not the only one with mixed emotions: emotions related to brands

Emotions play a central role in understanding youngsters' attitudes towards brands. We know from previous chapters that the adolescent brain is less capable of suppressing emotional triggers. Because the frontal lobe is still underdeveloped, it cannot sufficiently integrate the more rational information coming from the neocortex for decision making. Hence, Gen Y behaviour is even more based on emotional decisions. The developing adolescent and young adult brain is less capable of reflecting. Instead of thinking things over, their emotional centre dictates them to take immediate actions. Every parent of adolescents will recall scenes where they seemed unreasonable or unexpectedly burst into tears. Well, they can't help it. It has nothing to do with a bad character or bad intentions, it's in their brains.

These emotional reactions do not limit themselves to everyday life. In our research, we interviewed Gen Yers and older generations about the emotions that were evoked by their most and least favourite brands. When we compared the number of emotions that both groups feel when thinking about their favourite and least favourite brand, we noticed that youngsters generally experience more emotions than adults. In Figure 7.1 you will see that adolescents (younger than 20) are not only more emotional in general, their interaction with brands is also more coloured by their feelings.

The scores are averages on a 5-point scale on the question: when thinking about your most favourite brand, to what extent do you feel each of the following emotions:

- happy;
- disgusted;
- sad;
- angry;
- surprised;
- afraid.

So how do emotions influence teenage brand perceptions? What type of emotions do they experience? There are six basic emotions that are universally recognized: happiness, sadness, anger, fear, disgust and surprise. They can be distributed into two groups: the positive emotions and the negative emotions.[12] In our study, we also investigated the tonality of the stories when youngsters were speaking about their favourite brand. As expected, we found that consumers expressed far more positive emotions in their stories than negative ones. The results also showed that youngsters expressed up to 20 per cent

FIGURE 7.1　Emotionality of age groups (sum of all emotions)

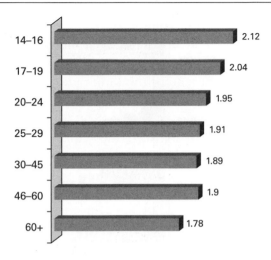

more positive emotions for clothing and mobile brands than older generations.

The same exercise was conducted for negative emotions where we found a striking result. We observed a higher intensity of negative emotions for youngsters even when they were talking about their favourite brand (see Figure 7.2). It seems that Generation Y sees the world more in black and white than the older generations. Given the fact that the emotional regulations systems of this target group are still in full expansion, this was no surprise. They simply do not have the cognitive power yet to put emotions into context.

We have been explaining why emotions for Gen Y are extremely important and that successful youth brands will arouse these emotions. But not all emotions are equally important. In Figure 7.3 you will see the frequency of expressed emotions for favourite and least favourite brands. It's clear on the whole that a feeling of **happiness** is most aroused by brands that touch the heart. Again, this is even more the case for Gen Yers. 'Surprise' is the second most expressed emotion for these stimulation addicts. Youngsters are triggered by new things and are more likely to take risk. They want to explore new things in order to find a new kick. Surprise is an emotion that has been successfully applied in communication. By incorporating humour caused by a surprising element or other unexpected executions, advertisers have successfully drawn attention in their campaigns.[13]

FIGURE 7.2   Levels of positive and negative emotions

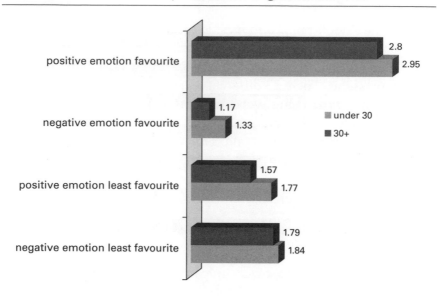

FIGURE 7.3   The six basic emotions associated with favourite and least favourite brands

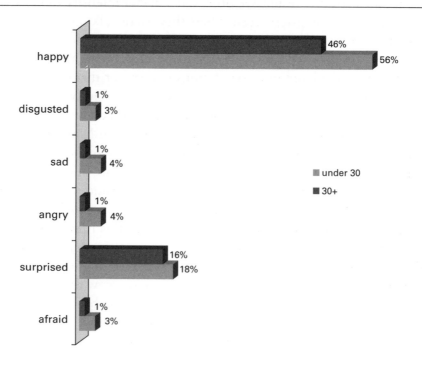

Facial coding to detect emotions

In Dan Hill's book *Emotionomics. Leveraging emotions for business success*, he explains that facial expressions are the most universal human way of expressing emotions. Even people born blind have the same expressions. These 23 different facial expressions correspond to the core emotions. Using webcams, Hill's company Sensory Logic analyses people's emotional responses – for instance to advertising – down to one thirtieth of a second. This allows the agency to measure the emotional engagement and profile of marketing stimuli and formulate advice to amend the material. Hill's facial measurement of 'happiness' includes four different types of smiles:

- true smile: strong natural smile seen around the eyes and mouth;
- robust smile: a broad social smile involving the mouth only;
- weak smile: a weak social smile involving the mouth only;
- micro smile: a unilateral (one side of the mouth) smile that is brief.[14]

In the following paragraphs, we will discuss how brands can appeal to positive emotions and how they can suffer from arousing negative emotions or benefit from removing the negatives.

How brands can tap into emotions

Because of the central role of emotions in youth behaviour, hot brands incorporate them in their marketing and communication strategy. Youngsters become emotionally attached to those that do well. Which types of emotions are most effective in creating this sense of attachment? As mentioned before, emotions are broadly categorized in two big groups: positive and negative emotions. In order to boost their general well-being, people try to increase positive emotions and minimize negative emotions. For brands this means that two strategies are possible: you can ensure that your brand is connected with positive feelings or create a brand that is powerful in taking away negative feelings.

Studies on emotional attachment to brands have found that evoking positive emotions is crucial for brand engagement.[15] Brands should induce affection or warm feelings like love, joy or happiness and peacefulness. They should also arouse passion. Gen Yers need to feel excited, delighted or captivated by the brand.

Using the five senses

How do you pave the way for this emotional attachment? One important strategy is transmitting emotions through the five senses, as Martin Lindstrom has stressed in his book *Brand Sense*.[16] Remember, the limbic brain system is adding emotions based on the sensory observations of the visceral brain.

Scents

Special attention needs to be paid to smell. There is a direct connection between our emotion brain centre (the amygdale-hippocampus) and the olfactory region of the brain. Scent is never filtered out: it is instinctive and involuntary. Gen Yers' nose is therefore always directly pushed into evoked emotions and memories. For many products they can easily recall how they smell and re-experience the stimulated emotion. Think of the artificial scents of Play-Doh modelling compound that bring back childhood memories. Certain perfumes or deodorant scents remind us of the girls we have loved or dad shaving to go to work. Giving your brand a scent that is linked to a positive emotion can enforce your emotional branding.[17] Sony Style stores have a vanilla and mandarin orange scent that was specially designed for them and is supposed to relax shoppers and make them feel more comfortable in the store. The scents used in Abercrombie stores to connect with teenaged girls are even available at the checkout and actively sold by the store personnel.[18]

Sound

Another sense that is particularly useful in addressing adolescents is sound. Youngsters use music as powerful emotion regulators. Music creates emotions. Movie soundtracks are the best proof of this. A thriller or romantic movie without the music score creating the required atmosphere and emotions would lead to bad box office. Response to rhythm and rhyme, melody and tune is so basic and so constant across all cultures that they must be part of our evolutionary heritage. Although the neuroscience and psychology effects of music are widely studied, they are still little understood. We do know that the affective states produced through music are universal. By incorporating music in advertising or directly in the product (think of a mobile phone with MP3 function but also a water boiler that whispers at a certain tone), an emotional state can be evoked. Many teenage-clothing retailers play loud rhythmic thumping music to get the shoppers' hearts pumping faster. A faster heartbeat will stimulate our brain to survey the environment in order to find out where the excitement comes from. Since the emotional brain dominates in teenagers' behaviour, they will link the arousal to the clothes surrounding them and automatically feel more attracted to them.[19] In the 1970s Scherer and Oshinsky tested different sounds on subjects and even then had found that apart from tempo, even pitch level and amplitude modulations of sounds can evoke other emotions (see Table 7.1).

TABLE 7.1 Sounds and emotions

TEMPO	slow	sadness, boredom, disgust
	fast	activity, surprise, happiness, pleasantness potency, fear, anger
PITCH LEVEL	low	boredom, pleasantness, sadness
	high	surprise, potency, anger, fear, activity
AMPLITUDE MODULATION	small	disgust, anger, fear, boredom
	large	happiness, pleasantness, activity, surprise

SOURCE: Gardner MP. Mood states and consumer behaviour: a critical review. *Journal of Consumer Research* 1985 Dec; 12. featured in: Gobé M, *Emotional Branding. The new paradigm for connecting brands to people.* 2nd rev edn (1st edn 2002). New York: Allworth Press; 2009.

How loitering teens inspired Fanta

Fanta, the Coca-Cola brand that targets teens, has a marketing strategy that makes full use of the teens' addiction to gaming. Inspired by the ultrasonic alarms that shopping malls and cities were using against loitering teens, Fanta developed a mobile app that would remain inaudible

Continued...

How loitering teens inspired Fanta   *Continued*

to parents or other adults over 20. The alarms produce high-pitched sounds that only young people are able to hear. In growing older, your hearing naturally gets worse. Ogilvy advertising turned the technology that treats teens like mosquitos upside down and created the Fanta Stealth Sound System. The app allows teens to communicate on their cell phones without adults hearing them. Individual high frequencies in the app are tagged to represent phrases such as 'cool', 'uncool' and 'let's get out of here'. Electronic music pioneer Martyn Ware, founder of Heaven 17 and The Human League, developed the sound tags.

Fanta combined great youth insights for this campaign, such as the importance of the teenagers' mobile phone in social connections, with their desire to talk freely without being overheard by adults. Initially launched in the UK, Fanta Stealth Sound System immediately hit over 530,000 downloads. It was launched in the rest of Europe in the summer of 2009.[20]

Visual appeal: shape and colours

Emotions can more easily be triggered by visuals than by text. The saying 'a picture is worth a thousand words' illustrates this beautifully. Gillette razors convey the efficiency of their innovative blades not by verbally explaining but by using the handle as a messenger for the blade. The Mach 3 handle had three grips symbolizing the blades, the Fusion razor (using five blades) has... five ribbed grips on top of the handle. Emotions are often difficult to express in words. On the other hand, making a simple drawing like an emoticon can be so much more meaningful than a written text. Therefore it is better to use one strong visual than a larger text in your communication to youngsters. Clothing retailers targeting Gen Y are often masters in creating emotions visually because they immediately witness sales effect for every effort they make. Urban Outfitters, for example, practically rebuild their stores every few months to remain a shopping adventure for youth. H&M regularly change the billboard-sized graphics in the store. Both Abercrombie & Fitch and sister store for teens Hollister create visually engaging worlds with, for instance, a real-time camera showing the waves crashing on Huntington Beach with California time ticking on the screen.[21]

Just like sounds and scents, colours trigger very specific automatic responses in the cerebral cortex. They can activate thoughts, memories and particular behaviour. Yellow, for instance, is right in the mid range of wavelengths that our eyes can detect. It is the brightest colour and thus the one that most easily attracts our attention. It is no coincidence that road signs and police scene-markers often use the colour and it's also how the *Yellow Pages* got colour marked. Generally, colours with long wavelengths (such as red) are arousing and stimulating and those with short wavelengths (like blue) lower blood pressure, pulse and respiration rates.[22] If you have often wondered why so many global brands at the top of Gen Y's wishlist (Coca-Cola, Levi's, Vodafone, H&M, Mars, Diesel, the list goes on...) use the dominant colour red in their logo, now you know.

Even product design affects emotions. The Gillette handle described above was a good example. Think of the Apple designs. The fact that their designers take inspiration from previous decades, as illustrated in the chapter on brand uniqueness, is addressing the needs of Gen Y consumers to anchor themselves with authentic designs that transpose cultural values into the 2010s.

Branding on negative emotions

Capitalizing on negative emotions seems a less suitable brand strategy for Generation Y. There are some common practices of using negative emotions in branding towards youngsters. A first is within the context of controversial advertising where negative emotions or shock tactics have widely been used as a legitimate creative technique to grab attention. Controversial advertising is generally created by transgressing a certain moral code or by showing things that outrage the moral or physical senses such as in the case of provocation or disgust. Arousing the negative emotions would then stimulate cognitive processing which would result in better ad recall. Especially when looking at the negative emotion 'disgust' we notice that a lot of ad executions use this emotion to reach youngsters, thinking it has a different and more positive effect on this age group.[23] But in studies of De Pelsmacker and Van den Bergh provocation seems to be an emotion that occurs to the same extent in all consumer segments. Provocation in advertising actually leads to less product category and brand name recognition and to a more negative attitude towards the advertisement. Nevertheless, it does not seem to affect the attitude towards the brand, nor the intention to buy the product. Still, although it's not hurting the brand, it won't help the brand's impact on Gen Y either.[24] This was confirmed in a study among young females in which

90 emotional fashion advertisements representing 56 different clothing brands were tested. Two emotional dimensions had a positive effect on ad attitude: hypo-activation (restful, soothed, drowsy) and pleasure (social affection, desire). The third dimension consisting of negative emotions such as anger, fear, irritation or tension had no effect at all on evaluation of the ads.[25]

Removing negative feelings

When negative emotions for the young have a clear link with your products or brand, removing the bad feelings can be a much better emotional brand strategy. When the US retailer Target observed the conversations of first-year students on Facebook, they found out that moving away from the parental cocoon to small boxy dorm rooms, often co-occupied with complete strangers, is a period of anxiety and worry for Gen Yers. So when Target, a brand with a strong hip identity among younger consumers planned their back-to-school campaign, they decided to go for social media marketing focusing on the negative emotions of freshmen. Instead of starting a commercial storyline through sponsoring on Facebook, Target launched a group for social interactions. The page was given the theme of 'Dorm Survival Guide' and much attention went to dorm room essentials such as comforters, pillowcases and furniture but the real focus was only one thing: offering aid. Target stimulated member posts including pictures of their dorm rooms and let them talk before trying to sell anything. The online ads linked to the Facebook interactive platform and not to Target's e-commerce site, for instance. Discounts and promotions were kept off the sponsored page to avoid a too-commercial tone of voice. The TV campaign's tagline 'Hello, Goodbuy' was deliberately not used on the site and actual members of the group posted real dorm room videos and photos. Once the user-generated discussion got started, Target gave the students advice on design for small rooms, recipes for the odd ingredients likely to be in student refrigerators and a personality test tied to their furniture. The provided content served as social currency that students could share on their profile pages with their friends, resulting in more group members. In less than three months, Target's back-to-school group hosted 37 discussion groups, received 409 dorm pictures and 483 posts. The contrast with Wal-Mart's attempt to reach Gen Y couldn't be bigger. A few weeks after Target started its Facebook campaign, Wal-Mart opened their back-to-school Facebook page too. 'Roommate Style Match' had the same goals as Target's Dorm Survival Guide: connecting college students with dorm-related products and information. Afraid of Gen Y's criticisms on the retailer's corporate policy, Wal-Mart did not include a discussion board or ways to upload pictures but merely offered the possibility for one-way Wall Posts. Instead of receiving good comments on the bargains and goods, the wall was still flooded with comments like 'Wal-Mart is toxic to communities and livelihoods'. Bloggers noticed these anti-Wal-Mart posts on Facebook and added their voices to the conversation, which resulted in even more negative posts. The fact that Wal-Mart, with a brand image of inexpensive and untrendy wares, was actually giving style and fashion advice to students on their Facebook page was seen as ridiculous and completely unauthentic.[26]

The sales results of both campaigns showed that although both retailers simultaneously came up with a comparable idea to reach Gen Yers, successful social media marketing really depends on the right execution and strategy. The three essential steps in social media marketing, as described by Steven Van Belleghem in his book *The Conversation Manager* were smoothly followed by Target. First observe the existing conversations, then facilitate these conversations and finally add social currency by participating.[27] Wal-Mart did not follow these steps but offended the youth and Facebook community with its top-down approach, while not really listening to the conversations. Two other differences: Target recognized the negative emotions of first-year students and helped them to remove these worries. They understood how to stick close to their existing and unique hip and cool brand DNA ensuring they remained authentic. The advice reflected the self-image of first-year students feeling insecure. Wal-Mart tried to copy Target's approach, ruining their brand authenticity and then used Gen Y's medium in the wrong way.

Another frequent usage of negative emotions can be found in health care and prevention campaigns targeting Gen Yers. Although this is one of the more successful applications, advertising in this area often comes across as 'too moralizing'. Youngsters are already confronted all day with information on what's good and not good for them and too often this information is not turned into behaviour. Cancer Society of Finland applied a different approach built around their knowledge of youth culture and the importance of emotions.

Have you test-driven your coffin yet?

Cancer Society of Finland fights against adolescent smoking. Its purpose is to prevent youngsters from starting to smoke as well as promote and support quitting. An important part of the work is to influence the attitudes of youngsters. In order to carry out successful anti-smoking promotion, Cancer Society of Finland applies the latest theories and practices of youth marketing. It invests in youth research to understand the youth culture, different subcultures, and their attitudes towards smoking.

Traditionally, health promotion has been too rational, telling us the facts about future health risks. Youngsters know smoking is bad for their health and yet they smoke anyway. Completely different reasons – or emotions – make them want to experiment with smoking. 'Understanding the psychological and social processes – the way smoking makes them feel about themselves and related to their peers – is the key', explains communication researcher and consultant Sanna-Mari Salomäki from Kuule. She has been researching adolescent smoking as a consultant for the Cancer Society for years.

An example of a successful anti-smoking campaign is the Coffin Shop 'pop-up store' (see Figure 7.4). A real coffin painted in pink toured the shopping malls and events across Finland. Youngsters had a chance to try out how it feels to lie in a coffin and got their picture taken. Promo persons were dressed in pink carnival-style costumes. Traditional hymns were remixed in a modern way for background music. There was a table with a white tablecloth, candles and flowers. Coffee was served. Pink balloons and LPs composed by the 'Pink Cantor' were distributed as well as stickers, posters and flyers to direct youth to the campaign website **fressis.fi**. There, they could download their pictures and watch the pictures of others. The website also offered information on smoking and how to quit. Outside, an old-fashioned, tuned funeral car and pink crosses were promoting the Coffin Shop.

Researcher Salomäki studied the campaign. Why was the Coffin Shop campaign such a success? Because it appealed to Gen Yers on an emotional level. The first reaction was surprise and curiosity. Why is there a pink coffin in a shopping mall? You don't expect to see such a thing there. It was attracting attention and got youth interested. Secondly, the campaign was very experiential. Seeing a pink coffin is kind of cool. But testing a real coffin seriously awoke feelings. It was a unique experience. You had a once in a lifetime chance to lie in a coffin – alive – and get out of it again. It was an experience youngsters would remember for a long time, maybe even for the rest of their lives. It was a very personal and touching experience. Some wanted to have the coffin open, some closed. The coffin is a very strong symbol – and a bit exciting too. However, the pink colour

Continued...

Have you test-driven your coffin yet? *Continued*

FIGURE 7.4 The pop-up coffin shop

made the coffin feel less scary. Many wanted to go in together with a friend. It was also about overcoming your own fears and showing off your courage. Youngsters wanted to tell their friends about their experience and share their picture. It was also touching to see your friend or girl/boyfriend in the coffin. The experience really made concrete that smoking kills. People had an immediate urge to talk about their experience and feelings with the promo persons and health experts. They also wanted to share their thoughts on their own smoking or the smoking habits of their loved ones as well as quitting. Some refused to go into the coffin because they felt it was unnatural for the living or it was considered a bad omen.

Continued...

Have you test-driven your coffin yet?   *Continued*

But isn't this just repeating the fear tactics of traditional health promotion? 'We use many different messages for different target groups and across time. And this time the message was "only one out of two dies because of smoking". Youth lives here and now, they don't think about future illnesses. We wanted to concretize that a smoker will end up in a coffin sooner than a non-smoker', Salomäki says.

The campaign evoked an interesting and provoking conflict of emotions that appealed strongly to the target audience. The campaign succeeded in communicating to the target group on an emotional level and made them feel that smoking kills. The pink coffin continued its successful journey from shopping malls to the *Big Brother* show. And it was finally auctioned. According to the legend, it ended up in the living room of a she-vampire... In this way the anti-smoking campaign became a phenomenon and part of the Finnish popular culture.[28]

Hijacks, hate and videotapes: when negative buzz takes over

For most brands and products association with positive emotions clearly is the favourable strategy. However, this is not always completely within the span of control of a marketer or brand manager. Sometimes your brand evokes negative feelings that weren't intended. The Wal-Mart example in this chapter is a good illustration. Like all evoked emotions, the negative ones will certainly lead to negative buzz. We only need to look at the numerous hate groups on Facebook or other social networks to understand how negative feelings stimulate consumers to spread the word. Predicting what will lead to negative emotions is hard. There are three main reasons why consumers start disliking a brand.[29]

A first source of negative feelings is a physical characteristic of the brand. Think of youngsters who get angry because their mobile phone is refusing to make a connection to the internet or who are disappointed because their expensive beauty product did not have the desired effect. Brands have few other options in this case than listening to the criticisms and learning from them for later product development.

Brand hate can also have a more symbolic cause. In the chapter on self-identification we discussed how youngsters build their identities by connecting with brands that are associated with their social or aspired lifestyle group. Similarly, they will reject brands that are connected with their non-groups. This often results in strong negative feelings towards the brand. The British sportswear label Lonsdale inadvertently became the victim of such a symbolic rejection. A couple of years ago the brand became very popular among European extreme-right-supporting teenagers. A carefully placed bomber jacket could leave the letters "nsda" visible in the Lonsdale logo on sweaters. NSDA is an acronym standing for National-Sozialistische Deutsche Arbeiter and one letter short of NSDAP, Hitler's Nazi party.[30] Soon, the brand became a symbol of neo-Nazism in Europe. In the Netherlands, Belgium, France and Germany, Lonsdale was associated with teenagers of extreme-right sympathies. The brand was even banned in certain schools and nightclubs because of this reason.

Lonsdale reacted to this development by sponsoring anti-racist events and campaigns and by refusing to deliver products to known neo-Nazi retailers. In 2003, the 'Lonsdale Loves All Colours' campaign was launched, emphasizing non-white fashion models, along with increased support for initiatives that combat racism.[31] These moves to distance the brand from neo-Nazi associations, combined with the police's increased awareness of the fashion and symbols used by neo-Nazis, have made the brand less popular in far-right crowds. Although brands are seldom hijacked by a certain subculture, this example shows that it is important to keep track of your brand's role in identity formation. Extreme-right youth are brand sensitive since they are also far right on the 'Me (I'm better)'-axis in our tribal mapping. Brands help them to stand out from others and often they find symbolic links with your brands you haven't even noticed yourself. New Balance sneakers for instance, with a large N on the side, appealed to them because the N was seen as shorthand for 'Nazi'. The German brand Thor Steinar, founded in 2002, was an immediate hit in the right-wing scene due to its connection with Nordic mythology, which is an important element in Nazi ideas on racial purity. In 2009, when the label was sold to International Brands General Trading – a company based in... Dubai – Neo-Nazi groups suddenly called for a boycott of the brand.[32]

Brand hijacking through social media

Brand hijacking happens when Gen Yers appropriate the brand for themselves and add meaning to it. Social media such as Facebook,

YouTube and Twitter in combination with the marketing savvy-ness of Gen Y have fuelled this trend. Many companies are com-pletely out of touch with these kinds of online conversation and have no online reputation management at all. Brand hijacks don't always have to be a negative thing. The AMC series *Mad Men*, a TV broad-cast revolving around the advertising world in the 1960s, saw its cast virtually hijacked by a number of Twitter users that were impersonat-ing some of the series' characters on the microblogging service. AMC wasn't involved at all but the impersonators were so good that a fake Don Draper, the lead character in the series, had almost 2,000 followers. AMC first issued a takedown to Twitter and most of the accounts got suspended. But after uprising negative commotion on Twitter and in the press, AMC came to their senses and reinstalled the accounts.

Sometimes brand hijacks can even bring a new start for brands. Dr Martens shoes, initially intended as a gardening shoe for senior women, was hijacked by punk teenagers with ideological purposes and this made the brand a success.[33] Corona beer was a Mexican beer for Mexican people until it was discovered by US surfers on a surf trip who gave it a cool beach lifestyle connotation. It can now be found in 150 countries and is the fifth-best selling beer in the world.[34]

Corporate hate affecting brands

A final reason for Gen Y to hate a brand involves the company and corporate cultures and policies behind the brand. Brands are not solely intangible. They act in the real world through the actions of the com-pany behind the brands, such as the everyday execution of marketing strategies and overall activity related to social, ethical or political issues. Consumers do not make a distinction between a brand and the parent company. Negative feelings towards the company are easily transmitted to the brand.

In the beginning of 2010 this became painfully clear for the chocolate-wafer brand Kit Kat owned by one of the biggest global food com-panies, Nestlé. The hate campaign had its roots in Nestlé's reported impact on rainforests in Indonesia. Deforestation for the establish-ment of palm oil plantations is threatening a number of species, including the critically endangered orangutan. Palm oil is widely used throughout the world in a variety of food products and Nestlé is a major buyer of the product. The trigger for the sudden onslaught of negativity was a series of videos made by Greenpeace. One of them shows a guy at the office eating a Kit Kat snack but the chocolates are replaced by bleeding orangutan fingers. The video led to a huge storm of protest on the fan page of Nestlé on Facebook. Users changed their avatar to a transformed Kit Kat logo saying 'Killer' in the Kit Kat logo and typography. As a result, Nestlé reviewed its palm oil policy and stopped the contract with the Indonesian company Sinar Mas.[35]

Don't worry, be happy: arousing happiness through experiences

As we have discussed earlier in this chapter, brands that are capable of evoking feelings of happiness for Gen Y will definitely benefit from this strategy. Brands that arouse happiness help Gen Yers to forget about their daily stress. In the Wellbeing Project of MTV Networks International, the company studied the feelings of children and young people in 14 countries around the world. Only 43 per cent of the world's 16- to 34-year-olds said they were happy with their lives. Below the age of 16, teens were slightly happier. Young people in developing countries were at least twice as likely to feel happy as their globalized counterparts. More than 70 per cent of 16- to 34-year-olds in Argentina and Mexico said they were happy versus less than 30 per cent in the United States and the UK. Notably, the happier young people of the developing world were also the most religious. In India, nearly 60 per cent of 16- to 34-year-olds were both religious and happy. In Japan, where 76 per cent of youngsters were faithless, only 8 per cent said they were happy. Again it seems that Gen Yers in globalized nations were putting more pressure on themselves as individuals to achieve goals, to be better than average and to get good grades in school or to obtain the right job.[36]

In consumer research, academics have only just started to develop frameworks and scales to study the effects of brands on happiness. So the whole domain is still fairly unknown territory for marketers and researchers. Although some research found that consumption with a social or high-status impact such as car ownership correlates moderately positive with happiness, it tells us little about the role of brands.[37] From our own 5,000 brand stories, we have learned that

Gen Yers develop extreme devotional relationships with brands and feelings of happiness are certainly associated with their favourite brands. Religions such as Buddhism and Stoicism, however, taught us that striving for external goods or to make the world conform to your wishes is merely striving after wind. According to this religious view, happiness can only be found within, especially by breaking our attachments to external things.

Can't get no satisfaction: a formula to find happiness

In *The Happiness Hypothesis*, Jonathan Haidt lists a number of principles from ancient wisdom as well as modern neuroscience that could be helpful to our understanding of what will affect Gen Yers' feelings of happiness. The first one is called 'the progress principle', which basically means that pleasure comes more from making progress toward goals than from achieving them. That big promotion you anticipated, finishing a big project, dreaming of the printed version of this book during nocturnal writing.... The moment we finally succeed won't make us happier in the end. This is again related to the functioning of our brains. The front left cortex gives us a pleasurable feeling whenever we make progress towards a goal but we will only feel a short-term effect when the left prefrontal cortex reduces its activity after the goals have been achieved. In other words, it really is the journey that counts, not the destination.

The second notion is 'the adaptation principle'. If you only have 10 seconds to name the very best and very worst things that could ever happen to you, you will probably think of winning the lottery jackpot and becoming paralyzed from the neck down. Wrong again. We are very bad at forecasting emotions. We tend to overestimate the intensity and the duration of our emotional reactions. Within a year lottery winners and paraplegics have both returned most of the way to their baseline levels of happiness. Adaptation is partly linked to our neurons. Nerve cells respond to new stimuli but gradually they habituate, firing less to stimuli they have become used to. It's why Seth Godin got bored of seeing cows in the French landscape and started writing a book on the *Purple Cow*. It is change that contains vital information to preserve our bodies and life. Human beings not only habituate, they also recalibrate. Each time we hit a new target, we replace it with another. We always want more than we have, which will always bring us back to our brain's default level of happiness. Good fortune or bad; in the long run, both will bring you back to the same feeling of happiness.

Based on studying identical twins, some researchers found that about half of our happiness is determined by our genes. It might surprise you that the elderly are happier than the young even though the old have so many more health problems. But they adapt to most chronic health problems. Another finding in happiness research is that most environmental and demographic factors influence happiness very little. This results in a real formula for happiness:

Happiness = 50% S + 10% C + 40% V

With:

- S = your biological set point, predefined in your genes.
- C = life conditions that you don't have under control, circumstances such as socio-economic status, health, income, sex and others.
- V = voluntary activities you do yourself.

Pleasures versus gratifications

Knowing this, you will understand that with our brands and products, we will only be able to influence 40 per cent of Gen Y's feelings of happiness. Of course this makes it even more important to know what kind of activities will have the biggest impact on the 40 per cent. The tool that helped psychologists to find the answer to this conundrum is known as the 'experience sampling method', and was invented by the Hungarian-born co-founder of positive psychology Csikszentmihalyi. In his studies subjects carried a pager that beeped several times a day. At every beep thousands of people wrote down what they were doing and how much they were enjoying it. In this way he found out what people really enjoy doing, not just what they remember having enjoyed. The first one is physical or bodily pleasure: mostly eating and sex. But there was one thing that people valued even more than eating chocolate after sex: total immersion in a task that is challenging yet closely matched to one's abilities. This can be reached during physical movements such as skiing, driving fast or playing team sports. The state of 'flow' can also happen during solitary creative activities such as painting, writing or photography. The key aspects of getting into this flow are: a clear challenge that fully engages your attention; you have the required skills to meet the challenge; and you get immediate feedback on how you are doing at each step (compare with 'the progress principle' above).[38]

These findings explain why Gen Yers are so addicted to computer and video games. The three conditions to get into a mental state of flow are clearly present in most video games. If you want this generation to connect with your brands and products, keep this in mind. Two things make them happy: pleasures and gratifications (see Table 7.2).

TABLE 7.2   What makes Gen Yers happy?

pleasures:	delights that have clear sensory and strong emotional components (as we have described in the section about using the five senses to arouse emotions)
	they feel good in the moment BUT sensual memories fade quickly
gratifications:	engaging activities that relate to gen Y's interests and strengths and allow them to lose self-consciousness
	accomplish something/learn something/improve something/strengthen connections between people can lead to 'flow'

SOURCE: Haidt J. *The happiness hypothesis. Putting ancient wisdom and philosophy to the test of modern science.* 1st edn. London: Arrow Books; 2006.

Gratifications will often take place as 'experiences' and Gen Yers will have higher levels of happiness when experiencing something. This is not only thanks to the state of flow but also because experiences are mostly social happenings or activities connecting them with other people. A study from 2008 published in the *British Medical Journal* reported that happiness in social networks spread from person to person like a virus. The happiness memes of even complete strangers will cheer us up. In the last part of this chapter we will discuss how these experiences can be supported by brands. First, we'll have a look at how the world's biggest brand, Coca-Cola, adapted the concept of happiness and made it the core of its marketing campaign.

Coca-Cola's 'Open Happiness' campaign and Expedition 206

Coca-Cola, the world's most valuable brand, is of course targeting a broader consumer group than only Generation Y. 'But the 13–30 age group certainly is a core target group for us', says Cristina Bondolowski, senior global brand director for Coke, in an interview with us. 'For Coke Red, global teenagers are very important. What's hot for them tends to change a lot and they are difficult to track. The complex variety of teen lifestyles is actually a rather recent phenomenon. They were never so individually expressed in the way they dress, communicate, shop and relate to brands as today.' Coca-Cola has its own permanent global teen research community, which allows Coke's marketers to follow 400 of them around the world. 'One of the things we have learnt, is that socially connecting with other people is what really makes teens happy.' The 'Open Happiness' campaign taps into this concept of happiness in the 206 countries where Coke is sold.

'The notion of happiness is actually nothing new for Coke', says Derk Hendriksen, senior global brand director for Coke Zero and Light. 'The brand has always been grounded in the core value of optimism and positive thinking in its history of 125 years.' To the brand, the 'Open Happiness' focus is just a contemporary way of expressing its identity. Coca-Cola's enduring positioning as the icon of universal happiness has certainly received successful responses from each new youth generation. 'Every five years a new teenage generation enters our brand franchise', explains Hendriksen, 'it is important to connect with them and teach them what our DNA stands for.' The 'Open Happiness' theme is giving the brand a more specific point of view when compared to its predecessor 'Coke's side of life'. 'It's a real call to action', says Hendriksen, 'we are inviting young people all over the world to be part of this movement.' When monitoring teens around the world, Coke found that they have to face a lot of uncertainty today, such as big climate disasters and economic crises. Next to that, they feel quite a big pressure to achieve in life: finding the right job, earning money, looking great, forming a relationship, dressing properly, getting good grades at school.... 'That's why we wanted this new angle on positivism to be much more direct than the "Coke side of life" campaign', explains Bondolowski. 'We want teens to learn how to enjoy the small everyday things in life. Coke fits naturally in this busy life: drink a Coke and feel uplifted to look at life in the positive and overcome the little challenges you daily face.' It's interesting that Coca-Cola had never used the word 'happiness' before although its campaigns have always been built around optimism and historically portray plenty of smiling people.

In 2010, Coke was spreading the optimist message and searching the globe for happiness with its Expedition 206 campaign. On New Year's Day, three youngsters, 'the happiness ambassadors', kicked off a 275,000-mile voyage to the 206 countries and territories where Coca-Cola is sold to seek and report on what makes people happy. Their stories could be followed in real-time on **www.expedition206.com** and a variety of social networks such as Facebook and Twitter. Fans could also interact with the team members and helped to decide where they would go next and what they would do. On every stop participants designed a special Coke bottle, which at the end of the expedition was displayed at the World of Coca-Cola in Atlanta. The team visited the Shanghai World Expo along with other marquee events that Coca-Cola sponsored throughout the year, such as the FIFA World Cup 2010 in South Africa. In May 2010, print, broadcast and online media coverage of Expedition 206 resulted in about 443 million media impressions and over 1,000 media stories in all corners of the world. The blog reached more than 50,000 page views per month and 78 per cent of the visitors were from outside the United States.

In late 2009, Coca-Cola aggressively used digital media for the first time. The company placed a vending machine at St Johns University in Queens New York during exam season. The idea was to bring a little bit of happiness to a woeful time such as the winter exams. The Happiness Machine delivered small moments of happiness for un-suspecting students including flowers, a pizza, balloon animals, free drinks, etc. Several hidden cameras captured the reactions. The video was released on the internet without any media support apart from just one Facebook status update to the Coke fans (more than 3 million at that time) and one tweet to Coke's 20,000 followers. Coke spent very little money on the execution in an attempt to prove they can make compelling content regardless of the budget. The video hit 1 million views in its second week and was ranked number 1 on viralvideo.com, which tracks buzz on online videos. The video was post-tested and scored in the top 1 per cent of all ads in Millward

Brown's global database and was the highest scoring English commercial ever tested by Coke in the United States. The scenes of real emotion were what drove the likeability of the ad. In the next phase the video was cut down into TV-sized portions and rolled out in other markets. Coke aroused excitement with a series of 'where will happiness strike next?' follow-up experiments.

In comparing the brand performance of Coca-Cola in its top 37 markets with the year before the launch of the 'Open Happiness' campaign, the company found a significant growth in 'exclusive love' for the brand among teens. One in three teens said Coca-Cola was their favourite brand and over 50 per cent of teens stated Coke was a brand they love.

Coca-Cola has been using the key element of music a lot in its long past but had lately been rather inactive on that front. With the 'Open Happiness' anthem and the song created for the World Cup in South Africa, Coke has regained interest in music as one of the tools to inject coolness in the brand. 'Other cool brands often use product innovation to stay hot', says Cristina Bonolowski, 'but at Coke the product is never going to change, so we have to find other ways of staying cool. Innovation in the way we communicate and emotions are both important for our brand to remain relevant for today's youth. We always say to our agencies: "we want something that only Coke can do".' Coca-Cola certainly has the power to put a song in play in a massive global way.

They also put much focus on local brand activations and events around the world. 'We want to let youth experience our products and brand on magic moments for them,' amplifies Derk Hendriksen. 'These can be music related events, for example the Coke Emergency Refreshment Nurses in the Benelux, but also other occasions like Carnival in Brazil or the NCAA Basketball events in the United States.' During the dark Christmas days, the Coca-Cola train of trucks brings happiness and light around the world and the brand is doing the same in other parts of the world with Ramadan or Chinese New Year. For FIFA's World Cup in South Africa in 2010, Coke had the rights to feature the trophy travelling the world and endorsed this happening with events around the world where participants could take a picture with the trophy and celebrity soccer players. 'The positive emotions people feel on these unique occasions are transferred to our brand and we always combine these moments of interaction with experiential sampling of our product', says Hendriksen. 'The unique aspect of Coke is the great refreshing taste. People love it, but can't describe it like anything else, it just tastes like... Coke, so you have to try it and experience it. This sensory feeling together with, of course, other enduring brand elements like the icon shape of the bottle are important differentiators for Coca-Cola.'

Apart from Coke's uniqueness and the 'Open Happiness' vision, the other components of the CRUSH model are important too. 'It's our everyday quest to stay relevant for youth', says Derk Hendriksen. 'As there are always new generations, it's a job that's never done.' Coca-Cola tries to capture today's spirit and has been proven to adapt its message of positivism to each new generation. Just think of the emotional reactions to the 'give a little love' *Grand Theft Auto* game-style commercial broadcasted during the Superbowl or the Happiness Factory movies. 'There are two countries in the world where Coke is the absolute number one coolest brand for Generation Y and where we are beating strong youth franchises like Nike and Apple: Belgium and South-Africa', says the senior global brand director. 'When we analysed those markets, we found that in these spots we are really committed to grassroots marketing interacting within youth's lives through experiential marketing.'

In 2008, Coke ran the 'Pemberton' campaign in which the brand's origin, heritage and history are told together with the fact that there are no added preservatives nor artificial flavours in Coca-Cola. It was quite a literal interpretation of stressing brand authenticity. 'It is important to remind our consumers that we offer a great-tasting product that has been served with consistent care and quality for 125 years', says Derk Hendriksen. 'It's that added reassurance that Coca-Cola is a brand that they can trust and enjoy throughout their lives from generation to generation.'

At The Coca-Cola Company, youth lifestyle segmentations are also high on the radar. 'It is important to understand the different tribes and lifestyle segments to engage our brands in their world', comments Hendriksen. 'We have to know what they are doing and what kind of media they're interacting with. Coke Zero, for instance, is positioned towards the more progressive and independent youngsters who embrace novelties and are not consuming what their parents are. They could be skaters or snowboarders for example.' The Zero sub-brand has built relevant connections with youth by endorsing the Winter X games in France in 2010.[39]

Magic moments:
brands endorsing happy happenings

Events can make a powerful contribution to an emotional branding strategy because they connect the social Gen Yers with peers and let them experience gratifications. Events give brands an opportunity to showcase their strengths in a festive and emotionally charged atmosphere. The fun and happiness that youth experience at events can create a bond with the brand. Brands that are able to fulfill Gen Y's need of fun and entertainment and understand how to cater for their pursuit of happiness will enjoy a better connection with them. When youth engage with brands at events products and brands are often featured as part of the experience through product trials. Brands will leave a memorable understanding of the brand values, resulting in youth affiliating the product with the created atmosphere. Experiential and emotional marketing creates brand advocacy and drives word-of-mouth communication.[40] The strengths of event marketing are derived from four features:

- the personal live and multi-sensory experience of brand values;
- the interactive and personal dialogues between participants, spectators and brand representatives;
- self-initiation: voluntary participation and thus higher involvement;
- dramaturgy bringing the brand image to life and capturing the imagination of consumers.[41]

Events have been known to increase Gen Y's emotional attachment to the brand and that's why many youth brands engage in them. Think of the Red Bull Flugtag, Diesel-U-Music Tour, Microsoft Xbox championship, etc. Since music is still one of the most universal youth passions many youth event activities are linked to music events. Merely sponsoring an event is old school and wouldn't work with the critical Gen Y target group anymore. If the brand owns the event, then the experience becomes a reflection of the brand.[42]

Since events use a pull strategy within marketing communications, the effectiveness will depend on Gen Y's motivation to participate voluntarily in them. This motivation is largely influenced by the situational involvement that can be stirred through investing in traditional promotional tools such as TV and online ads, flyers, etc. Almost 70 per cent of the motivation to participate is explained by this awareness building. Other important motivators are:

- Content involvement: Gen Y's interest in the activity that is at the heart of the event's dramaturgy. Of course it is important to connect with the popular leisure interests of Gen Yers and let them experience fun, excitement and challenges in actions that cannot be realized in everyday life.

- Category and brand involvement: if youth is more involved with the category and approves of the organizing brand, they will be more likely to participate. It will be easier for sports, mobile phones or game console brands to reach a big Gen Y audience than for an insurance company or bank.

- Community involvement: this refers to an individual youngster's desire to belong to a particular community, lifestyle group or tribe.[43]

Coca-Cola has been using the Emergency Refreshment (ER) nurses for four years now on all major summer music festivals and events in the Benelux. They offer sun lotion, massages, frozen T-shirts or just a cold fire-hose shower to refresh youngsters visiting the music festivals. The campaign is endorsed with sponsoring festival reports, advertising and branded content on screen and online on youth music channel TMF and through social network pages that contain a blog, videos and pictures of Nurse Selma. In MTV Networks' research, 87 per cent of Gen Yers said that there was a perfect fit between the Coca-Cola brand and TMF's own Award event.[44]

In Germany, Sony Computer Entertainment endorsed the MTV Campus Invasion, a series of festivals at German universities (see Figure 7.5). National and international acts such as the Kaiser Chiefs attracted more than 30,000 music-loving students and young adults. Sony wanted to promote the new *Singstar* release for Playstation 3 and boost the awareness of the 'SingStore', the online download platform for *Singstar* content. A promotional plan with TV trailers, an online microsite, cut-ins during the live broadcasts and off-air integration of sponsor logos supported the live event. Sony had an on-the-ground presence with an own *Singstar* stage used for open student karaoke performances during the concert breaks, a *Singstar* booth and promotion teams. Key themes for the *Singstar* franchise such as experiencing music and having fun were perfectly transported and emotionalized in this sponsorship of MTV's Campus Invasion.

FIGURE 7.5   MTV Campus Invasion in Germany

Magic stores

Apart from magic moments on events, Gen Yers can also experience gratification in a special retail environment. Attitudes towards fashion retailers are mainly influenced by youth's shopping experience. During consumer interactions with the store's physical environment and atmosphere, its employees and its offerings, bonds are created between the brand and Generation Y consumers.[45] Pop-up stores, bars or restaurants that promote a brand or product line for a short time are one of the latest ways of creating an environment that is highly experiential for Gen Y consumers. Upscale fashion brand Comme des Garcons was the first to discover that it sparks off excitement and surprise through its temporary nature, intentionally springing up and disappearing quickly. Martini opened bars selling Martini-based cocktails for two weeks on one spot before popping-up in another secret place. Promotion often depends solely on word-of-mouth and viral marketing. Pop-up concepts appeal to the stimulation junkie characteristic of Gen Y and it's no surprise that they are the demographic group that shows the biggest interest in this guerilla marketing approach.[46]

Levi's has permanently reserved the storefront of its most expensive retail space in London's Regent Street for art exhibitions. A group of musicians and artists have been picked by the brand to be the faces of its new brand campaign.[47] In *Brand Lands, Hot Spots and Cool Spaces* Christian Mikunda demonstrates the power of mood management in building strong brands. All Nike Towns, the flagship stores of the US sports brand, have a system of futuristic mini lifts in a prominent central position. They transport Nike T-shirts and shoes from the underground storage to the different store floors. The see-through acrylic glass capsules float through the store and then theatrically slide open, providing a visual attraction to everyone who is visiting the store.[48]

Conclusion

As experience shows, Gen Yers love campaigns that are capable of triggering positive emotions or relieving stress or other negative feelings. If your brand is capable of arousing happiness through its offer, marketing or communication, it will definitely touch the hearts of the youth generation. The key to emotional branding is maximizing the sensory appeal as well as bringing your brand alive through experiences in events or retail environments. Since emotions and happiness spread like a virus, an intelligent use of social media marketing will boost the feelings of Generation Y. Still, never forget that this is their medium in the first place, so it should be used with care by keeping the three steps in mind: observing, facilitating and participating.

Hot takeaways for cool brand builders

- Gen Y are an emotional consumer generation, which is reflected in their shopping behaviour and brand preference.
- Brands have two routes to tap into emotional branding: connecting with and arousing positive emotions or taking away negative ones.
- By addressing youth's five senses, and especially scent, sound and design a brand puts EQ (emotional quotient) in its offer to Generation Y.
- Happiness is the most important emotion evoked by hot brands because this emotion caters for youths' needs of hedonism and escapism.
- Hot brands know how to deliver gratifications instead of pleasures.
- Gratifications are challenging experiences, in-store or at events, that require one's full attention and socially connect Gen Yers to peers.

Conclusion

From our daily experience with both advertisers and youth, we know that the word 'cool' is as dangerous as it is useful in discussions on building brands that are appealing to Generation Y. The second you tell a Millennial kid you are cool, you can be very sure that, well, you are not. They decide themselves what's cool. It's not a characteristic you can deliberately plan or chase. You have to earn the status of 'cool brand'. When you are capable of attaining this status, your brand's coolness will translate into buying preference and long-term loyalty. In this book, we have created the mnemonical CRUSH framework that might be helpful to protect your brands from losing their relevancy for the new consumer generation. In other words: to stay hot. The brand-building model, combining coolness, realness, uniqueness, self-identification with the brand and happiness, is based on years of interacting with Millennials through qualitative and quantitative research as well as the everyday creation of compelling content and brand solutions for them.

To stay hot, cool brands need to connect on a deep and individual emotional level with Generation Yers. Cool brands make them happy. Youth will engage with brands that feel as close to them as their best friends. The metaphor of an engagement is actually very useful in visualizing the different steps youth marketers can consider in this branding process. Marketing and branding to the previous Generation X could be compared to an arranged marriage. Individual preferences were restrained by the generation's desire to belong to the predominant 'achievers' predilection. Image was important and Gen Xers were prepared to pay dowries to be seen with the right bride/brand. You will probably expect that we will now compare Gen Y branding to the other extreme of speed dating... wrong. If you scratch the surface of what is commonly described as a cool and trendy phenomenon, the truth will reveal that the average duration between the initial meeting of a partner and accepting a marriage proposal for Gen Yers today is 2 years and 11 months. Between proposal and wedding, there's another 2 years and 3 months! For strategic brand management this means: if you don't want to surf on hypes and fads and want to avoid your brand's obsolescence, it takes a lot more branding efforts than just a speed date with these critical youngsters.

With Gen Y, you first need to deserve trust and affection. Successful Gen Y brands don't dictate or shout, but empower and leave control in the hands of youth. The main difference between shouting and having a conversation is actually: listening. Those brands that are devoted to listening to the assertive voice of this generation will find their relationship gaining strength.

Generation Y has been dubbed 'the echo boomer generation', because of the big resemblance with their parents and the strong ties between child and parent. With Gen Yers – and Gen Xers will frown now – their parents' opinion is highly valued in every important choice they make. Considering the boomerang and hotel mum and dad trend, as a youth marketer, you should never forget the parental voice.

In the first phase of traditional courtship, men might show off by sending love letters, poems and singing romantic songs. For a Gen Y brand, continuously bringing compelling content and cool utilities linked to the brand's unique vision is an important first step to be noticed and raise awareness. Content is youth's social currency and they talk about the brands they perceive as unique and buy brands they hear recommended by peers. Since youngsters are sceptical about a brand's uniqueness, it is only through consistent positioning in all details that you will manage to break through the clutter in a credible way and acquire their attention. To stay on youth's stimulus-oriented radar, brands need to adapt to changing tastes and offer variety and choice. You might think that Apple iPhone does the trick with just one model, but they are actually selling a cool tool to access an enormous daily updated variety of apps and Apple introduced four generations of the device in less than four years. Cool youth brands know how to develop this well-balanced area of tension between recognizable consistency and regular novelty and surprise. Your brand has to reward this triumph-craving generation's efforts in life and support their busy lifestyle.

Once your brand is able to catch Gen Y's interest, the next step is to enduringly confirm that you share the same interests. As with romance, it is by finding out what partners have in common that flirting moves to the next phase of bonding. Winning youth brands show us every day how their vision is related to the passions of the lifestyle groups they are targeting. Those brands that represent the identity aspects that youngsters want to accentuate and fit in with the aspired crowd behaviour will be able to establish a relationship. Self-identification with brands is by far the most important step in remaining a hot brand. Just like lovers often mirror their body language, great youth brands echo Gen Y's passion points. Yet, remember again that it's not about shouting you have the same passions. Youth should experience with their own eyes that you fit in their lives.

This brings us to the next step in the courtship: dating. Couples go out together for a meal, a party, a film or shopping. For our emotional consumer generation, spending magic moments together with a brand will arouse feelings of happiness. When a boy and a girl engage in thrilling activities together, like a roller coaster ride or rafting, psychologists have found that the excitement involved with the activity is transposed to the person they are with and their relationship. For brands this works in exactly the same way. Positive emotions evoked on brand-initiated or endorsed events will strengthen the bond Gen Yers have with your brand. Brands should surpass the delivery of short-term pleasures and think of challenging gratifications that will leave a long-lasting impression.

In an era with more divorces than marriages, there's one main breeding ground for long-term relationships: honesty and authenticity. After all, you can pretend you have a lot in common for a while. Or lovesickness sometimes makes you blind to reality. But in the long run, your true personality traits and behaviour will inevitably be revealed. Only Gen Y brands that don't imitate or fake their personality and stay true to their DNA will earn a sustainable place in the heart of this savvy generation.

This metaphor of courtship and relationship building is of course just another angle to look at the five strategic brand CRUSH dimensions we have developed for this book.

We wish you good luck in approaching this demanding new consumer market. Remember, the future of your company is depending on how strong your connection with these kids will turn out to be. Addressing the needs and wants of this new consumer generation will be of a much higher importance for your brands than it was to understand Generation X. The size of the articulate Gen Y cohort is substantial. The influence of this generation on society, economics, politics and business will be comparable to the impact of their Baby Boomer parents in the past three decades. As Gen Yers are only starting to enter job markets and creating households, you ain't seen nothing yet....

We hope you have enjoyed this book as a stirring source of strategic Gen Y branding. Frequent updates will be available on the companion website and blog **www.howcoolbrandsstayhot.com**. It is also a good place to share your own experiences or campaigns and interact with the authors as well as other passionate youth brand builders.

Appendix 1
A word from
the research team

The CRUSH © study was fielded between 29 October 2009 and 3 December 2009. All questionnaires were completed online, and the research was conducted in Belgium, the Netherlands, France, Germany, Spain, Sweden and the UK. The total sample size was 6,994 respondents, of which 40% (N = 2,820) were male and 60% (N = 4,174) were female. The sample was composed of 2,474 respondents from the Talk to Change community, a market research panel maintained by InSites Consulting. Of the Talk to Change sample, 51% (N = 1,259) were aged 14–29, while 49% (N = 1,215) were aged 30–65. With the participation of MTV Europe, an additional 4,489 respondents were recruited by means of a pop-up that was shown on the MTV websites in the countries listed above. The pop-up directed interested website visitors to the online survey. Of the participants recruited through the MTV websites, 89% (N = 3,987) were aged 14–29, while 11% (N = 502) were 30+.

The CRUSH © branding model was tested by means of path analysis. Path analysis is a regression-based technique designed to test hypothesized directional relationships between variables. This is a complicated way of saying that path analysis can be used to evaluate theories about how different kinds of brand attitudes (in this case, the constructs in the CRUSH model) lead to overall evaluations of brand (in this case, Brand Leverage).

The model (see Figure A1.1) starts with the foundation of perceptions of the brand as cool, real, unique, self-brand identification (perceived overlap between one's own personality and the brand's personality) and of positive emotions engendered by thoughts of the brand. These five dimensions are all included as independent variables in two separate regression models, one explaining brand conversations, and one explaining brand image. The results from this first set of analyses indicate that seeing a brand as cool, real, unique and having greater identification with the brand and feeling more positive emotions when thinking about the brand, are associated with having more conversations about the brand as well as having a better image of the brand.

FIGURE A1.1   The CRUSH branding model

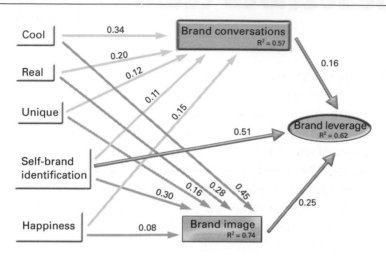

The second set of analyses consisted of a single regression analysis examining the joint impact of brand conversations, brand image and brand identification on brand leverage, which is defined as the overall strength of the brand in the consumer's mind. These three variables are all included as direct predictors of brand leverage because of their importance and indeed centrality to brand evaluation for the modern consumer. The results from this analysis show that more conversations about the brand, a better image of the brand and greater identification with the brand are all associated with greater brand leverage, in other words: with a stronger brand.

The sum of these analyses provide support for the CRUSH © branding model that is the backbone of this book. By proposing a theoretical explanation of the ways in which strong brands are formed in consumers' minds, and then evaluating and testing the relationships between the hypothesized constructs and brand strength, this research provides marketers with a useful and validated framework to better understand key drivers of brand strength, especially among young consumers.

Michael Friedman, Niels Schillewaert and Annelies Verhaeghe
ForwaR&D Lab, InSites Consulting
More information can be found on: **www.insites.eu**

Appendix 2
The Staying Alive
Foundation

Who we are

The Staying Alive Foundation is a global HIV/AIDS charity that empowers young people. We give out small sums of money to young people who we believe in – who we trust – and who we are genuinely inspired by. These young people have one thing in common – they're fighting to conquer HIV and AIDS in their local communities in the most creative and innovative ways. To date, the Foundation has raised over $3 million, allowing it to support over 193 grants to 126 organizations' projects in 50 countries. We are 100 per cent donor funded and rely on donations from organizations and private companies to continue the work we do. We believe that promoting awareness and prevention of the virus is our greatest hope of turning the tide of this epidemic.

What we are about

We are FIRST FUNDERS. Our grant-giving strategy is unique; we fund young people with little or no previous funding. As well as providing small cash grants, we also provide them with local mentors and training to help them get their projects off the ground and develop them as they go forward.

We only fund projects run by YOUNG PEOPLE. We're not ageist! But we recognize the importance of peer-to-peer education when it comes to changing the dynamics of this epidemic. We want young people to go into their communities and educate their peers using language and methods that resonate with their peers.

We believe in the power of ONE. The Staying Alive Foundation recognizes that one person really can make a difference in his/her wider community. We know that the power of the individual can mobilize others into taking action.

So: funding the un-funded, funding young leaders, and understanding the power of every one of our grantees.

More information can be retrieved on: **www.staying-alive.org.**

Notes

Chapter 1   Defining generation Y

1   Di Falco A, Gibbs D, Corcoran A. *MTV generation V.2*. London: MTV Networks Europe; 2009

2   Doherty M. *Millennials could be your next growth opportunity* [Online]. 2 Apr 2010 [accessed 5 Apr 2010]; Available from: **http://www.mediapost. com/publications/?fa=Articles.showArticle&art_aid=125415**

3   Mason M. *The pirate's dilemma. How youth culture is reinventing capitalism*. New York: Free Press; 2008

4   Urwin R. Generation Y. Attracting, engaging and leading a generation at work. *White paper series Drake International* 2006; 3(1): 1–20

5   Taylor P, Keeter S. *Millennials. A portrait of generation next. Confident. Connected. Open to change* [Online]. 24 Feb 2010 [accessed 28 Mar 2010]; Available from: **http://www.pewresearch. org/millennials**

6   Van den Bergh J. Building an online social identity. In: Cooreman G (ed). *MCDC*. Ghent (Belgium): InSites Consulting; 2009 Sept: 49–53

7   Van Belleghem S, Van den Branden S. *Global social media study* [Research]. Ghent (Belgium): InSites Consulting; Mar 2010

8   Kimball D. *My parents joined Facebook. Personalized clubhouses and divergent social norms online* [Online]. 18 May 2009 [accessed 28 Mar 2010]; Available from: **http://blogs.law.harvard.edu/digitalnatives/ 2009/05/18/my-parents-joined-facebook-personalized-clubhouses-and- divergent-social-norms-online/**

9   Taylor P, Keeter S. *Millennials. A portrait of generation next. Confident. Connected. Open to change* [Online]. 24 Feb 2010 [accessed 28 Mar 2010]; Available from: **http://www.pewresearch.org/ millennials**

10   Goodstein A. Interview with Neil Howe in Ypulse Daily Update [Online]. 18 Mar 2010 [accessed 28 Mar 2010]; Available from: **http://www.ypulse.com/ypulse-interview-neil-howe-president- lifecourse-associates**

11   Rosen LD. *Rewired. Understanding the iGeneration and the way they learn*. New York: Palgrave MacMillan; Apr 2010

12   Urwin R. Generation Y. Attracting, engaging and leading a generation at work. *White paper series Drake International* 2006; 3(1): 1–20

13   Vandyck T. Duizenden doen mee aan urenlang sneeuwballengevecht in Washington DC (Thousands of people participate in endless snowball fight in Washinton DC). *De Morgen* 8 Feb 2010: 13

14   Rose H. *Youthopia. A study of hopes and dreams*. London: Viacom Brand Solutions International; Nov 2010

15   Verhaegen B. *18–30 in Belgium and Europe. The New Pragmatics*. Belgium: Presentation for VMA; 7 Nov 2006

16   Taylor P, Keeter S. *Millennials. A portrait of generation next. Confident. Connected. Open to change* [Online]. 24 Feb 2010 [accessed 28 Mar 2010]; Available from: **http://www.pewresearch.org/ millennials**

17   Schupak HT. Teen survey. Courting the next wave of customers. *JCK* 2008 Mar:106

18   Rand N. The 'peace and plenty' generation: understanding teenagers' lives. *Advertising & Marketing to Children* 2003 Oct–Dec: 45–52

19   *Instilling confidence in tweens hinges on parent communication* [Online]. 31 Mar 2010 [accessed 1 Apr 2010]; Available from: **http://www. prnewswire.com/news-releases/instilling-confidence-in-tweens-hinges-on-parent-communication-89586617.html**

20   Roberts S. *Facing a financial pinch, and moving in with mom and dad* [Online]. 21 Mar 2010 [accessed 27 Mar 2010]; Available from: **http://www.nytimes.com/2010/03/22/nyregion/22singles.html**

21   Rolfe J. The stay at home generation. *Young Consumers: Insight and Ideas for Responsible Markers* 2005; 6(3): 14–17

22   Van den Bergh J, Claus D. *VRT VOLT study* [Research]. Ghent (Belgium): InSites Consulting; Mar 2008

23   Giedd J, Blumenthal J, Jeffries NO, Castellanos F, Liu H, Zijdenbos A, *et al*. Brain development during childhood and adolescence: a longitudinal MRI study. *Nature Neuroscience* 1999; 2(10): 861–63

24   Feinstein S. *Secrets of the teenage brain. Research-based strategies for reaching and teaching today's adolescents*. San Diego (CA): The Brain Store; 2004

25   Baird AA, Gruber SA, Fein DA, Maas LC, Steingard RJ, Renshaw PF, *et al*. Functional magnetic resonance imaging of facial affect recognition in children and adolescents. *Journal of the American Academy of Child and Adolescent Psychiatry* 1999; 38(2): 195–99

26   Spear LP. The adolescent brain and the college drinker: biological basis of propensity to use and misuse alcohol. *Journal of Studies on Alcohol Supplement* 2000; 14: 71–81

27   Feinstein S. *Secrets of the teenage brain. Research-based strategies for reaching and teaching today's adolescents*. San Diego (CA): The Brain Store; 2004

28 Andersson J. *H&M* [Interview]. 26 April 2010

29 Morgan N. *Blame my brain. The amazing teenage brain revealed.* London: Russel Cobb; 2007

30 Morgan N. *Blame my brain. The amazing teenage brain revealed.* London: Russel Cobb; 2007

31 Irwin T. *Diesel launches social media campaign* [Online]. 11 Mar 2010 [accessed 12 Mar 2010]; Available from: **http://www.mediapost.com/ publications/?fa=Articles.showArticle&art_aid=124018**

32 *Teens spend free time texting* [Online]. 4 Feb 2010 [accessed 30 Mar 2010]; Available from: **http://www.marketingcharts.com/interactive/ teens-spend-free-time-texting-11869/**

33 Di Falco A, Gibbs D, Corcoran A. *MTV generation V.2.* London: MTV Networks Europe; 2009

34 Twenge JM. *Generation Me. Why today's young Americans are more confident, assertive, entitled – and more miserable than ever before.* New York: Free Press; 2006

35 Yarrow K, O'Donnell J. *Gen BuY. How tweens, teens and twenty-somethings are revolutionizing retail.* San Francisco: Jossey-Bass; 2009

36 Penman S, McNeill LS. Spending their way to adulthood: consumption outside the nest. *Young Consumers* 2008; 9(3): 115–69

37 Loechner J. *Gen X and Millennials driving recovery* [Online]. 25 Mar 2010 [accessed 29 Mar 2010]; Available from: **http://www.mediapost. com/publications/?fa=Articles.showArticle&art_aid=124696**

38 Niedzviecki H. *Hello I'm special. How individuality became the new conformity.* San Francisco: City Lights; 2006

39 Byfield S. Snapshots of youth: the lives of late teens across the world. *Advertising & Marketing to Children* 2002 Jul–Sep: 15–20

40 Di Falco A, Gibbs D, Corcoran A. *MTV generation V.2.* London: MTV Networks Europe; 2009

41 Greene J. *How Nike's social network sells to runners* [Online]. 6 Nov 2008 [accessed 26 Mar 2010]; Available from: **http://www.businessweek. com/print/magazine/content/08_46/b4108074443945.htm**

42 Christensen O. Changing attitudes of European Youth. *Advertising & Marketing to Children* 2002 Apr–Jun: 19–32

43 McCarthy C. *The dark secrets of Whopper sacrifice* [Online]. 3 Apr 2009 [accessed 5 Apr 2010]; Available from: **http://news.cnet. com/8301-13577_3-10211898-36.html?tag=mncol**;txt

44 Dover D. *A bad day for search engines: how news of Michael Jackson's death travelled across the web* [Online]. 26 Jun 2009 [accessed 27 Mar 2010]; Available from: **http://www.seomoz.org/blog/a-bad-day-for-search-engines-how-news-of-michael-jacksons-death-traveled-across-the-web**

45 *Michael Jackson* [Online]. 6 Jul 2009 [accessed 27 Mar 2010]; Available from: **http://infodisiac.com/blog/2009/07/michael-jackson/**

46 Dumon P. Grenzen aan de betrouwbaarheid (Limits to the reliability). *De Morgen* 26 Feb 2010: 35

47 Van Belleghem S, Van den Branden S. *Global social media study* [Research]. Ghent (Belgium): InSites Consulting; Mar 2010

48 Van Belleghem S, Van den Branden S. *Global social media study* [Research]. Ghent (Belgium): InSites Consulting; Mar 2010

49 Mason M. *The pirate's dilemma. How youth culture is reinventing capitalism*. New York: Free Press; 2008

50 Doherty M. *Millennials could be your next growth opportunity* [Online]. 2 Apr 2010 [accessed 5 Apr 2010]; Available from: **http://www.mediapost.com/publications/?fa=Articles. showArticle&art_aid=125415**

51 Twenge JM. *Generation Me. Why today's young Americans are more confident, assertive, entitled – and more miserable than ever before.* New York: Free Press; 2006

52 Twenge JM, Campbell WK. *The Narcissism epidemic. Living in the age of entitlement.* New York: Free Press; 2009

53 Halpern J. *Fame Junkies. The hidden truths behind America's favorite addiction.* New York: Houghton Mifflin Company; 2007

54 Sandoval G. *Teen iPad destruction – 'what was the point of that?'* [Online]; 5 Apr 2010 [accessed 6 Apr 2010]; Available from: **http://news.cnet.com/8301-31001_3-20001729-261.html**

55 Niedzviecki H. *Hello I'm special. How individuality became the new conformity*. San Francisco: City Lights; 2006

56 Halpern J. *Fame Junkies. The hidden truths behind America's favorite addiction.* New York: Houghton Mifflin Company; 2007

57 Taylor P, Keeter S. *Millennials. A portrait of generation next. Confident. Connected. Open to change* [Online]. 24 Feb 2010 [accessed 28 Mar 2010]; Available from: **http://www.pewresearch.org/ millennials**

58 Twenge JM. *Generation Me. Why today's young Americans are more confident, assertive, entitled – and more miserable than ever before.* New York: Free Press; 2006

59 Medeiros G, Walker C. *GenWorld. The new generation of global youth* [Research]. Chicago: Energy BBDO; 2005

60 Meeus R. De dag waarop iedereen kon gamen (The day everybody could play a videogame). *De Morgen* 2010 Mar 26: 34

61 Van den Bergh J, De Ruyck T. *Brand authenticity study for Levi's Europe* [Research]; Ghent (Belgium): InSites Consulting; Nov 2008

62 Christensen O. Changing attitudes of European youth. *Advertising & Marketing to Children* 2002 Apr–Jun: 19–32

63 Van den Bergh J, De Ruyck T. *Brand authenticity study for Levi's Europe* [Research]; Ghent (Belgium): InSites Consulting; Nov 2008

64 *Puma new shoe box by Yves Behar/Fuse project.* [Online] 14 Apr 2010 [accessed 21 Apr 2010]; Available from: **http://www.designboom. com/weblog/cat/8/view/9828/puma-new-shoe-box-by-yves-behar-fuse-project.html**

65 Taylor P, Keeter S. *Millennials. A portrait of generation next. Confident. Connected. Open to change* [Online]. 24 Feb 2010 [accessed 28 Mar 2010]; Available from: **http://www.pewresearch.org/ millennials**

66 Namiranian L. *Brand engagement. Teenagers and their brands in emerging markets.* ESOMAR World Research Paper, London; Sept 2006

67 *Pepsi refresh project.* [accessed 30 Mar 2010]; Available from: **http://www.refresheverything.com/**

68 Germinsky L. *Eva Longoria says Yo Sumo* [Online]. 2 Apr 2010 [accessed 4 Apr 2010]; Available from: **http://www.tonic.com/article/ eva-longoria-inside-out-yo-sumo-more-than-desperate-housewife/**

69 Rand N, The 'peace and plenty' generation: understanding teenagers' lives. *Advertising & Marketing to Children* 2003 Oct–Dec: 45–52

70 Rose H. *Youthopia. A study of hopes and dreams.* London: Viacom Brand Solutions International; Nov 2010

71 Nelis H, van Sark Y. *Puber brein, binnenstebuiten (Adolescent brain, inside out).* Utrecht (The Netherlands), Antwerp (Belgium): Kosmos Uitgevers; 2009

72 Foehr UG. *Media multitasking among American youth: prevalence, predictors and pairings.* Menlo Park (CA): The Henry J. Kaiser Foundation; 2006 Dec: 1–36

73 Johnson S. *Everything is bad for you.* New York: Riverhead Books; 2005

74 De Bruyckere P, Smits B. *Is het nu Generatie X, Y of Einstein? (Is it generation X, Y or Einstein?).* Mechelen (Belgium): Plantyn; 2009

75 Patel K. *MTV will have a 'Beavis and Butt-head' iPad App and much more* [Online]. 28 Mar 2010 [accessed 5 Apr 2010] Available from: **http://www.businessinsider.com/mtv-will-have-a-bevis-and-butt-head-ipad-app-and-much-more-2010-3**

76 McCrindle M. *Understanding Generation Y.* North Parramatta: Australia: The Australian Leadership Foundation; Dec 2001

77 Verhaegen B. *18–30 in Belgium and Europe. The New Pragmatics.* Belgium: Presentation for VMA; 7 Nov 2006

78   Twenge JM. *Generation Me. Why today's young Americans are more confident, assertive, entitled – and more miserable than ever before.* New York: Free Press; 2006

79   Christensen O. Changing attitudes of European Youth. *Advertising & Marketing to Children* 2002 Apr–Jun: 19–32

80   Reisenwitz TH, Iyer R. Differences in generation X and generation Y: implications for the organization and marketers. *The Marketing Management Journal* 2009; **19**(2): 91–103

Chapter 2   Developing a brand model for the new consumer

1   Dale R. *Tumour in the whale.* A collection of modern myths. London: WH Allen; 1978

2   Snowden D, Stienstra J. *Stop asking questions. Understanding how consumers make sense of it all.* Proceedings of the ESOMAR Congress; 8 Sept 2007; Berlin (Germany)

3   Zaltman G. *How customers think. Essential insights into the mind of the market.* Boston, MA: Harvard Business School Press; 2003: 211–13

4   Hein K. *Teen talk is, like, totally branded* [Online]. 6 Aug 2007 [accessed 1 Apr 2010]; Available from: **http://kellerfay.com/news/Brandweek_8_6_07.pdf**

5   Van den Bergh J, Lagae M, Vandenbranden S. *MTV Cool brand awards study: emotions & conversations.* Ghent (Belgium): InSites Consulting, Jun 2010

6   Okazaki S. The tactical use of mobile marketing: how adolescents' social networking can best shape brand extensions. *Journal of Advertising* 2009 Mar; **49**(1): 12–26

7   Claus D. *Conversation diary* [Research]. Ghent (Belgium): InSites Consulting; Feb 2010

8   Van den Bergh J, Lagae M, Vandenbranden S. *MTV Cool brand awards study: emotions & conversations.* Ghent (Belgium): InSites Consulting, Jun 2010

9   Andersson J. [Interview]. *H&M.* 26 Apr 2010

10   Van den Bergh J, Friedman M, Verhaeghe A, Schillewaert S. *Developing the CRUSH branding model.* Ghent (Belgium): InSites Consulting; 2010

11   Friedman M, Schillewaert S, Ahearne, Lam S. *Brand leverage study* [Research]. InSites Consulting and Houston University; 2009

12 Jorgensen DB, Gam A. [Interview]. Bestseller. 19 Apr 2010
13 Kalliokulju S. [Interview] Nokia. 28 Apr 2010
14 Söder P, Wahlstrom E. [Interview]. DDB Stockholm & MTV Sweden. 26 Apr 2010

Chapter 3   What cool means to brands

1   Danesi M. *Cool. The signs and meanings of adolescence*. Toronto: University of Toronto Press; 1994

2   Van den Bergh J, Claus D. *The meaning of cool*. Ghent (Belgium): InSites Consulting & MTV Networks; 2007

3   Coates D. *So very cool in more ways than one* [Online]. 12 Feb 2010 [accessed 14 Feb 2010]; Available from: **www.Ypulse.com**

4   Van den Bergh J, Claus D. *The cool sneaking formula*. Ghent (Belgium): InSites Consulting & MTV Networks; 2008

5   Van den Bergh J, Friedman M, Verhaeghe A, Schillewaert S. *Developing the CRUSH branding model*. Ghent (Belgium): InSites Consulting; 2010

6   Wilmoth P. *Turning silver into gold* [Online]. 3 Dec 2006 [accessed 15 Feb 2010]; Available from: **http://www.theage.com.au/news/in-depth/turning-silver-gold-into/2006/12/02/1164777841650.html**

7   Bellantonio J. Image makers. *Orange County Business Journal* 2002 Sept 16

8   Kerner N, Pressman G. *Chasing cool. Standing out in today's cluttered marketplace*. New York: Atria Books; 2007

9   MTV Networks Cool Brand Awards Research, conducted by InSites Consulting.

10 Van den Bergh J, Claus D. *The cool sneaking formula*. Ghent (Belgium): InSites Consulting & MTV Networks; 2008.

11 Brenemark T. [Interview] DDB Stockholm. 26 Apr 2010

12 Nancarrow C, Nancarrow P, Page J. An analysis of the concept of cool and its marketing implications. *Journal of Consumer Behaviour* 2002 Jun; 1(4): 311–22

13 Olson EM, Czaplewski AJ, Slater SF. Stay Cool. *Marketing Management* 2005 Sep–Oct: 14–7

14 Blasberg J, Vishwanath V. Making cool brands hot. *Harvard Business Review* 2003 Jun: 20–22

15 Van den Bergh J, Claus D. *The meaning of cool*. Ghent (Belgium): InSites Consulting & MTV Networks; 2007

16   Elliott S. Sprite recast as spark in a bottle [Online]. *The New York Times*. 11 Feb 2010 [accessed 15 Feb 2010]; Available from: **http://mediadecoder.blogs.nytimes.com/2010/02/11/sprite-recast-as-spark-in-a-bottle/?scp=1&sq=Sprite%20Recast&st=cse**

17   De Pauw E. Movies en make-up. [Movies and make-up]. *De Morgen* 20 Feb 2010: 56

18   Van den Bergh J, Lagae M. *Cool today, gone tomorrow? Generation Y and loyalty*. Ghent (Belgium): InSites Consulting & MTV Networks; 2009

19   Lukovitz K. *Doritos bags enable virtual 3-D concert experience* [Online]. 6 Jul 2009 [accessed 16 Feb 2010]; Available from: **http://www.mediapost.com/publications/?fa=Articles. showArticle&art_aid=109223**

20   Hall K. *The big ideas behind the Nintendo Wii* [Online]. 16 Nov 2006 [accessed 16 Feb 2010]; Available from: **http://www.businessweek.com/ technology/content/nov2006/tc20061116_750580.htm**

21   Van den Bergh J, Lagae M, De Vuyst P. *Branded solutions tracking* [Research]. InSites Consulting for MTV Networks; 2010

22   GfK Data provided with permission of Procter & Gamble. Belgium: Nov–Dec 2009

23   Mortimer R. Bling bling branding with strictly no mention of 'cool'. *Brand Strategy*. 2002 Oct: 10–11

24   Nancarrow C, Nancarrow P, Page J. An analysis of the concept of cool and its marketing implications. *Journal of Consumer Behaviour* 2002 Jun; 1(4): 311–22

25   Gladwell M. *Annals of style. The coolhunt* [Online]. 17 Mar 1997 [accessed 16 Feb 2010]; Available from: **http://www.newyorker.com/ archive/1997/03/17/1997_03_17_078_TNY_CARDS_000378002**

26   Southgate N. Coolhunting with Aristotle. *International Journal of Market Research* 2003; 45(2): 167–89

27   Rogers EM. *Diffusion of innovations*. New York: Free Press; 1962

28   Metcalfe B. Metcalfe's law: a network becomes more valuable as it reaches more users. *Infoworld* [Online]. 2 Oct 1995 [accessed 12 August 2010]; Available from: **www.infoworld.com**

29   Reed D. The law of the pack. *Harvard Business Review* 2001 Feb: 23–4

30   Domensino C. [Interview]. 27 Feb 2010

31   Van den Bergh J. *European MC DC survey* [Research]. InSites Consulting; summer 2009

32   Verhaeghe A. *Qualitative report for Johnnie Walker* [Research]. InSites Consulting with permission of Diageo Benelux; 2008

33   Martel A. [Interview]. Diageo Benelux; 22 Feb 2010

34 Gloor P, Cooper S. *Coolhunting. Chasing down the next big thing*. New York: AMACOM Books; 2007

35 Van den Bergh J, Van Heddegem M. *Co-creating a new newspaper for generation Y*. [Research]. InSites Consulting for Corelio; 2009

36 Centre for Information about Media. *Circulation of newspapers* [Online]. 2009 [accessed 17 Feb 2010]; Available from: **http://www.cim.be**

37 VBSI. *Golden age of youth research challenges assumptions about the meaning of youth* [Online]. 10 Oct 2008 [accessed 17 Feb 2010]; Available from: **http://www2.prnewswire.com/cgi-bin/stories. pl?ACCT=104&STORY=/www/story/10-07-2008/0004899039&EDATE=**

38 Noxon C. *Rejuvenile. Kickball, cartoons, cupcakes and the reinvention of American grown-up*. New York: Three Rivers Press; 2006

39 ESA [Online]. *Industry facts*. 2009 [accessed 17 Feb 2010]; Available from: **www.theesa.com/facts**

40 Higham W. *Old is the new young* [Online]. 17 Mar 2010 [accessed 3 May 2010]; Available from: **http://www.adweek.com/aw/ content_display/community/columns/other-columns/ e3iff897d5a72be7303195a70be8209cf9d**

41 Noxon C. *The rejuvenile phenomenon from a to z* [Online]. 2010. [accessed 18 Feb 2010]; Available from: **www.rejuvenile.com**.

Chapter 4 The real thing: brand authenticity

1 *Don Draper's presentation for Kodak* [Online]. 16 Apr 2008 [accessed 23 Feb 2010]; Available from: **http://blogs.amctv.com/ mad-men/2008/04/don-drapers-kodak-presentation.php**

2 Eng J. *Kirstin Chenoweth, Jon Cryer win first Emmys* [Online]. 20 Sept 2009 [accessed 23 Feb 2010]; Available from: **http://www.tvguide.com**

3 Bryant A. *Ratings: viewers go mad for Mad Men* [Online]. 17 Aug 2009 [accessed 23 Feb 2010]; Available from: **http://www.tvguide.com**

4 Our journal *Madipedia* [Online]. 9 Sept 2009 [accessed 23 Feb 2010]; Available from: **http://www.madisonavenuejournal.com/2009/09/08/ our_journal_madipedia/**

5 Derbaix M, Decrop A. Authenticity in the performing arts: a foolish quest? *Advances in Consumer Research* 2007; 34: 75–80

6 Millet K, Van den Bergh B, Pandelaere M. *First things first? The value of originality*. Belgium: Faculty of Business and Economics of the KULeuven; 2008

7   Beverland MB. *Building brand authenticity. 7 Habits of iconic brands.* Basingstoke (UK): Palgrave Macmillan; 2009

8   Elber L. *Mad Men makes a splash bigger than its ratings* [Online]. 23 Oct 2008 [accessed 24 Feb 2010]; Available from: **http://www.usatoday.com/life/television/2008-10-23-2948376121_x.htm**

9   *Sesame Street: Mad Men* [Online]. [accessed 24 Feb 2010]; Available from: **http://www.youtube.com/watch?v=YgvKCfZqxrQ&feature=fvst**

10 Gilmore JH, Pine II BJ. *Authenticity. What consumers really want.* Boston (MA): Harvard Business School Press; 2007

11 Van den Bergh J, De Ruyck T. *Authenticity for gen Y.* [Research]. Ghent (Belgium): InSites Consulting; 17 Feb 2009

12 Rose RL, Wood SL. Paradox and the consumption of authenticity through reality television. *Journal of Consumer Research* 2005 Sep; 32: 284–96

13 Botterill J. Cowboys, outlaws and artists: The rhetoric of authenticity and contemporary jeans and sneaker advertisements. *Journal of Consumer Culture* 2007; 7(105): 105–25

14 Peterson RA. In search of authenticity. *Journal of Management Studies* 2005 Jul; 42(5): 1083–98

15 Beverland MB. Crafting brand authenticity: The case of luxury wines. *Journal of Management Studies* 2005 Jul; 42(5): 1003–29

16 Mol JM, Wijnberg NM. Competition, selection and rock and roll: the economics of Payola and authenticity. *Journal of Economic Issues* 2007 Sep; XLI(3): 701–14

17 Ganz C. *Rocking literally: the story behind 'Take on Me', 'Head over Heels' video parodies* [Online]. 10 Oct 2008 [accessed 25 Feb 2010]; Available from: **http://www.rollingstone.com/rockdaily/index.php/2008/10/16/rocking-literally-the-story-behind-take-on-me-head-over-heels-video-parodies/**

18 Botterill J. Cowboys, outlaws and artists: The rhetoric of authenticity and contemporary jeans and sneaker advertisements. *Journal of Consumer Culture* 2007; 7(105): 105–25

19 Beverland MB. *Building brand authenticity. 7 Habits of iconic brands.* Basingstoke (UK): Palgrave Macmillan; 2009

20 Janoff B. Off the wall and in the black. *Brandweek* 2006 9 Oct; 47(37): 40–61

21 Beverland MB. *Building brand authenticity. 7 Habits of iconic brands.* Basingstoke (UK): Palgrave Macmillan; 2009

22 Gilmore JH, Pine II BJ. *Authenticity. What consumers really want.* Boston (MA): Harvard Business School Press; 2007

23 Pandelaere M, Sampermans D, Verbruggen T. Various student dissertations and research. Ghent (Belgium): Department of Marketing Ghent University; 2007–08

24 Pandelaere M, Millet K, Van den Bergh B. *Attitudinal effects of first exposure*. [Working paper]. Ghent (Belgium): Faculty of Business and Economics, University of Ghent; Nov 2008

25 Millet K, Van den Bergh B, Pandelaere M. *First things first? The value of originality*. Leuven (Belgium): Faculty of Business and Economics Leuven University; 2008

26 Gilmore JH, Pine II BJ. *Authenticity. What consumers really want*. Boston (MA): Harvard Business School Press; 2007

27 *Flat Eric's cruise to the top* [Online]. 20 Mar 1999 [accessed 24 Feb 2010]; Available from: **http://news.bbc.co.uk/2/hi/ entertainment/299803.stm**

28 *Flat Eric* [Online]. [accessed 24 Feb 2010]; Available from: **http://muppet.wikia.com/wiki/Flat_Eric**

29 Van den Bergh J, De Ruyck T, Van Kemseke D. *Even better than the real thing. Understanding generation Y's definition of authenticity for the Levi's brand*. Proceedings of the ESOMAR qualitative conference; Marrakech (Morocco); 16 Nov 2009

30 Fishman TC. Manufakcture. *New York Times Magazine* 9 Jan 2005: 40–44

31 *Foreign branding* [Online]. [accessed 25 Feb 2010]; Available from: **http://en.wikipedia.org/wiki/Foreign_branding**

32 Campbell B. *What do hard rock, ice cream, and do-it-yourself furniture have in common?* [Online]. [accessed 25 Feb 2010]; Available from: **http://www.clicknation.com/snoof/stuff/umlaut.pdf**

33 Beverland MB, Lindgreen A, Vink MW. Projecting authenticity through advertising. Consumer judgments of advertisers' claims. *Journal of Advertising* 2008 Spring; **37**(1): 5–15

34 Ritson M. Want brand authenticity? Be authentic. *Marketing* 2008 14 May: 21

35 Van den Bergh J, De Ruyck T. *Authenticity for generation Y*. [Research]. Ghent (Belgium): InSites Consulting; 2008

36 Millet K, Van den Bergh B, Pandelaere M. *First things first? The value of originality*. Leuven (Belgium): Faculty of Business and Economics Leuven University; 2008

37 Brown S, Kozinets RV, Sherry JF Jr. Teaching old brands new tricks: retro branding and the revival of brand meaning. *Journal of Marketing* 2003; **67**(3): 19–33

38 Blackshaw P. The six drivers of brand credibility. It's time to tell credible stories. *MM* 2008 May/June: 51–4

39   Phelvin P, Wallop H. *Innocent smoothies accused over environmental marketing* [Online]. 1 Aug 2008 [accessed 26 Feb 2010]; Available from: **http://www.telegraph.co.uk/news/2484148/Innocent-Smoothies-accused-over-environmental-marketing.html**

40   Sibun J. *Not such a smooth ride for Innocent* [Online]. 2 Aug 2008 [accessed 26 Feb 2010]; Available from: **http://www.telegraph.co.uk/finance/newsbysector/retailandconsumer/2794173/Not-such-a-smooth-ride-for-Innocent.html**

41   Northedge R. *Slaughter of the Innocent? Or is Coke the real deal?* [Online]. 12 April 2009 [accessed 26 Feb 2010]; Available from: **http://www.independent.co.uk/news/business/analysis-and-features/slaughter-of-the-innocent-or-is-coke-the-real-deal-1667412.html**

42   Van den Bergh J, De Ruyck T, Van Kemseke D. *Even better than the real thing. Understanding generation Y's definition of authenticity for the Levi's brand.* Proceedings of the ESOMAR qualitative conference; Marrakech (Morocco); 16 Nov 2009

43   Van den Bergh J, De Ruyck T, Van Kemseke D. *Even better than the real thing. Understanding generation Y's definition of authenticity for the Levi's brand.* Proceedings of the ESOMAR qualitative conference; Marrakech (Morocco); 16 Nov 2009

Chapter 5   We all want unique brands

1   *Moonwalk (dance)* [Online]. [accessed 11 April 2010]; Available from: **http://en.wikipedia.org/wiki/Moonwalk_(dance)**

2   Trout J. *Differentiate or die. Survival in our era of killer competition.* 2nd edn. Hoboken, NJ: John Wiley & Sons; 2008: 27–29

3   Mason M. *The pirate's dilemma. How youth culture is reinventing capitalism.* New York: Free Press; 2009: 704

4   Michelsen C. The truth about NPD. *Brand Strategy* 2008 May: 44–45

5   Andersson J. [Interview] *H&M.* 26 April 2010

6   Cullinane S. *The old new* [Online]. 21 Sept 2005 [accessed 16 April 2010]; Available from: **http://news.bbc.co.uk/2/hi/uk_news/magazine/4265374.stm**

7   Mason M. *The pirate's dilemma. How youth culture is reinventing capitalism.* New York: Free Press; May 2009: 70–71

8   Diaz J. *1960s Braun products hold the secrets to Apple's future* [Online]. 14 Jan 2008 [accessed 16 Apr 2010]; Available from: **http://gizmodo.com/343641/1960s-braun-products-hold-the-secrets-to-apples-future**

9   Bogusky AM, Winsor J. *Baked in. Creating products and businesses that market themselves.* Chicago, IL: Agate publishing; 2009: 116–17

10   Twenge JM, Campbell WK. *The Narcissism epidemic. Living in the age of entitlement*. New York: Free Press; 2009

11   Neff J. *Scientists prove the 'Axe effect' is real. Sort of* [Online].
     7 Jan 2009 [accessed 16 Apr 2010]; Available from:
     http://adage.com/print?article_id=133621

12   *Axe clean your balls* [Online]. 11 Jan 2010 [accessed 16 Apr 2010]
     Available from: **http://www.mahalo.com/axe-clean-your-balls**

13   Ciminillo JA. Elusive Gen Y demands edgier marketing. *Automative News* 2005 Apr; **79**(6411): 28B

14   Kostecki E. *Brand extension to the youth and young adult markets*.
     Thesis submitted in fulfilment of the requirements for the degree of
     Bachelor of Science. LN Stern School of Business, New York
     University; May 2005: 43–49

15   Neigher J. *Dr. Martens: The doctor is still in* [Online]. 4 April 2010
     [accessed 13 Apr 2010]; Available from: **http://articles.latimes.com/
     2010/apr/04/image/la-ig-0404-martens-20100404**

16   Van den Bergh J, De Ruyck T, Van Kemseke D. *Even better than the
     real thing. Understanding generation Y's definition of authenticity for
     the Levi's brand*. Proceedings of the ESOMAR qualitative conference;
     Marrakech (Morocco); 16 Nov 2009

17   Ballantyne R, Warren A, Nobbs K. The evolution of brand choice.
     Brand Management 2006 Jun; **13**(4/5): 339–52

18   MacMillan D. What's in a name? *Business Week* 2007 9 Jul: 18

19   Day A. The right kit for the game. *Brand strategy* 2003 Nov: 28

20   Lindstrom M. *Buyology. How everything we believe about why we
     buy is wrong*. London: Random House Business Books; 2008

21   Jones CRM, Fazio RH. Associative strength and consumer choice
     behaviour. In: Haugtvedt CP, Herr PM, Kardes FR (eds). *Handbook of
     consumer psychology*. New York: Psychology Press; 2008: 437–59

22   Loewe EM. Wireless world. *Display & Design Ideas* 2007 Mar; **19**(3):
     60–62

23   Nosek BA, Banaji MR. The go/no-go association task. *Social
     Cognition* 2001; **19**(6): 625–64

24   Riesenbeck H, Perrey J. *Power brands. Measuring, making, managing
     brand success*. Weinheim (Germany): Wiley-VCH; 2007: 41–42

25   Friedman M, Van den Bergh J, De Wulf K, Vantomme D.
     Implicit measurement of brand distinctive assets for energy drinks
     [Research]. Ghent (Belgium): InSites Consulting; April 2010

26   Wu Y, Ardley B. Brand strategy and brand evolution: welcome to the
     world of the meme. *The Marketing Review* 2007; **7**(3): 301–10

27 Bauerlein V. *Vitaminwater tries winking. New campaign hints at brand's repute in some circles as a hangover remedy* [Online]. 5 April 2010 [accessed 14 April 2010] Available from: **http://adage.com/globalnews/article?article_id=143166http://online.wsj.com/article/SB10001424052702303450704575160280077022428.html?mod=googlenews_wsj**

28 Madden N. *Coke launches Spritea to bolster brand among Chinese youth* [Online]. 7 April 2010 [accessed 14 April 2010]; Available from: **http://adage.com/globalnews/article?article_id=143166**

29 Dodes R. *Levi aims for high-end halo* [Online]. 14 April 2010 [accessed 14 April 2010]; Available from: **http://online.wsj.com/article_email/SB20001424052702303695604575182252816707936-IMyQjAyMTAwMDEwNDExNDQyWj.html**

30 Aaker DA, Joachimsthaler E. *Brand leadership*. New York: The Free Press; 2000: 168–73

31 Wu Y, Ardley B. Brand strategy and brand evolution: welcome to the world of the meme. *The Marketing Review* 2007; 7(3): 301–10

Chapter 6   Self-identification with the brand

1 *Tattoo* [Online]. [accessed 9 Mar 2010]; Available from: **http://en.wikipedia.org/wiki/Tattoo**

2 *Gang tattoos. Unique gang identifiers for street and prison gangs* [Online]. [accessed 9 Mar 2010]; Available from: **http://www.gangsorus.com/tattoos.html**

3 Thomas A. *Youth Online. Identity and literacy in the digital age*. New York: Peter Lang Publishing; 2007

4 Hall SG. *Adolescence: its psychology and its relation to physiology, anthropology, sociology, sex, crime, religion, and education*. New York: Appleton; 1904

5 Erikson EH. *Identity: youth and crisis*. London: Faber & Faber; 1968

6 Van Gorp J. *Youth, identity and consumption, a research model*. Proceedings of the 7th Conference of the European Sociological Association 'Rethinking Inequalities'; Torun: Poland; 9–12 Sept 2005

7 Verhaeghe A, Van den Bergh J, Colin V. *Me, myself and I. Studying youngsters identity by combining visual ethnography and nethnography*. Proceedings of the ESOMAR Qualitative 2008 Conference; Istanbul: Turkey; Nov 2008

8 Macdonald N. The Graffiti subculture. Making a world of difference. In: Gelder K (ed). *The Subcultures Reader*. 2nd edn. Abingdon, Oxon: Routledge; 2005: 313–25

9   Hoogervorst D. *Graffiti in reclame, hoe authentiek is that? (How authentic is graffiti in advertising?)* [Online]. 3 Feb 2010 [accessed 21 Mar 2010]; Available from: **http://youngmarketing.web-log.nl/ youngmarketing/2010/02/graffiti-in-rec.html**

10 Brown BB, Klute C. Friendships, cliques and crowds. In: Adams GR, Berzonsky MD (eds). *Blackwell Handbook of Adolescence.* Oxford (UK): Blackwell Publishing; 2003: 330–48

11 Bourdieu P. *Distinction. A social critique of the judgment of taste.* New York: Routledge; 1986

12 Thornton S. *Club cultures. Music, media and subcultural capital.* Oxford: Blackwell Publishers; 1995

13 Maule A, Head N, Moroney L. *Consumers, trends and trendsetters. Do we speak to the sheep or the sheepdog?* Proceedings of the ESOMAR Worldwide Qualitative Research Conference; Cannes: France; Nov 2004

14 Van den Bergh J. *Subcultures and internet. Speech on Talkie Walkie Event, Ladda*; Ghent: Belgium; 22 Mar 2007

15 Beek J. *UKTribes*, Channel 4 Television; London: 2010

16 Hullegie J. *Urban Art Guide. Adidas heeft het begrepen (How Adidas understands youth)* [Online]. 13 May 2009 [accessed 21 March 2010]; Available from: **http://youngmarketing.web-log.nl/youngmarketing/ 2009/05/urban-art-guide.html**

17 Cova B, Cova V. Tribal marketing: the tribalisation of society and its impact on the conduct of marketing. *European Journal of Marketing* 2002; **36**(5/6): 595–620

18 Verhaeghe A, Van den Bergh J, Colin V. *Me, myself and I. Studying youngsters identity by combining visual ethnography and nethnography.* Proceedings of the ESOMAR Worldwide Qualitative 2008 Conference; Istanbul: Turkey; Nov

19 Hoogervorst D. *1 limo, 1 rapper, 3 dames & het Axe-effect. (1 limo, 1 rapper, 3 ladies and the Axe-effect)* [Online]. 27 Aug 2009 [accessed 21 March 2010]; Available from: **http://youngmarketing.web-log.nl/ youngmarketing/2009/08/1-limo-1-rapper.html**

20 Tuten TL. Deconstructing identity: an exercise to clarify the determinants of brand legitimacy. *Marketing Education Review* 2007 Spring; **17**(1): 57–61

21 Andersson J. [Interview]. *H&M*. 26 Apr 2010

22 Quester P, Beverland M, Farrelly F. Brand-personal values fit and brand meanings: exploring the role individual values play in ongoing brand loyalty in extreme sports subcultures. *Advances in Consumer Research* 2006; 33: 21–27

23   Van den Bergh J, Verhaeghe A. *Lifestyle research report*. [Research].
     Ghent (Belgium): InSites Consulting for MTV Networks; 2008

24   Arning C, Tappy E. *Hip-hop: subculture of super brand. How
     understanding hip-hop culture can inform effective marketing
     communications*. Proceedings of the ESOMAR worldwide Qualitative
     2003 Research Conference; Venice, Italy; Nov

25   James L. *American brandstand 2004* [Online]. [accessed 16 Mar 2010];
     Available from: **http://www.brandchannel.com/images/Papers/
     245_brandstand04_final.pdf**

26   Arning C, Tappy E. *Hip-hop: subculture of super brand. How
     understanding hip-hop culture can inform effective marketing
     communications*. Proceedings of the ESOMAR worldwide Qualitative
     2003 Research Conference; Venice, Italy; Nov

27   Levine R. *It's American brandstand: marketers underwrite performers*
     [Online]. 7 Jul 2008 [accessed 15 Mar 2010]; Available from:
     http://www.nytimes.com/2008/07/07/business/media/07music.html

28   Hampp A, York EB. *How miracle whip, plenty of fish tapped Lady
     Gaga's 'telephone'* [Online]. 13 Mar 2010 [accessed 16 Mar 2010];
     Available from: **http://adage.com/madisonandvine/article?article_
     id=142794**

29   Van Belleghem S, Van den Branden S. *Social media study*. [Research]
     Ghent, Belgium: InSites Consulting; Jan 2010

30   Baumeister RF. The Self. In: Gilbert DT, Fiske ST, Gartner L (eds).
     The handbook of social psychology. New York: McGraw-Hill; 1998

31   Valkenburg PM, Schouten AP, Peter J. *Jongeren en hun
     identeitsexperimenten op internet, Jaarboek ICT en samenleving
     (Youngsters and their identity experiments online)*. In: de Haan J, van't
     Hof C (eds). *Jaarboek Ict en* Samenleving. Amsterdam: Boom;
     2006:47–58

32   Boyd D. Why youth loves social network sites: the role of networked
     publics in teenage social life. In: Buckingham D (ed). *Youth, identity
     and digital media*. Cambridge, MA: The MIT press; 2008

33   Hoogervorst D. *Coke Zero vindt je dubbelganger op Facebook (Coke
     Zero finds your lookalike on Facebook)* [Online]. 4 Dec 2009
     [accessed 21 March 2010]; Available from: **http://youngmarketing.
     web-log.nl/youngmarketing/2009/12/coke-zero-vindt.html**

34   Thomas A. *Youth Online. Identity and literacy in the digital age*.
     New York: Peter Lang Publishing; 2007

35   Verhaeghe A, Van den Bergh J, Colin V. *Me, myself and I. Studying
     youngsters identity by combining visual ethnography and
     nethnography*. Proceedings of the ESOMAR Qualitative 2008
     Conference; Istanbul, Turkey; Nov

36 Back MD, Stopfer JM, Vazire S, Gaddis S, Schmukle SC, Egloff B, Gosling SD. Facebook profiles reflect actual personality, not self-idealization. *Psychological Science* 2010; 21: 372–74

37 *Cosplay* [Online]. [accessed 9 Mar 2010]; Available from: http://en.wikipedia.org/wiki/Cosplay

Chapter 7   Happiness: Gen Y's adoration for branded emotions

1   Emoticon [Online]. [accessed 7 Apr 2010]; Available from: http://en.wikipedia.org/wiki/Emoticon

2   Haidt J. *The happiness hypothesis. Putting ancient wisdom and philosophy to the test of modern science*. London: Arrow Books; 2006

3   Maclean PD. Some psychiatric implications of physiological studies on frontotemporal portion of limbic system (visceral brain). *Electroencephalography and Clinical Neurophysiology* 1952; 4(4): 407–18

4   Ledoux J. *The emotional brain. The mysterious underpinnings of emotional life*. London: Phoenix; 1998

5   Gladwell M. *Blink: the power of thinking without thinking*. New York: Little Brown; 2005

6   Marcus G. *The sentimental citizen*. Pennsylvania: Pennsylvania State University Press; 2002

7   Fox E, Russo R, Georgiou GA. Anxiety modulates the degree of attentive resources required to process emotional faces. *Cognitive, Affective & Behavioural Neuroscience* 2005; 5(4): 396–404

8   LeDoux J. Emotion, memory and the brain. *Scientific American* 1994 June: 50–57

9   Rimé B, Finkenhauer C, Luminet O, Zech E, Philippot P. Social sharing of emotions: new evidence and new questions. In: Stroebe W, Hewstone M (eds). *European Review of Social Psychology* 1998; 3: 145–89. Chichester: Wiley and Sons

10 LeDoux J. Emotion, memory and the brain. *Scientific American* 1994 June; 50–57

11 Dobele A, Lindgreen A, Beverland M, Vanhamme J, Van Wijk R. Why pass on viral messages? Because they connect emotionally. *Business Horizons* 2007 1 Jul; 50: 291–304

12 Izard CE. Basic emotions, relations among emotions, and emotion-cognition relations. *Psychological Review* 1992; 99: 561–65

13   LeDoux J. Emotion, memory and the brain. *Scientific American* 1994 June; 50–57

14   Hill D. *Emotionomics. Leveraging emotions for business success.* 3rd edn. Philadelphia, PA: Kogan Page; 2009

15   Thomson M, MacInnis D, Whan Park C. The ties that bind: measuring the strength of consumers' emotional attachment to brands. *Journal of Consumer Psychology* 2005; **15**(1): 77–91

16   Lindstrom M. *Brand sense. Sensory secrets behind the stuff we buy.* 2nd edn. London: Kogan Page; 2010

17   Gobé M. *Emotional branding. The new paradigm for connecting brands to people.* 2nd edn. New York: Allworth Press; 2009

18   Yarrow K, O'Donnell J. *Gen BuY. How tweens, teens and twenty-somethings are revolutionizing retail.* San Francisco: Jossey-Bass; 2009

19   Yarrow K, O'Donnell J. *Gen BuY. How tweens, teens and twenty-somethings are revolutionizing retail.* San Francisco: Jossey-Bass; 2009

20   *Fanta mobile app keeps the adults out of earshot* [Online]. 2 Dec 2008 [accessed 9 Apr 2010]; Available from: **http://www.ogilvy.co.uk/ogilvy-advertising/index.php/2008/12/02/fanta-mobile-app-keeps-the-adults-out-of-earshot/**

21   Yarrow K, O'Donnell J. *Gen BuY. How tweens, teens and twenty-somethings are revolutionizing retail.* San Francisco: Jossey-Bass; 2009

22   Gobé M. *Emotional branding. The new paradigm for connecting brands to people.* 2nd edn. New York; Allworth Press; 2009

23   Dahl DW, Frankenberger KD, Manchanda R. Does it pay to shock? Reactions to shocking and nonshocking advertising content among university students. *Journal of Advertising Research* 2003; **43**(3): 268–80

24   De Pelsmacker P, Van den Bergh J. The communication effects of provocation in print advertising. *International Journal of Advertising* 1997; **15**(3): 203–21

25   Kim HS. Examination of emotional response to apparel brand advertisements. *Journal of Fashion Marketing and Management* 2000; **4**(4): 303–13

26   Voight J. Social marketing do's and don'ts [Online]. 8 Oct 2007 [accessed 9 Apr 2010]; Available from: **http://www.adweek.com/aw/magazine/article_display.jsp?vnu_content_id=1003654896**

27   Van Belleghem S. *The conversation manager.* Leuven (Belgium): Lannoo Campus; 2010

28   Salomäki SM. [Interview]. *Kuule and the Cancer Society of Finland.* 23 Apr 2010

29 Romani S, Sadeh H, Dalli D. When the brand is bad, I'm mad! An exploration of negative emotions to brands. *Advances in Consumer Research* 2009; 36: 494–501

30 *Neo-Nazi teenagers fight in British boxing's No 1 brand* [Online]. 9 Apr 2005 [accessed 11 Apr 2010]; Available from: **http://www.timesonline.co.uk/tol/news/world/article379031.ece**

31 Van den Berg S. *Branded youths* [Online]. 7 Feb 2005 [accessed 8 Apr 2010]; Available from: **http://www.dailynews.co.za/index.php?fArticleId=2401151**

32 *Neo-Nazi group calls for Thor Steinar boycott. On the wrong side of the right* [Online]. 27 May 2009 [accessed 8 Apr 2010]; Available from: **http://www.spiegel.de/international/germany/0,1518,627114,00.html**

33 Alves A. *Social media and brand hijacking* [Online]. 3 Sept 2008 [accessed 9 Apr 2010] Available from: **http://www.asourceofinspiration.com/2008/09/03/social-media-and-brand-hijacking/**

34 Thomas G. *Brand hijack: when unintended segments desire your brand* [Online]. [accessed 10 Apr 2010]; Available from: **http://www.emorymi.com/thomas2.shtml**

35 Nestlé. *Statement on palm oil* [Online]. Apr 2010 [accessed 10 Apr 2010]; Available from: **http://www.nestle.com/MediaCenter/SpeechesAndStatements/AllSpeechesAndStatements/statement_Palm_oil.htm**

36 Rose H. *The Wellbeing Project* [White paper]. MTV Networks International; Nov 2006

37 Bettingen JF, Luedicke MK. Can brands make us happy? A research framework for the study of brands and their effects on happiness. *Advances in Consumer Research* 2009; 36: 308–14

38 Haidt J. *The happiness hypothesis. Putting ancient wisdom and philosophy to the test of modern science.* London: Arrow Books; 2006

39 Bondolowski C, Hendriksen D. [Interviews] *The Coca-Cola Company.* 30 Apr and 4 May 2010

40 Smilansky S. *Experiential marketing. A practical guide to interactive brand experiences.* London: Kogan Page; 2009

41 Wohlfeil M, Whelan S. Consumer motivations to participate in event-marketing strategies. *Journal of Marketing Management* 2006; 22: 643–69

42 Preston N. Do brands hit the right note with Gen Y? *B&T Magazine* 2008 11 Apr: 22–25

43 Wohlfeil M, Whelan S. Consumer motivations to participate in event-marketing strategies. *Journal of Marketing Management* 2006; 22: 643–69

44 MTV Networks The Netherlands. *Campaign Evaluation Coca-Cola Nurses*. The Netherlands: MTV; 2009

45 Yalcin YDM, Eren-Erdogmus I, Demir S. Using associations to create positive brand attitude for generation Y consumers: application in fashion retailing. Suleyman Demirel University Turkey. *The Journal of Faculty of Economics and Administrative Sciences* 2009; **14**(2): 261–76

46 Niehm LS, Fiore AM, Jeong M, Kim HJ. Pop-up retail's acceptability as an innovative business strategy and enhancer of the consumer shopping experience. *Journal of Shopping Center Research* 2007; **1**(2): 1–30

47 Wood Z. *Levi's looks to art to win denim war* [Online]. 2 Apr 2010 [accessed 10 Apr 2010]; Available from: **http://www.guardian.co.uk/ business/2010/apr/02/levis-art-denim-war-jeans/**

48 Mikunda C. *Brand lands, hot spots and cool spaces. Welcome to the third place and the total marketing experience*. London: Kogan Page; 2007

Index

(italics indicate a figure or table)

With over 1,000 titles in printed and digital format, **Kogan Page** offers affordable, sound business advice

www.koganpage.com

The sharpest minds need the finest advice.
Kogan Page creates success.

www.koganpage.com